Marginalization in China

Marginalization in China

Recasting Minority Politics

Siu-Keung Cheung, Joseph Tse-Hei Lee, and
Lida V. Nedilsky

palgrave
macmillan

MARGINALIZATION IN CHINA
Copyright © Siu-Keung Cheung, Joseph Tse-Hei Lee, and
Lida V. Nedilsky, 2009.

All rights reserved.

First published in 2009 by
PALGRAVE MACMILLAN®
in the United States—a division of St. Martin's Press LLC,
175 Fifth Avenue, New York, NY 10010.

Where this book is distributed in the UK, Europe and the rest of the world,
this is by Palgrave Macmillan, a division of Macmillan Publishers Limited,
registered in England, company number 785998, of Houndmills,
Basingstoke, Hampshire RG21 6XS.

Palgrave Macmillan is the global academic imprint of the above companies
and has companies and representatives throughout the world.

Palgrave® and Macmillan® are registered trademarks in the United States,
the United Kingdom, Europe and other countries.

ISBN: 978–0–230–61423–9

Library of Congress Cataloging-in-Publication Data is available from the
Library of Congress.

A catalogue record of the book is available from the British Library.

Design by Newgen Imaging Systems (P) Ltd., Chennai, India.

First edition: July 2009

10 9 8 7 6 5 4 3 2 1

Printed in the United States of America.

CONTENTS

List of Illustrations		vii
Acknowledgments		ix
Notes on Contributors		xi
One	Introduction: Recasting Minority Politics in China Siu-Keung Cheung, Joseph Tse-Hei Lee, and Lida V. Nedilsky	1
Two	Reaching out for the Ladder of Success: "Outsiders" and the Civil Examination in Late Imperial China Wing-Kin Puk	21
Three	Banditry, Marginality, and Survival among the Laboring Poor in Late Imperial South China Robert J. Antony	35
Four	Politics of Faith: Christian Activism and the Maoist State in South China Joseph Tse-Hei Lee	49
Five	The Transnational Redress Campaign for Chinese Survivors of Wartime Sexual Violence in Shanxi Province Yuki Terazawa	67
Six	The Chinese Underclass and Organized Crime as a Stepladder of Social Ascent Ming Xia	95
Seven	Feminization, Recognition, and the Cosmological in Xishuangbanna Anouska Komlosy	123

Eight	Re-Presenting Women's Identities: Recognition and Representation of Rural Chinese Women Sharon R. Wesoky	145
Nine	"This Is My Mother's Land!" An Indigenous Woman Speaks Out Siu-Keung Cheung	165
Ten	Making Rights Claims Visible: Intersectionality, NGO Activism, and Cultural Politics in Hong Kong Lisa Fischler	187
Eleven	Institutionalizing the Representation of Religious Minorities in Post-1997 Hong Kong Lida V. Nedilsky	211
Twelve	The Limits of Chinese Transnationalism: The Cultural Identity of Malaysian-Chinese Students in Guangzhou Kam-Yee Law and Kim-Ming Lee	237
Glossary		253
Index		257

ILLUSTRATIONS

Maps

4.1	Chaozhou Prefecture	53
7.1	Yunnan Province	125
7.2	Xishuangbanna Dai Autonomous Prefecture	126

Figures

7.1	Sculpture in Jinghong's main square, 2005	129
7.2	Zhuzagapam upon dying. Mural on village temple's outer wall, 2005	137

Tables

3.1	Number of bandits by age	40
3.2	Number of robberies by Chinese lunar month	43
6.1	Drug-related criminals and registered drug addicts	112

ACKNOWLEDGMENTS

We began this collaboration in the summer of 2005, with a gathering of scholars from Hong Kong, Macao, Singapore, and the United States considering whether there is anything Chinese in the way minorities have been recognized in Chinese-dominant polities. Since that provocative beginning, we have incurred numerous institutional and personal debts.

Hong Kong Shue Yan University, including the Centre for Qualitative Social Research under the Department of Sociology, provided a home for our endeavor. Consistently generous and welcoming, Shue Yan University housed and hosted the participants of our 2006 symposium. Its faculty, specifically Harold Traver, Lee Ying Wa, Li Xiuguo, and Ho Wai Shing, functioned as symposium coorganizers, while its students were symposium helpers. Karen Ting-Nga Ng helped to format the final manuscript. Finally, Shue Yan University and Pace University provided the financial support necessary to complete the final manuscript for publication.

The contributors to this volume include participants of the 2006 symposium, guest speakers Stephen Chan of Lingnan University, Joseph Cheng of the City University of Hong Kong, and Tak-Wing Ngo of Leiden University, who helped focus discussion at the symposium, and authors of the case studies contained herein. Careful and considerate preparation by all ensured that each stage of collaboration was both pleasurable and rewarding. Finally, the editors would like to thank those who sustained them in their daily work. In Chinese, the readiness to *xiangru yimei* (相濡以沫) guided us throughout our joint effort.

CONTRIBUTORS

Robert J. Antony is Associate Professor of History at the University of Macao. His publications include *Pirates in the Age of Sail* (New York: W. W. Norton, 2007); *Like Froth Floating on the Sea: The World of Pirates and Seafarers in Late Imperial South China* (Berkeley, CA: Institute for East Asian Studies, 2003); and coedited with Jane Kate Leonard, *Dragons, Tigers, and Dogs: Qing Crisis Management and the Boundaries of State Power in Late Imperial China* (Ithaca, NY: East Asia Program, Cornell University, 2002).

Siu-Keung Cheung is Assistant Professor of Sociology and Coordinator of the Centre for Qualitative Social Research at Shue Yan University in Hong Kong. He is the author of *Gender and Community under British Colonialism: Emotion, Struggle, and Politics in a Chinese Village* (New York: Routledge, 2007).

Lisa Fischler is Assistant Professor of Political Science at Moravian College in Bethlehem, Pennsylvania. She has authored a number of book chapters on the women's movement in Hong Kong, including "Women's Activism during Hong Kong's Political Transition" in Eliza W. Y. Lee (ed.) *Gender and Change in Hong Kong: Globalization, Postcolonialism, and Chinese Patriarchy* (Honolulu: University of Hawai'i Press, 2003). Her current research involves globalization and gender in Chinese societies.

Anouska Komlosy is the Curator of Asian Ethnography at the British Museum. She has published several studies on Yunnan province in southwestern China where she has carried out long-term fieldwork. She has a special interest in Dai (Tai) Studies as well as in gender and identity understandings across borders.

Kam-Yee Law is Associate Professor of Social Sciences at the Hong Kong Institute of Education and the executive editor of *The Hong Kong*

Journal of Social Sciences. He coedited with Kim-Ming Lee, *The Economy of Hong Kong in Non-economic Perspectives* (Hong Kong: Oxford University Press, 2004) and edited *The Chinese Cultural Revolution Reconsidered: Beyond Purge and Holocaust* (New York: Palgrave, 2003).

Joseph Tse-Hei Lee is Professor of History and Codirector of the East Asian Studies Program at Pace University in New York. He is the author of *The Bible and the Gun: Christianity in South China, 1860–1900* (New York: Routledge, 2003).

Kim-Ming Lee is Lecturer in Social Studies at the Community College of City University of Hong Kong. He recently coedited with Kam-Yee Law, *The Economy of Hong Kong in Non-economic Perspectives* (Hong Kong: Oxford University Press 2004).

Lida V. Nedilsky is Associate Professor of Sociology at North Park University in Chicago. Her article, "The Anticult Initiative and Hong Kong Christianity's Turn from Religious Privilege," *China Information* 22, no.3 (2008), reflects her interest in the related processes of personal, spiritual, and ideological formation. Currently she is researching how Christians in Hong Kong understand the religious and political development of their own children.

Wing-Kin Puk is Instructor of History at the Chinese University of Hong Kong. He has authored several studies on Ming-Qing social and economic history.

Yuki Terazawa is Associate Professor of History at Hofstra University in Hempstead, New York, and has authored several studies on the transmission of Western biomedical science in Meiji Japan and the issue of comfort women in the Second World War.

Ming Xia is Professor of Political Science at the College of Staten Island, the City University of New York. He is the author of *The People's Congresses and Governance in China: Toward a Network Mode of Governance* (New York: Routledge, 2008) and *The Dual Developmental State: Development Strategy and Institutional Arrangements for China's Transition* (London: Ashgate, 2000).

Sharon R. Wesoky is Associate Professor of Political Science at Allegheny College in Meadville, Pennsylvania. She is the author of *Chinese Feminism Faces Globalization* (New York: Routledge, 2001).

CHAPTER ONE

Introduction: Recasting Minority Politics in China

SIU-KEUNG CHEUNG,
JOSEPH TSE-HEI LEE, AND LIDA V. NEDILSKY

Managing diversity is a modern enterprise. When a highly centralized state seeks to consolidate its rule it needs to mandate uniformity on some of its vast and diverse population, and to permit variety and difference on others. These needs for uniformity and variety are in tension with each other, and the state must strike a balance between them. The situation in China for the past few hundred years is no exception. The Chinese state has responded to a wide range of political, social, and economic pressures by constantly redefining the terms of citizenship. For example, demographic pressures of the seventeenth–nineteenth centuries forced imperial authorities to maintain unity and stability by labeling as social outcasts some highly mobile communities such as salt merchants, the Hakka, fishing communities, bandits, and pirates. As the Communist state came to power in 1949, it instituted a rigid system of control based on the Marxist ideology of "class" in order to manipulate the direction of social and geographic mobility. This powerful system of control contributed to nation- and state-building throughout the Maoist era (1949–1976). But faced with the challenges of industrialization and globalization in the late twentieth and early twenty-first centuries, the Chinese Communist state encountered new pressures for change, namely eroding mechanisms of state control, rising inequality, corruption, ethnic tensions, and emerging popular discontent in post-1997 Hong Kong. In March 2008 street riots in Tibet and adjoining provinces with significant Tibetan populations revealed starkly the difficulty in admitting an alternative to national unity in the People's Republic of China. The Chinese state has yet to formulate effective strategies for coping with the concerns of its differentiated groups of citizens, and to accommodate the divergent modes of recognition for citizens' rights.

While similar demographic, political, and economic pressures have helped sustain a decades-long debate about minority experience and identity politics in North America, Chinese polities have until recently been neglected in the discussion. A Chinese alternative to Western systems of recognition politics has yet to be articulated. How has membership worked in Chinese polities from the past to the present? What are the contemporary trends in defining political, social, and economic memberships in contemporary China? And how do these trends offer an alternative to similar conditions in today's world? *Marginalization in China: Recasting Minority Politics* addresses these questions by documenting persistent prejudices against marginal groups from late imperial China to the present, and the moral claims groups have mustered in response. Female farmers, religious faithful, migrant workers, and criminal elements have historically been marginalized by the Chinese state and society. Because their very existence questions the long-standing representations of productive, norm-observant, and loyal community members, they have been denied access to the institutions that have determined their life chances, including civil service examinations, urban residence permits, and inheritance rights. In those instances of recognition by the state, when marginal groups have attracted formal attention, attention has been fueled by the desire to control and recast their images.

How such groups came to constitute minorities in China is the focus of our discussion. Besides analyzing the state's policies over marginal groups, this book explores how over time the Chinese state responded to pressures from marginal groups by classifying the population into different social segments and providing graded terms of citizenship. As time passed, marginal groups gradually identified themselves as minorities, articulating demands for equal opportunity and compensation for past unequal treatment. Moreover, the groups internalized and refashioned state-imposed labels according to their own needs. Because moral and political judgments have undergirded the formation of minorities, this study seeks to highlight the processes by which marginal groups have been drawn into a Chinese-style politics of recognition—the call to stand up and be counted.

Why Do Minorities Matter?

The concept of minority is essential for understanding the accommodation of diversity in Chinese polities. Yet no single term for minority exists in the Chinese language, as will be demonstrated later in this chapter. This study uses the concept in both its theoretical forms, numeric and social, to underscore the dynamic claims-making process involved in giving the term "minority" its meaning. On the one hand, determining the relative number as deficient enables both the state and a particular marginal group to justify differential treatment. On the other hand, the minority's association with persistent marginality, especially its distance from political and economic power, serves to maintain tension between state and society, and between rival groups. Minority seldom refers to a group that is negligibly few. Under such circumstances a group finds it nearly impossible to assert its claim and to articulate its existence in society (Kymlicka, 1995; Kymlicka and He, eds., 2005). On the contrary, existence matters only when the group in question constitutes itself into a recognizable collective with a discernible identity, culture, and set of practices. This is particularly true when its common claims for rights potentially threaten the state's project of social and political integration.

Minority carries through both these meanings, numeric and social in combination, a particular conceptual significance. Minority implies being at once part of and alternative to society. It means living in common with other groups while maintaining national, ethnic, racial, linguistic, religious, gender, sexual, class, and other differences based on ascriptive ties. One is typically born into a preexisting group with an associated status. This means that minority can be understood as a fundamental and common capacity to fashion an alternative and specific identity. Consequently, status as a minority also implies a growing rigidity of group membership and group interest.

Yet ascribed status is only half the story. While the condition of difference may appear fundamental, inequality that results from state-imposed discrimination and labeling stands alongside social groups' actions to gain the attention and recognition of the state. The composition of minority—and with it the majority—is achieved, promoted and represented via political and cultural means (Gladney, ed., 1998b: 7). In other words, minority and majority are made through the everyday actions of living, struggling, striving people. Both are conscious choices vividly illustrated in the policy decisions of the Chinese state. Groups' demands for ending discrimination and improving social status are an additional, integral part of making minorities. Either through calls for equality of opportunity via a common and uniform term of citizenship or through calls for advantageous terms specific to a group, minorities make demands based on their conceptions of justice and desert.

Rights claims have come on the heels of dramatic shifts in the state's project to distribute among and unify official members of the populace. Their articulation has, moreover, emerged with the growing space for exploration of self-identity, expression of resistance, appeal for compensation, and basic urging for recognition made in moral terms (Taylor, 1989; Connolly, 1995; Gutmann, 2003). Technologies such as the Internet and cell phones have certainly facilitated the mechanics of self-expression as well as visibility of claims makers (McCaughey and Ayers, eds., 2003). Over time, certain bounded groups have come to be associated with specific issues of the economic, cultural, and religious minorities. Groups and their interests become rigid in our imaginations, bringing minority back to its ascribed rather than achieved status conception. While asking ourselves who we are may have brought us to see shared interests and to pursue justice, the pursuit of minority recognition is not just an interest-making process. Making minorities is equally an identity-making process. When demanding rights, minorities open the door to their own redefinition. Rather than just entrenching a neat, timeless identity, they risk with every entreaty calling into question their preexisting identity. Self-reflection, in turn, brings minority members back to what the philosopher Kwame Anthony Appiah (2005) calls the "ethics of identity," through which members judge what they are in their personal and political lives.

In the face of minority mobilization and action, managing and placating minorities through state policies is now a key to flourishing civil society and democracy on the domestic front, and to social harmony and political stability throughout the world (Keating and McGarry, eds., 2001; Connor, 1999). Global institutions actively push for common standards of administrative practice and classification. The United Nations, in which the People's Republic of China assumed a permanent seat from the Republic of China in 1971, and the World Bank, which it joined in 1980, promote the idea of minority rights alongside that of basic human rights (Foot, 2000). Nongovernmental organizations (NGOs) located within and extending beyond state boundaries, furthermore, facilitate the spread of global norms. This global action provides minorities with new room to maneuver in their struggle for formal recognition, autonomy, and even independence from the immediate control of the state. Such transnational activism can be seen in

Yuki Terazawa's account of Chinese survivors of wartime rape, Sharon R. Wesoky's analysis of women NGOs in China, and Lisa Fischler's study of women activists in Hong Kong.

Despite the dynamic and varied constitution of any given minority, state and global governing structures often take cultural difference as the basis for minority status and differential rights. Such an approach of fixing upon cultural practice can easily oversimplify and freeze the cultural reality (Wu, McQueen, and Yamamoto, eds., 1997). As shown in Wing-Kin Puk's study of social outcasts in late imperial China, Anouska Komlosy's examination of the Dai in Yunnan province, Siu-Keung Cheung's critique of the British colonial land rights in Hong Kong, and Kam-Yee Law and Kim-Ming Lee's survey of Malaysian-Chinese students' identity, it is clear that any formal recognition of minorities tends, for the sake of administrative convenience, to entrench cultural difference. By using rigid standards of measure and glossing over any internal diversity, the state is bound to reinforce inequality. This often leads to misrecognition and ghettoization, a situation described by Charles Taylor (1994: 75) as "imprisoning someone in a false, distorted and reduced mode of being." Rather than avoiding misrecognition, some scholars urge avoiding recognition altogether. Recognition of cultural difference as a general model of citizenship arguably works to the advantage of a new system of global control. This new system supports the multiplicity of difference not so much as a means of self-determination but as a way to fragment and thus manage society from a position of power outside the state (Hardt and Negri, 2004). These traps underscore for us once again the importance of looking at the dynamic process behind making minorities, and of appreciating its potential to tease our imagination and to seek an alternative to any of our preconceptions (Connolly, 1995: xv–xvi).

Why Study Minorities in China?

On the surface, China appears a homogeneous society. With the numerical and political dominance of ethnic Han Chinese in the People's Republic of China (92 percent), Taiwan (98 percent), Hong Kong (98 percent), Macao (95 percent), and Singapore (77 percent), managing diversity seems less a problem in Chinese polities than elsewhere. Perhaps for this reason it has taken scholars some time to consider pluralism and Chinese societies in the same breath. Exploring Chinese strategies of accommodating minorities as part of the state-building process, especially the competition among entrenched social groups for political inclusion and the Chinese practice of naming, counting and differentiating marginal groups, has been secondary to scholarly concern with the expansion of state power and changes in state-society relations (for exceptions, see Harrell, ed., 1995; Antony and Leonard, eds., 2002). As Dru Gladney argues (1998a), this oversight of China's minority (née ethnic) experience has come at a cost since minority studies can provide a lens through which to gauge the majority. But in China today, the powerful force of marketization, the rise of inequality, and the spread of neoliberalism have led to the outbreak of conflicts and the struggle for citizenship among people outside the political establishment.

In fact, diversity exists across Chinese polities. States with Chinese-majority populations have publicly acknowledged and institutionalized difference for the purpose of administrative control. This can be discerned in the Communist designation of fifty-five official minorities (*shaoshu minzu*) and five official religions along Stalinist modes of recognition, in the distinctions between native place central to self-identity and state-imposed ethnic labels that assume cultural difference (Faure and Siu, eds., 1995), in the differences among Mandarin-speaking citizens from outside provinces (*waishengren*), native-born Taiwanese-speaking citizens (*benshengren*) and aboriginals in Taiwan (Jordan, Morris, and Moskowitz, eds., 2004), as well as in Hong Kong, Macao, and Singapore's efforts to manage their postcolonial populations. Diversity is a highly politicized issue in these places, especially when globalization intensifies large-scale migration, cross-cultural exchange, and identity formation.

As there is growing appreciation for China's diversity, globalization and marketization pose new challenges to Chinese societies and any conception of uniformity. Not just ethnic minorities but marginal groups labeled and limited in ways resembling ethnicity constitute today's recognizable minorities. Neoliberalism promoted through economic interchange emphasizes distinguishing between the deserving and undeserving poor in terms of productivity, education, and entrepreneurial initiative. Hong Kong citizens, for example, regard the enterprising individual as the ideal citizen against whom others are measured (Ku and Pun, eds., 2004). In the People's Republic of China, even this enterprising ideal is graded as state and society differentiate between the entrepreneurial urbanite (*qianyi*) and the permanently floating population (*liudong renkou*) drawn to cities by the promise of work (Solinger, 1999).

The normative order of the day, whether in a Chinese or Anglo polity, appears to be that every person is an agent of his or her destiny. In reality, Aihwa Ong (2006) points out, where such an order is still in formation, where it exists as an exceptional idea or exceptions are made to this ideal, its application is uneven and inconsistent. Take, for example, the discourse of *suzhi*, or "embodied human quality." Ranking the relative quality of human beings might find reception among market-oriented students and professionals, writes Andrew Kipnis (2007), but it also echoes orientations to hierarchy, inequality, and authoritarianism sharply at odds with the liberal marketplace. Instead, *suzhi* resonates with systems of belief in China's recent and distant pasts. Likewise, disputing the loss of pensions in China's industrial rust belt and seeking legal redress against unpaid wages in today's booming sunbelt, Chinese laborers communicate their status in terms employed under socialism, namely the masses (*qunzhong*), as well as newer concepts, the weak and disadvantaged (*ruoshi qunti*) (Lee, 2007). The first term, *qunzhong*, suggests majority and the second term, *ruoshi qunti*, implies minority. But both these expressions convey the contemporary notions of marginalization and recourse under exploitation. Taken together, they indicate the inconsistency of appropriating the ideas of weakness and worthiness among Chinese citizens today.

China scholars have responded to contemporary conditions of structural change and citizen action by compiling several important collections on minority politics in Chinese societies. These studies reveal two analytical approaches. The first approach follows in the footsteps of an earlier generation of researchers, notably Elizabeth J. Perry, to examine social groups prominent in Communist Chinese experience but in the context of the transformation of China's market economy (Goldman and Perry, eds., 2002; Perry and Selden, eds., 2003). In *State and Society*, for instance, Peter Hays Gries and Stanley Rosen move beyond the conventional focus on what were under communism representatives of the working class to reveal how particular interests such as laborers, peasants, and military personnel themselves have experienced market transformation and anticipated questions of post-Communist import (Gries and Rosen, eds., 2004). The politics of class has morphed into competition among interest groups, where workers once automatically privileged by the state must now produce an active voice that their interests might be heard and their needs met. Their study documents the rising fortunes of some and the descent into poverty and violence for others.

The second approach compares the rise of identity politics in Western democracies with similar movements in Chinese society, as shown in the studies of Anges Ku and Ngai Pun (Ku and Pun, eds., 2004), as well as Scott Simon (Jordan, Morris, and Moskowitz, eds., 2004: 67–88). Ethnicity, gender, and sexual orientation serve as rallying points for recognition. Likewise informed by Western trends, recent Chinese neoliberal critiques place identity and citizenship issues squarely in the context of globalizing systems of calculation. Economic rationales that guide investment, production, and wealth accumulation are applied as standards in the political arena, shaping conceptions of good versus bad citizens.

Marginalization in China: Recasting Minority Politics, in contrast, brings together the interest-bearing with the identity-forming notions of minority that other scholars have studied separately. It does so, moreover, with the engaged, active Chinese state as well as citizen in mind. At the political level, it examines both the bureaucratic and cultural processes around the designation and politicization of minority groups in historical and contemporary China. At the grassroots level, it looks at minority formation through lived experiences and self-conceptions along class, gender, religious and ethnic lines, and the efforts of related minorities to appeal for the normalization of their status. Sensitive to the expansive private sphere as well as the role of international NGOs and cross-border exchange with Hong Kong post-1997, this collection argues that the constructed identities offer values alternative to the established political and social order, and directly challenge the state's claim to legitimacy and ideological control.

Chinese Minorities as Graded Terms of Citizenship

This collection of essays takes the Chinese state, through its policies of labeling and institutionalizing graded terms of citizenship, as a crucial component of making minorities. More so than the conventional focus on minority as an ethnic entity or on minority as a postsocialist invention, this state-centered perspective investigates the application of culturally and historically specific approaches to any conceptualization of inequality. In late imperial China, for instance, the government bureaucracy created minority status based on the state's judgment of a group's allegiance, authenticity, or contribution. Such state-imposed gradations were institutionalized as ascribed statuses. In Communist China, the state invented a complex system of differentiation to deal with the separate worlds of countryside (the realm of landlords, rich peasants, middle peasants, poor peasants, hired laborers) and city (the realm of capitalists, workers, hawkers, teachers, clerks). The state politicized these distinctions when it labeled people as revolutionary martyrs, revolutionary comrades, leftists, rightists, bad elements, and counterrevolutionaries. It further institutionalized this link between citizenship and stratification through its practice of distributing both opportunities and responsibilities among its citizens. Especially under Mao Zedong, graded citizenship was built through the centrality of decision making. Under the pretense of nation-building and socialist revolution, the state imposed the household registration system, the neighborhood surveillance system, and specific agricultural and industrial production quotas. The state had to rely on a bureaucratic mechanism of management burdened with minute attention to details in order to govern a diverse population.

Several studies of modern China throw light on the logic, practice, and consequence of this graded citizenship. As Sydney White (1998) notes, state policies have oscillated between emphasis on a unified nation and policies of affirmative action. But in both instances, the state's role in planning and distribution has yielded categories of ascription along with the usual quotas and supply channels.

Dorothy Solinger (1999) challenges Western conceptions of ascribed status by arguing that from the mid-twentieth to the early twenty-first century, the Chinese state deliberately maintained the hereditary status of peasants, and hardened the difference between countryside and city as well as between rural and urban dweller. Whether in Qing, Republican, or Communist China, the state created the systems of communal surveillance (*baojia*) and household registration (*hukou*) to check geographic mobility and to police its subjects. Under Communist rule, the system of household registration merged with state-imposed class status. It was also combined with a set of rigid policies designed to limit physical mobility to formal assignment only. This produced what Solinger calls "ethnic" labels binding country dwellers across China (27). The pairing of political label and resource distribution has considerably affected the life chances of Chinese minorities.

In *Competitive Comrades*, Susan Shirk (1982) examines the collapse of Chairman Mao's vision of cooperation across peoples and interests, and singles out the state's control over access to education as a key component of defining social and political distinction. In Mao's vision of "virtuocracy," where individuals are awarded future consumption opportunities, status, and power based on moral virtues of a political movement, "[every high school student] had to come to grips with his or her class label–if it was a liability, to compensate for it, if it was an asset, to take advantage of it" (76). Class labels helped Mao identify the enemies and allies of the state. In the 1960s, Mao pushed for an affirmative action policy channeling students of politically reliable classes into the university. As a result, the children of workers, peasants, cadres, soldiers, revolutionary martyrs, national minorities, and Overseas Chinese benefited from the state's support in the social mobility game. We might add that the children of capitalists, industrialists, counter-revolutionaries, and Christians suffered miserably. This ascriptive and behavioral definition of class was designed to promote state-sponsored mobility in a very narrow field of opportunity, where the alternative was physical relegation to the countryside. Thus, the Maoist state not only established graded citizenship among a large number of high school applicants for the university, but also maintained a sharp distinction between urban residents and rural folk in all life chances.

Lessons from these studies of Chinese citizenship show the limitations of understanding ascribed minority as the experience of inequality from birth associated with gender, ethnicity, or religion. Ascription of minority in China reveals starkly the state's agency. The Chinese state has till now made rural workers an ascribed—both inherited and fixed—status. Likewise through its power to limit access to the civil service examination, to higher education and to jobs in the prosperous coastal cities, the bureaucratic state has made birthplace itself an ascribed status. This state-imposed ascribed status is an important element in the making of minorities in China.

In addition, rights consciousness is another powerful element that gives rise to a minority. But to speak of "rights" in the Chinese context, argues Lin Chun (2006), is to ignore the lived reality. It refers to norms for which Chinese have articulated an alternative that may yet prove liberating in the face of continued, albeit "human rights," imperialism. The socialist legacy of "rightful claims" in China is mingled with a historically significant conception of popular mandate: equal pay for equal work, right to work, education and healthcare, and people's livelihood (*minsheng*). Others share in the view that the Chinese conceptualization of rights differs significantly from that of the West. As James D. Seymour (1985) explains, human rights encompasses freedom of information, legal equality, rights for the handicapped, right to sexual preference, right to mobility, right to family, freedom of religion, among many others. The language of rights in the West thus suggests some measure of equality already exists in citizens' imaginations. The contemporary Chinese state, in contrast, has enforced graded citizenship and preferential policies among the populace in the name of equality of collective rights, and so normalizing inequality.

But Ching Kwan Lee (2007) reminds us of Karl Marx's insights that the growth of rights consciousness among China's working class population has resulted from regular collective actions rather than common deprivation. Through collective actions, minorities can mobilize themselves and hold the community together and prevent it from falling apart. Therefore, rights consciousness can and does provide a lens through which to investigate the formation of minority identity and the minorities' strategies of mobilization and empowerment.

Case Studies in This Volume

Incorporating the fundamental lesson of philosopher Charles Taylor's "politics of recognition"—that state and society meet to define complex systems of membership—*Marginalization in China: Recasting Minority Politics* places state and grassroots efforts side by side to show negotiation of minority identity and rights. It singles out the politics of minority recognition as a key to understanding the growing awareness of political, social, and economic rights in China. Awareness of one's rights is as important as awareness of one's marginality, and these two processes together have constituted the integral parts of minority politics.

The concept of politics of recognition, through its close association with philosophical and political discussions of what is good and possible, lends itself to fierce academic critique. This study employs the concept to illustrate the competitive strategies that social minorities have used to empower themselves and gain legitimacy from the state. In Chinese polities the meeting of state and society in negotiating terms of citizenship has been ongoing from the late imperial period to the present. The lessons of E. P. Thompson (1964) are helpful in seeing this process as modern, part of the context of political and economic transition, and not just contemporary. Thus, this study emphasizes the "making" of minority, with a social location for any moral production process generated by state and social groups. It argues that the state and society engage beliefs, expectations, and norms in making demands of the other, and deciding matters of distribution and justice. Not only intellectuals (Goldman, 2005), moreover, but grassroots people push abstract ideals such as justice. The result of this negotiation is a sense of moral consciousness embracing the notion of collective good.

With an eye for this moral dimension, all the chapters in this book address the features of three interrelated processes: the construction of minority status, the response (typically resistance) to state-produced labels, and the lived experience of minority in China. The first feature concerns the making of minority as a distinct element in society. Throughout its modern history, the Chinese state has imposed rigid behavioral standards to marginalize certain social, economic, and ethnic groups. In the process, it developed an elaborate political mechanism to label, restrict access to resources, and reduce the threat of different groups to the established order. Social minorities, in turn, appropriated the state's rhetoric and its mechanisms of control to reconstitute themselves. The second element of the politics of recognition in China is the ongoing resistance against the implications of the state's labels. Social minorities develop competitive strategies to challenge the existing order created by the state, and wield resources, intended or unintended, in order to address the political, social, and economic pressures that limited their life chances in specific contexts. The third element of the politics of recognition has to do with how minorities' own understanding of their marginality shapes their lived experience. When struggling for recognition and the opportunity to legitimately define their life chances, social minorities confront state-imposed ideas of marginality's meaning. The push for political voice transforms what it is to be marginal in China today.

What is gained and lost in the course of battle? Clearly, China's diversity exists even as the state often masks it with a unified cultural face. But looking at the cultural production through individual cases raises the question: are we not all becoming minorities? That we experience our marginality in relation to others should not come as a surprise. But it has certain consequences. In a world of fragmentations, where it is not necessarily the state that can and does proffer recognition, we may find ourselves caught in a "citizenship gap," vulnerable to manipulation (Brysk and Shafir, eds., 2004; Hardt and Negri, 2004). At the same time, to offset this negative, we develop an awareness of, empathy for the other. Moreover, we ourselves create the circumstances where we are not bound except by our own terms. Increasingly we relate to the concept of minority.

Wing-Kin Puk reconceptualizes the civil service examination as an instrument of control rather than open access to officialdom. Puk points out that labeling "salt merchants," "Dan," and "Hakka" became a bureaucratic procedure in the complicated politics of resource competition in imperial Chinese local society. Only the well-established land settlers of specific localities, in contrast to these unsettled groups, were allowed to sit for the examination. Consequently, the seventeenth-century salt merchants, eighteenth-century fishing communities, and nineteenth-century Hakka continuously struggled for more seats in the civil service examination that promised a chance at merit-based mobility. They sought to transform their social status by integrating into the settled communities and ascending the "ladder of success."

Robert J. Antony looks at the struggle for recognition among the laboring poor in late imperial China. Antony argues that dramatic social and economic changes in late eighteenth and early nineteenth centuries sowed the seeds of intense class conflicts along the South China coast. Because of demographic pressure and shortage of resources, the laboring poor sought survival through banditry. The Chinese imperial state failed to address the root causes of social and economic grievances, but it developed a complicated and highly bureaucratic procedure to criminalize and discipline the poor. As a result, the poor village communities chose banditry as the predatory and protective strategy for survival.

In Maoist China, the state's policies regulating people's daily life were not received with a sense of relief. This was particularly true for the Christian minorities. Joseph Tse-Hei Lee reconstructs the historical experience of the Chaozhou-speaking Christians in Guangdong province, and shows that these Christians employed different survival strategies to avoid, bypass, and challenge the state's control over the local church organizations and religious activities. These strategies included using existing lineage networks to create highly diffused and autonomous religious communities, retreating to Christian villages in the countryside, proselytizing among the victims of Mao's socialist campaigns, and turning to overseas Chinese Christians for support.

Yuki Terazawa shares the stories of Chinese comfort women who survived the Anti-Japanese War in Shanxi province. According to Terazawa, these survivors of wartime rape endured stigma through physical segregation and economic marginalization in their home villages. But in the 1990s they ended many decades of silence, and came out to petition the Japanese government for public apology and compensation. Although the Chinese government remains indifferent to these victims' claims, control over the physical mobility of Chinese citizens has loosened during the era of reform. This has enabled war victims to network with transnational support groups and travel to Tokyo to give testimonies in Japanese courts.

By extending the historical perspectives on economic minorities shown in the studies by Wing-Kin Puk and Robert J. Antony, Ming Xia fixes upon the labeling of the underclass. For the underclass in China today, economic marginalization entails social and political marginalization as well. The unemployed or migrant laborer is the blind-floater and criminal, unrepresented in the political order. For some, the world of organized crime under the new political order may bring the windfall of cash and other riches that can buy legitimacy and a change of status. Yet, for the majority of the underclass, there is now even less leverage with which to claim political solutions to their destitution.

But for the Dai in Xishuangbanna, Yunnan province, the state's attempts to impose a compliant and accommodating identity on this widely recognized ethnic group are countered with the Dai's own efforts at identity claims-making. Anouska Komlosy explores the feminizing project from both sides—the local authorities' marketing campaigns to promote ethnic tourism and the Dai's use of feminine imagery to propagate an alternative notion of Dai culture. When dealing with a powerful and modernizing Chinese state, the Dai's strategies of resistance, which have both local people and land feminized, require compensation at least according to Dai moral sensibilities.

Within the context of an emerging market economy and inflow of global development dollars, NGOs such as *Nongjianü* (Rural Women) have been promoting identity formation and recognition among rural women since the 1990s. Sharon R. Wesoky draws out the distinctive ways state, NGO agents, and their clients come together in symbiotic fashion to constitute the moral character and ethical claims of today's rural women. The paradox is that these organizations neither promote an image of individual consumerism nor any post-Communist utopian solution to the economically marginal and undereducated female.

In contemporary Hong Kong, a former British colonial policy of recognizing land claims raises the question of long-standing misrecognition. The colonial policy in Hong Kong's New Territories only legitimated male villagers' claims to land ownership. Siu-Keung Cheung reconstructs the story of Deng A-Mei, a female indigenous villager, whose right to inherit her mother's land was not recognized by the Hong Kong government that succeeded the British. Deng A-Mei's launch of a legal challenge to the patriarchy established by the British has led to many years of court contestation. For Deng A-Mei it has neither brought recognition of person nor recognition of legal claims as a woman without sons.

International conferences set in postcolonial Hong Kong have provided opportunities for diverse NGOs to negotiate women's rights and livelihood entitlements. Political scientist Lisa Fischler documents how NGOs through a United Nations annual forum on women and a World Trade Organization protest employ varied constructions of gender to press for formal recognition of their moral claims. In Fischler's Hong Kong as in Wesoky's mainland China, evidence shows that despite limited response to these claims by legislators and state officials, discussions and struggles over rights shape informal recognition of women's marginal status by a broader public composed of both local and transnational audiences.

Among Hong Kong's religious minorities, return to Chinese sovereignty in 1997 has meant an invitation to participate in the new "Hong Kong people ruling Hong Kong" formula. Sending representatives to the committee that elects Hong Kong's chief executive, writes sociologist Lida V. Nedilsky, has proven a complicated issue where members negotiate and contest the terms of participation. Like the Chaozhou Christians in South China a half-century before, the focus of Joseph Tse-Hei Lee's study, Hong Kong religious minorities meet the co-optation of religious community with a measured response. While perceptions of costs and benefits to validating a postcolonial order influence how representatives are sent, such calculations alone do not suffice. The legacy of independent religious institutions from the colonial era has also shaped the terms of participation.

Kam-Yee Law and Kim-Ming Lee, in the final chapter, investigate the transnational dimension of identity negotiation between overseas Chinese and their mainland counterparts. By examining the construction of "Chinese" identity among a group of Malaysian-Chinese students at Jinan University in Guangzhou, Law and Lee show that Chinese authorities have long distinguished themselves with policies of nurturing patriotic sentiment and social networks among overseas Chinese communities. Despite continued efforts, and despite students' subjective claims to a strong Chinese identity, the Malaysian-Chinese studying at Jinan still find themselves, as other ethnic groups, "outsiders" in mainland China.

Politics of Recognition: Chinese-Style

Taken together, these case studies underscore two recurring and related themes. Consistent across the historic and the contemporary, the Chinese mainland and Hong Kong, movement and dialectic have both been involved in making minorities. Our cases represent a geographic bias toward Chinese coastal experiences that may explain for group sensitivity to inequality, both sparking contestation and affording resources to manage conflict. As demonstrated in the analyses of Wing-Kin Puk, Robert J. Antony, and Joseph Tse-Hei Lee, respectively, an outward orientation inspired by geography and physical mobility could compete with the pull of a highly bureaucratic state in dynastic and Maoist times. It afforded greater interaction with the wider world, the possibility of external interest, and the potential for external support. The Chinese state historically discouraged mobility for these very reasons. Yet the promise of a better economic and social future was enough to challenge the state-imposed geographical and social immobility. And when the bureaucratic intervention in daily life became a serious threat as shown in Joseph Tse-Hei Lee's account of Chaozhou Christians, reverse migration from the cities to the countryside was a coping mechanism against the Communist state.

Globalization today complicates these preexisting "Chinese" patterns of minority politics by adding further actors, pressures, and options. The contemporary underclass, as Ming Xia shows, is as much the result of inequality of opportunity caused by neoliberal economic reform as it is a matter of long-standing population flows and their moral backlash. Likewise, minority recognition for overseas Chinese at Jinan University, as addressed in Kam-Yee Law and Kim-Ming Lee's chapter, and recognition of religions through formal association in Hong Kong, as documented by Lida V. Nedilsky, refer back to the long-standing conception of difference based on transnationality. But today marginal groups have a new option to seek transnational solutions for the problems of inequality. Women especially, as Yuki Terazawa, Sharon R. Wesoky, and Lisa Fischler point out, find sympathetic collaborators among NGOs equipped to offer help from outside. As a result, every type of minority politics is local, national, and transnational.

This resort to transnational solutions points to a second, related theme of dialectic underscored by the prevalence of gender-specific cases of minority politics in China. As NGOs give voice to the voiceless, they reveal long-standing barriers for the subjectivity necessary to demand recognition. This creates the impression that after many decades of women's liberation in China, it is still impossible for rural women to articulate and organize in a way that is self-transformative. On the other hand, NGOs' mobilization and advocacy highlight the moral question of what is lost in feminine diversity by lumping together people around the concept of gender politics.

But Siu-Keung Cheung's account of Deng A-Mei's struggle for land rights in Hong Kong and Anouska Komlosy's work on the ethnic Dai women in Xishuangbanna point to other convergences of ideas that foment self-reflection and contestation. Cheung and Komlosy reject the politics of patriarchy and suggest an imaginary space for individual and group contestation. Their studies question the state's efforts at labeling and categorizing minorities, and reveal how much further state and society have to go in pursuit of justice. As captured so vividly in the person of Deng A-Mei, recognition is not a matter of resolving different voices and claims but a matter of appreciating difference itself. Added to the mix, argues Lisa Fischler, is the role of public awareness as a force influencing this dynamic process. Recognition politics is not the end of the process. It functions as a significant consideration in evaluating the making of minorities. Public and informal recognition may even be morally superior to formal recognition by the state, as it avoids essentializing group boundaries and claims, and sustains the continuing process of negotiation.

In the final analysis, this book highlights the experience of minorities in Chinese politics. Much as Aihwa Ong (2006: 22) underscores that inclusion of noncitizens in the human family is an ethical question we all live with in a globalized world, this book emphasizes that solidarity among minority-conscious people across national boundaries is a key ethical concern for a China seeking coexistence in this globalized world. Concerned as it has been with the movement of people and ideas so characteristic today, China may yet offer an alternative suited not only to its authoritarian sensibilities but one with wider appeal to other polities. State-initiated conceptions of minority open the door to engagement at all levels of governance as recognition is demonstrated at the intersection between state and society. Here, negotiated terms are expressed and challenged by people sharing a common context. What the following chapters show are the complexities, the political, economic and socio-cultural processes, and the logic of Chinese-style politics of recognition.

Bibliography

Antony, Robert J., and Jane Kate Leonard, eds. 2002. *Dragons, Tigers and Dogs: Qing Crisis Management and the Boundaries of State Power in Late Imperial China*. Ithaca, NY: East Asia Program, Cornell University.

Appiah, Kwame Anthony. 2005. *The Ethics of Identity*. Princeton, NJ: Princeton University Press.
Brysk, Alison, and Gershon Shafir, eds. 2004. *People Out of Place: Globalization, Human Rights, and the Citizenship Gap*. New York: Routledge.
Connolly, William E. 1995. *The Ethos of Pluralization*. Minneapolis, MN: University of Minnesota Press.
Connor, Walker. 1999. "National Self-Determination and Tomorrow's Political Map." In Alan Cairns, John C. Courtney, Peter Mackinnon, and Hans J. Michelmann, eds. *Citizenship, Diversity and Pluralism: Canadian and Comparative Perspectives*, 163–176. Montreal, Canada: McGill-Queen's University Press.
Faure, David, and Helen Siu, eds. 1995. *Down to Earth: The Territorial Bond in South China*. Stanford, CA: Stanford University Press.
Foot, Rosemary. 2000. *Rights beyond Borders: The Global Community and the Struggle over Human Rights in China*. Oxford: Oxford University Press.
Gladney, Dru C. 1998a. *Dislocating China: Muslims, Minorities and Other Subaltern Subjects*. Chicago, IL: University of Chicago Press.
———. ed. 1998b. *Making Majorities: Constituting the Nation in Japan, Korea, China, Malaysia, Fiji, Turkey, and the United States*. Stanford, CA: Stanford University Press.
Goldman, Merle, and Elizabeth J. Perry, eds. 2002. *Changing Meanings of Citizenship in Modern China*. Cambridge, MA: Harvard University Press.
Goldman, Merle. 2005. *From Comrade to Citizen: The Struggle for Political Rights in China*. Cambridge, MA: Harvard University Press.
Gries, Peter Hays, and Stanley Rosen, eds. 2004. *State and Society in 21st-Century China: Crisis, Contention, and Legitimation*. New York: Routledge.
Gutmann, Amy. 2003. *Identity in Democracy*. Princeton, NJ: Princeton University Press.
Hardt, Michael, and Antonio Negri. 2004. *Multitude: War and Democracy in the Age of Empire*. Cambridge, MA: Harvard University Press.
Harrell, Stevan, ed. 1995. *Cultural Encounters on China's Ethnic Frontiers*. Seattle, WA: University of Washington.
Jordan, David, Andrew Morris, and Marc Moskowitz, eds. 2004. *Minor Arts of Daily Life: Popular Culture in Taiwan*. Honolulu, HI: University of Hawai'i.
Keating, Michael, and John McGarry, eds. 2001. *Minority Nationalism and the Changing International Order*. Oxford: Oxford University Press.
Kipnis, Andrew. 2007. "Neoliberalism Reified: *Suzhi* Discourse and Tropes of Neoliberalism in the People's Republic of China." *Journal of the Royal Anthropological Institute* 13: 383–400.
Ku, Agnes, and Ngai Pun, eds. 2004. *Remaking Citizenship in Hong Kong: Community, Nation and the Global City*. New York: Routledge.
Kymlicka, Will. 1995. *Multicultural Citizenship: A Liberal Theory of Minority Rights*. Oxford: Oxford University Press.
Kymlicka, Will, and Baogang He, eds. 2005. *Multiculturalism in Asia*. Oxford: Oxford University Press.
Lee, Ching Kwan. 2007. *Against the Law: Labor Protests in China's Rustbelt and Sunbelt*. Berkeley, CA: University of California Press.
Lin, Chun. 2006. *The Transformation of Chinese Socialism*. Durham, NC: Duke University Press.
McCaughey, Martha, and Michael D. Ayers, eds. 2003. *Cyberactivism: Online Activism in Theory and Practice*. New York: Routledge.
Ong, Aihwa. 2006. *Neoliberalism as Exception: Mutations in Citizenship and Sovereignty*. Durham, NC: Duke University Press.
Perry, Elizabeth J., and Mark Selden, eds. 2003. *Chinese Society: Change, Conflict and Resistance*. New York: Routledge.

Seymour, James D. 1985. *China Rights Annals: Human Rights in the People's Republic of China from October 1983 through September 1984*. Armonk, NY: M. E. Sharpe.
Shirk, Susan. 1982. *Competitive Comrades: Career Incentives and Student Strategies in China*. Berkeley, CA: University of California Press.
Simon, Scott. 2004. "From Hidden Kingdom to Rainbow Community: The Making of Gay and Lesbian Identity in Taiwan." In David Jordan, Andrew Morris, and Marc Moskowitz, eds. *Minor Arts of Daily Life*, 67–88.
Solinger, Dorothy. 1999. *Contesting Citizenship in Urban China: Peasant Migrants, the State, and the Logic of the Market*. Berkeley, CA: University of California Press.
Taylor, Charles. 1989. *Sources of the Self: The Making of the Modern Identity*. Cambridge, MA: Harvard University Press.
———. 1994. "The Politics of Recognition." In Amy Gutmann, ed. *Multiculturalism: Examining the Politics of Recognition*, 25–73. Princeton, NJ: Princeton University Press.
Thompson, E. P. 1964. *The Making of the English Working Class*. New York: Pantheon Books.
White, Sydney D. 1998. "State Discourses, Minority Policies, and the Politics of Identity in the Lijiang Naxi People's Autonomous County." In William Safran, ed. *Nationalism and Ethnoregional Identities in China*, 9–27. Portland, OR: Frank Cass.
Wu, David Y. H., Humphrey McQueen, and Yamamoto Yasushi, eds. 1997. *Emerging Pluralism in Asia and the Pacific*. Hong Kong: Hong Kong Institute of Asia-Pacific Studies, Chinese University of Hong Kong.

CHAPTER TWO

Reaching out for the Ladder of Success: "Outsiders" and the Civil Examination in Late Imperial China

Wing-Kin Puk

Introduction

The civil examination was the most important ladder of success in late imperial China; passing the examination and earning a degree was a way to achieve status without being born to it. As might be expected, the examination, or series of examinations, was extremely rigorous, and competition was fierce. While in theory the examination was open to everyone, Ho Ping-Ti's monumental study showed that in fact it was not the case. During the Ming dynasty (1368–1644) 47.5 percent of the *jinshi*, the highest degree, went to candidates from families where no one, for three preceding generations, had possessed even the most elementary degree. By the Qing dynasty (1644–1911) this percentage had dropped to 19.1 (Ho, 1964: 107–125). The more limited their success rate, the more likely that participants from previously uneducated and marginalized groups were being excluded. In this case, how did marginalized social groups gain access to the ladder of success?

To answer the question, this chapter focuses on three social groups: migrant salt merchants in the city of Yangzhou in the seventeenth century, Hakka immigrants in Guangdong province in the nineteenth century, and the fishing people known as the Dan in coastal Guangdong in the eighteenth century. Salt merchants were the wealthiest people in China during the Ming and most of the Qing, the Dan were among the most underprivileged, and the Hakka fell somewhere in between. Despite radical socioeconomic differences, all three groups were regarded as outsiders against the backdrop of a more-or-less established community. Their existence created "awkwardness" for the government, which can be examined in the context of the imperial civil examination.

This chapter illustrates how the politics of minorities operated in late imperial China. It was the government's concern over social hierarchy, rather than any discourse on ethnicity or race, that created obstacles for all three groups. It was within the official Confucianist framework of ruler and subject that each of the three groups were permitted or denied access to the examination and the privileges of social mobility.

The Confucian Hierarchy and Social Mobility

Compared to continental Europe, late imperial China stood out as a unified polity with strong political authority and weak social stratification. The Chinese nobility were much fewer in number than their European counterparts and had little, if any, political power. The civil imperial examination opened the door of officialdom to *almost* everyone. By regarding this unique historical landscape as the working of Confucianism, one risks reifying Confucianism and simplifying the state-society relationship in late imperial China. Nevertheless, to understand the tensions between social mobility and hierarchy in late imperial China, it is necessary to address some of the key concepts and terminologies of Confucianism.

Confucius spoke of social hierarchy in terms of "rites" (*li*) (Hsü, 1932: 90–127; Fung, 1952: 66–75; Hall and Ames, 1987: 168–173). Based on their position in the network of social relations, people had roles and obligations to fulfill as they went about their daily rituals. Thus a son needed to show filial piety to his parents, a father, benevolence to his children, a minister, loyalty to his emperor, and so on. The central value regulating the behavior of people of all ranks was "benevolence" (*ren*), which was believed to be biologically inherent in everyone. Mencius, the early Confucianist philosopher, spoke of the sense of "compassion," of "shame," of "courtesy and modesty," and of "right and wrong" as being the germ of "benevolence," "dutifulness," "observance of the rites," and "wisdom," respectively. And "man has these four germs just as he has four limbs" (Lau, 1984: 67). A social order thus established is by no means egalitarian, but neither is it oppressive, because it assumes mutual obligation. Moreover, such a social order denies territorial or racial boundaries. Differences in ethnicity scarcely matter; what matters more is the willingness or readiness to be brought into the hierarchy. As *the Book of Odes*, one of the Confucian classics, puts it (Xu, 1993: 449),

> The land under the sky
> Is all the king's domain;
> The people far and nigh
> Are under royal reign.

The inherent weakness in this Confucianist ideal was the assumption of common benevolence in every human being. This assumption legitimized the social hierarchy but also immediately destabilized it. Whereas John Locke, who also believed in man's "natural" morality, refuted divine and absolute sovereignty, looking to consent or contract to both legitimize and limit government power, Confucianism took the political and social order of ruler and ruled for granted, but offered no easy answers to abuses of power. Confucius himself was dubious about what should be done if those at the top failed to honor the moral obligations of their position (Lau, 1983: 25, 137).

Three hundred years later, Mencius had no doubts. He advocated violent revolution against corrupt sovereigns, saying that immoral behavior had made their position forfeit. He endorsed killing such a ruler, saying that it was not killing an emperor, but putting to death "a despised creature" (de Bary, Chan, and Watson, eds., 1965: 97). Moreover, Mencius maintained that while any sovereign could be put to death for violating his moral obligation to those he ruled, any common, ordinary person could become a sage by following the sages' ways (Lau, 1984: 245). From Mencius in the fourth century BCE, to Lu Jiuyuan in the twelfth century, and Wang Yangming in the sixteenth century, this left-wing branch of traditional Confucianism never ran short of charismatic leaders and their devotees. But rulers themselves were bound to reject Mencius's solution; the founding emperor of the Ming, for example, was known to have stated with fury: "Had this old man been alive today, he should not have been spared!" (Rong, 1989: 171).

Consequently, when Confucian political theory finally materialized into polity, Mencius's destabilizing left-wing elements were castigated.

Confucius's ambiguity was turned into an explicit endorsement of the absolute power of the ruler as the son of heaven, as well as of the primary importance of maintaining a hierarchy of the ruler and the ruled, the respected (*zun*) and the low (*bei*). This is why, for all its fairness and openness, the civil examination system could become extremely hostile to "outsiders." Those who had the misfortune to be perceived as outside the hierarchy could also be considered "alien" or "base," and denied access to the civil examination entirely. To see how this occurred, we will take a brief look at how the examination worked.

The Imperial Civil Examination and Household Registration

Throughout the Ming and Qing dynasties, the imperial civil examination operated in more or less the same way, with three tiers of examinations that ran parallel with the government's administrative structure. The first step was for a boy to enroll in a local government school (girls were denied access to both the examination and to formal schooling), and then to pass the Annual Examination (*suishi*) and the Qualification Examination (*keshi*). This qualified a student to take the tri-annual Provincial Examination (*xiangshi*), which was held in various provincial capitals. If he passed this examination, he received the *juren* degree and was allowed to sit for the tri-annual Metropolitan Examination (*huishi*) in Beijing, the capital. If he passed this last examination, he received the highest degree (*jinshi*) and became a government official.

An extremely lucky and capable boy could go from being nobody to becoming a *jinshi* in four years, with a government appointment, and the attendant honor. But if he failed in either the Provincial or the Metropolitan Examination, he had a three-year wait, since these examinations were held only once every three years. It was extremely common for a student to spend more than "ten years under a cold window," as the Chinese saying goes, preparing for the imperial examination, and even then, very few students passed it.

The difficulty of the examination was one matter, access to it was another. While the imperial civil examination was a series of extremely rigorous competitions, its entry point was the county or prefecture government school. It was here that those who were labeled by the state as "outsiders" ran into trouble. The imperial civil examination was closely tied to household registration (*huji*). Household registration was the Ming government's major mechanism of social control. It was designed to keep people in their place, both literally and figuratively. Families were registered under occupational and territorial categories that were supposed to remain fixed. While the occupational registration assigned taxes as well as the family's work, the territorial registration provided legitimate access to a local government school. A child from a family registered as a civilian household in District X would have access to the government school in that district. Access was still neither easy nor automatic, since he had to take a series of examinations before being enrolled. But for those who had settled in District X and were registered elsewhere (i.e., the "outsiders"), access to the government school was next to impossible. By incorporating the civil examination system with the household registration system, the government tied down individuals with administrative and occupational bonds, while granting or denying them access to the ladder of success.

Salt Merchants in the Ming Period: Migration and the Examination

Zhu Yuanzhang, founder of the Ming dynasty, mistrusted the market and was contemptuous of merchants, but he did not completely ban their movement from place to place. According to a decree in 1386, traveling merchants had to possess valid transit passes and at least 10,000 copper cash (Shen, ed., 1989: 350). Once merchants were allowed to move around, it was nearly impossible to keep them from migrating. The household registration system showed that people did settle in places other than their registered hometowns. Such migration, known variably as "claimed registration," "lodged registration," or "attached registration," was permitted by Ming law, as can be seen in a decree in 1451 and another one in 1501 (854, 859).

Ironically, registration of the living began with the burial of the dead. Once migrants (merchants or not) had settled outside their registered hometowns to marry, bear children, and die there, their graves became physical evidence of the legitimacy of their children's settlement. In Yangzhou, in 1531, Zhu Tingli, the Lianghuai Salt-control Censor, issued a placard to "sojourning" salt merchants over their funerals, which Zhu saw as inappropriate. Funerals for the wealthy tended to be lavish, for everyone else they tended to be cursory, and both burial styles went against the Confucian notion of a proper rite. Zhu allowed six months for deceased salt merchants to be sent back to their registered hometowns for burial; but then he allowed them to be buried in

Yangzhou as long as the funeral was conducted appropriately and without undue ostentation (Zhu, 1821: 17a–17b). Zhu Tingli's ambivalent order in 1531 marked the first step toward the official recognition of salt merchants' settlement in Yangzhou.

In 1567, when the emperor sent Pang Shangpeng to Yangzhou to reform the salt administration, Pang noticed that hundreds of "sojourning" salt merchant families had been settled in Yangzhou for generations (Pang, 1995: 129, 140):

> As for merchants from various provinces who claim registration locally, their families number by the hundreds. Their ancestors' graves climb the hills. They have spent several generations here, raised children and grandchildren, and have become Yang[zhou] people.

Although Pang Shangpeng still categorized salt merchants as sojourners who only had "claimed registration," he admitted that they were "Yang[zhou] people" and even suggested that a school be established and an examination quota reserved for their descendants. Unfortunately for the merchants, Pang Shangpeng's suggestion was not implemented. The Ming government would allow migrants to settle and be buried outside their registered hometowns, but denied their children access to schools in their "new" hometowns.

While household registration left a tiny legal crack for those who had relocated in the form of "claiming registration," the law on the imperial civil examination was more rigid. Examinees had to take each level of the examination in the seats of their registered county, prefecture, and province. Sitting for the examination in places other than one's registered place of origin was known as "falsifying registration" (*maoji*), and this was prohibited. For the Shanxi merchants in Yangzhou, such a policy, if enforced, would mean they had to travel hundreds of kilometers, back to Shanxi province, to sit for the examination, even though they might have been settled in Yangzhou for generations.

The regulation against "falsifying registration" was by no means toothless, and "sojourning" examinees were always at the mercy of officials' temper. Even with claimed registration, access to the examination was by no means certain. An excerpt from Xie Zhaozhe's writing illuminates the problem (Xie, ed., 1995: 499).

> The government recruits the literati through examination. From district and prefectural examination to provincial examination, the

ban on falsifying registration is applied, (even though it) is rather meaningless... In Linqing prefecture of Shandong province, nine-tenths [of the examinees] are Huizhou merchants with claimed registration... Last year a Provincial Education Commissioner tried hard to drive them out, to the extent that some of them were banned from sitting for the examination even though their grandfathers and fathers had acquired the *juren* degree in Shandong. This is really laughable. I was then serving in Linqing prefecture, and only with my strong opposition was this ban lifted.

While the insecurity of the situation for those with claimed registration persisted throughout the Ming and Qing periods, Shanxi merchants in Yangzhou were able to overcome it (Zhao et al., eds., 1976: 3480; Xie, ed., 1966: 1201–1202). During the Ming they acquired a quota known as the merchant registration (*shangji*). Huizhou merchants in Yangzhou, however, could not acquire a similar quota.

At least three circumstances might account for the Shanxi merchants' success and the Huizhou merchants' failure. First, in Hedong, the salt depot in Shanxi province, salt merchants had already established a special school and had a reserved quota for the civil examination. No such precedent existed in Huizhou. Second, Shanxi was farther from Yangzhou than Huizhou, which meant travel problems would be greater for Shanxi merchants' descendants. Third, and most importantly, Yangzhou and Huizhou both belonged administratively to the Southern Metropolitan Area, while Shanxi was not even a neighboring province. Because of this geographical issue, it was absurd to expect a student of Shanxi origin to travel across three provinces in order to take the examination. Although Huizhou and Yangzhou were two weeks apart in travel time, the government had no problem with this; and at least it made sense administratively.

The Huizhou salt merchants in Yangzhou did not submit quietly; they campaigned for their own school, and therefore an entry quota in the imperial civil examination. Their campaign began in the 1630s, but had little success until the downfall of the Ming dynasty (Xie, ed., 1966: 1202). Unsurprisingly, their campaign was strongly opposed by Shanxi and Shaanxi merchants, who did not want the competition. Lei Shijun, a member of the literati and a native of Jingyang in Shaanxi province, provided a detailed account of the Huizhou merchants' campaign in an essay that, although mild in tone and elegant in style, revealed his entrenched opposition to it (Xie, ed., 1966: 2041–2050).

According to Lei's essay, written in the 1620s, the Huizhou merchants nearly succeeded: the emperor had granted them permission for a school and a quota when the Salt Distribution Commissioner who had sympathized with their cause was transferred. The new Yangzhou Prefect, being himself a native of Shaanxi province, opposed the plan and the Huizhou merchants' cause was lost. Lei admitted that it was unfair for descendants of Shanxi and Shaanxi merchants to sit for the imperial civil examination in Yangzhou while descendants of Huizhou merchants had to travel all the way to Huizhou. Losing ground on the principle behind the decision, Lei stressed the financial difficulties: establishing a new school would cost the government tens of thousands of taels, an unaffordable burden. Instead of building another school, Lei suggested that the enrollment quota of the Yangzhou Prefecture School be increased, creating a new quota for the Huizhou merchants. This proposal would cost a few thousand taels, only a few taels for every salt merchant involved. Before this suggestion could be considered, war broke out with the Manchu armies. The Ming dynasty fell and the Manchu soldiers devastated Yangzhou in the notorious "ten days' massacre." Not until the early eighteenth century did the Huizhou merchants finally gain access to the imperial civil examination in Yangzhou.

The Hakka in Guangdong:
"Guest People" and the Examination

From 1661 to 1669, coastal Guangdong was a forbidden zone because of the Qing government's campaign against Zheng Chenggong's naval force in Taiwan. In 1669 the ban was lifted and the Qing government encouraged migration to the now depopulated coast. In Xin'an district where Hong Kong and Shenzhen are located today, "Guest people (kemin) from Jiangxi and Fujian provinces or from the prefectures of Huizhou, Chaozhou and Jiaying in Guangdong gradually came. They subscribed for military land and purchased civilian property" (Wang and Shu, eds., 2003: 833).

In this climate of massive migration, chaotic registration of land and population, and bankrupt local government, the Hakka or "guest people" came into being. By 1819, when the second gazetteer of Xin'an district was published, about 570 "local" and 270 "guest" villages were mentioned (Wang and Shu, eds., 2003: 751). The administrative labels tell us little about the genuine ethnic composition, cultural differences, and linguistic demarcation of these villages. The Hakka themselves might be from anywhere; the label only denoted their status as newcomers. But as far as the civil examination was concerned, the labels were very specific: local boys had access to the government school and Hakka boys did not.

Following the nationwide practice, the government school in Xin'an district offered initial examination for its newly enrolled students. The first twenty students with high scores were granted scholarship and became Scholarship Students (*linshansheng*), the next twenty became Added Students (*zengguangsheng*). A quota of eight was reserved for both groups in the Annual and Qualification Examinations, respectively; and in 1737, the quota was further increased to eleven, respectively (Wang and Shu, eds., 2003: 831–832). Meanwhile Hakka boys were still barred from attending the government school. They were still supposed to be educated in their registered hometowns and to take their examinations in their registered provinces.

The Qing government soon realized that this policy was unreasonable and unfair for the Hakka, but the remedy was too little, too late. In 1716, nearly five decades after the lifting of the coastal ban, Hakka boys all over the country finally got their quotas in each district: two civil and two military students, or four in all, in the Annual Examination, and two civil students in the Qualification Examination. Although smaller than the quotas of eight students for local students in the two Examinations, the Hakka quota represented significant progress as far as access to social mobility for the immigrants was concerned. In 1735, however, the Hakka quota was canceled. It was to take nearly seven decades before the Hakka quota was resumed in 1802 (Wang and Shu, eds., 2003: 833).

The 1802 decree allowed students of Hakka origin to enroll in the Guangzhou Prefecture government school. Although it was not clear how many Hakka students were admitted, a quota of two was reserved for them in the Annual and Qualification Examinations. Beginning in 1802, in every tri-annual Guangdong Provincial Examination, twenty-six local students (thirteen with scholarships and thirteen without) and two Hakka students from Xin'an district would have the chance to try their luck. Locals enjoyed more privileges than Hakka, with a quota ratio of 13:1. Considering that the ratio of local to Hakka villages was 2.2:1, the quota is even more unfair; not to mention that Hakka students from Xin'an were still denied access to the district government school and had to go to Guangzhou for schooling. Nevertheless, the 1802 decree must be seen as a great victory for the "guest" people of

Xin'an in that they had gained a limited access to the civil examination (Wang and Shu, eds., 2003: 833).

The Xin'an district gazetteer tells us nothing about how this victory was achieved, but Chan Wing-Hoi (2007: 25–45) asserts that it was the result of persistent lobbying by the Hakka in Xin'an. Liang Degong, leader of the Hakka community, repeatedly petitioned the government to create a quota for them. After the 1802 decree, Hakka in Xin'an established a lodge for their students in Guangzhou, known as the Common Virtue Examination Lodge (*Tongde shiguan*). As its name suggests, the Lodge was created for Hakka students who visited Guangzhou for both study and examination. The Hakka leaders in Xin'an were clearly aware of the potential return to this investment in education and human resources.

The Fishing People in Guangdong: Outcasts and the Examination

The Dan or fishing people of Guangdong were one of the most underprivileged groups in late imperial China; as such they have long been of interest to anthropologists and historians. Recently Helen Siu and Liu Zhiwei have studied their history in the Pearl River Delta in the context of state-making and social formation from the fourteenth century on. Their research shows that ethnic labels were created and an ethnic hierarchy was formed with the Dan at the bottom (Crossley, Siu, and Sutton, eds., 2005: 285–310). Anders Hansson (1996: 107–132) also devotes a section to the Dan in his study of Chinese outcasts. Drawing on their insights, the following analysis focuses on the Dan's access to the civil examination.

Throughout the Qing dynasty, the Dan became a target of social discrimination and economic exploitation. As late as the 1940s, fishing people on Cheung Chau Island of Hong Kong were subjected to public humiliation because of their "strange" accent, darker skin, and bare feet (Faure and Siu, eds., 1995: 105). The Dan were particularly vulnerable because of their poverty and the nature of their work: fish were bulky to store and rotted quickly unless one had access to the wholesale market to sell them or could afford the salt to preserve them. Compared with the local settlers, the Dan had no margin for bargaining with wholesalers. Even in the 1960s, fishing people in Hong Kong routinely fell prey to wholesalers' usury (Anderson, 1981: 77–78). The discrimination against Hakka people and salt merchants was certainly unfair, but it was nothing compared to how the Dan people were treated in the Qing era: they were not even allowed to live on land and they were forced to reside on their boats (Jing, 1993: 218–228, 233–236; Hansson, 1996: 107–132).

The plight of the fishing people even caught the sympathy of the emperor. In 1729, Qing Emperor Yongzheng decreed:

> The Guangdong people regard the Dan as base and low lots, and do not allow them to live on land. The Dan also dare not confront the local people, fearing their power, enduring in silence, crowding on their boats, and never enjoying the happiness of peaceful settlement throughout their lives. They deserve sympathy... those [Dan] who are capable of building houses or sheds on land should be allowed to live in villages near the shore and be registered together with the local people so that they can be easily monitored. Under no pretext should they be bullied or driven out by powerful local scoundrels. (Qing government, 1978: 1249)

It was only until 1729 that the fishing people were permitted to live on land and to be registered as commoners. Their access to schooling and the civil examination would also have begun then. Since most Dan barely made ends meet, legitimate access to schooling and the examination had no practical meaning for them. In any case, such access was lost about forty years later. In 1771 the government drew up new regulations, making it more difficult for previous outclasses to take the civil examination. The policy was based on Shaanxi Education Commissioner Liu Zun's memorial:

> The musician people in Shanxi and Shaanxi, the beggar people in Zhejiang... must wait for four generations after they have reported to the government renouncing their occupations, and during which time their own branches and their relatives must have no criminal record, before they will be allowed to purchase official titles or to take the civil examination.... The fishing people in Guangdong and the fishing people of the nine surnames in Zhejiang, and all other similar people in various provinces must be dealt with in the same vein. (Suerna et al., eds., 1995: 691)

If those who renounced a low-status occupation would be forced to live with its disadvantages for four generations to come, then a change in occupation was better kept a secret. The 1771 regulation officially denied the Dan people access to local schooling.

Hierarchy versus Universalism

In a forty-two-year period, the Dan were granted the right to live on land, and then denied access to the civil examination. Was Emperor Yongzheng benevolent or was his son Qianlong exceptionally harsh? Anders Hansson argues that Emperor Yongzheng did not perceive the Dan as shameful and "unclean" (1996: 127–128). Interestingly enough, Yongzheng was not known for his benevolence. In fact, his hatred and persecution of political rivals had made him notorious. For instance, he had decreed that two of his brothers, who had been his rivals for the throne, be renamed; thereafter his defeated brothers were addressed in the denigrating terms he had chosen for them (Zhao et al., eds., 1976: 316–317; Shen, 1997: 90–96). According to William Rowe, Emperor Yongzheng knew only too well that such behavior scandalized his subjects. Whenever possible, he was eager to publicize his benevolent acts. Moreover, in 1730, alarmed by the anti-Manchu rhetoric shown in Lü Liuliang's attempt to talk one of his military generals into rebellion, Emperor Yongzheng launched an extensive propaganda campaign to play down ethnic differences between Manchu and Han. He also invoked tailor-made Confucian classics to bolster the legitimacy of his Manchu government (Rowe, 2001: 294). As seen from this perspective, one can argue that if the Manchu rulers were no longer seen as "barbarians," other outsiders deserved better treatment. Against this political background, the Dan became the unexpected beneficiaries of Yongzheng's propaganda campaign.

Emperor Qianlong, on the other hand, was more relaxed and confident than his father Yongzheng. The eighteenth century was the zenith of the Qing empire. But economic prosperity not only added to the grandeur of the empire, it eroded the established social hierarchy. Even the most open-minded ministers valued hierarchy over fairness. William Rowe notes that Chen Hongmou, the eighteenth-century Chinese official famous for his pursuit of "statecraft" and "social management," emphasized the "heavenly goodness" (*tianliang*) of humanity, a concept derived from Mencius and discussed earlier, as the foundation of his social engineering project. Rowe objects to Susan Mann's argument that Chen Hongmou was among those who tried to arrest social mobility in order to halt its erosion of hierarchy. But Rowe admits that there existed "a variety of possible elements of rank-consciousness" in Chen's political thinking. Rowe sees in Chen "an awkward combination of quasi-egalitarian Confucian universalism with a frank recognition that status distinctions do exist in fact and are even, when properly regulated, of potential social utility" (Rowe, 2001: 2–3, 291, 293, 297).

Maintaining social hierarchy took precedence over empowering marginalized groups. While Chen Hongmou was not the architect of the government policy of restricting access to the civil examination to people from previous outclasses, he would probably have supported this plan. Maintaining the hierarchy of the ruler and the ruled, of the respected and the low, was a common principle upheld by the late imperial Chinese government. Mencius's moral universalism and egalitarian thinking, the fault line running through the Confucian social hierarchy, was carefully cemented over during the Qing. In the process, without employing the vocabularies of race and ethnicity, the imperial Chinese government created administrative labels for marginalized groups and drove them away from the ladder of success.

Bibliography

Anderson, Eugene. 1981. *The Floating World of Castle Peak Bay*. Ann Arbor, MI: University Microfilms International.

de Bary, Wm. Theodore, Wing-Tsit Chan, and Burton Watson, eds. 1965. *Sources of Chinese Tradition*, vol. 1. New York: Columbia University Press.

Chan, Wing-Hoi. 2007. "Zuowei zhongguo guozu shiye de kejia yanshuo: Cong xianggang kan jindai kejia wenhua rentong xingzhi de bianqian" (The discourse of Hakka as part of the project of the Chinese nation). In Lau Yee-Cheung, ed. *Xianggang kejia* (The Hakkas of Hong Kong), 25–45. Guilin: Guangxi shifan daxue chubanshe.

Crossley, Pamela, Helen F. Siu, and Donald S. Sutton, eds. 2005. *Empire at the Margins: Culture, Ethnicity, and Frontier in Early Modern China*. Berkeley, CA: University of California Press.

Faure, David, and Helen F. Siu, eds. 1995. *Down to Earth*. Stanford, CA: Stanford University Press.

Fung, Yu-Lan. 1952. *History of Chinese Philosophy*, vol. 1. Princeton, NJ: Princeton University Press.

Hall, David, and Roger Ames. 1987. *Thinking through Confucius*. Albany, NY: State University of New York Press.

Hansson, Anders. 1996. *Chinese Outcasts: Discrimination and Emancipation in Late Imperial China*. Leiden: E. J. Brill.

Ho, Ping-Ti. 1964. *The Ladder of Success in Imperial China: Aspect of Social Mobility, 1368–1911*. New York: John Wiley and Sons.

Hsü, Leonard Shihlien. 1932. *The Political Philosophy of Confucianism*. London: Curzon Press.

Jing, Junjian. 1993. *Qingdai shehui de jianmin dengji* (The hierarchy of the "base" people in the Qing society). Hangzhou: Zhejiang renmin chubanshe.

Lau, D. C. trans. 1983. *The Analects (Lun yü)*. Hong Kong: Chinese University Press.
———. trans. 1984. *Mencius*, vol. 1. Hong Kong: Chinese University Press.
Pang, Shangpeng. 1995. *Baiketing zaigao* (An excerpt from the Pavilion of Hundred Compromise). 1599 edition, in *Siku quanshu cunmu congshu* (Books' titles recorded in the complete books of the four imperial repositories), vol. 129. Liuyingxiang, Tainan: Zhuangyan wenhua shiye.
Qing government. 1978. *Daqing shizong xian huangdi shilu* (The veritable records of Emperor Shizong of the great Qing). Reprint. Taipei: Xinwenfeng.
Rong, Zhaozu. 1989. *Rong zhaozu ji* (The collected works of Rong Zhaozu). Jinan: Qilu shushe.
Rowe, William. 2001. *Saving the World: Chen Hongmou and Elite Consciousness in Eighteenth-Century China*. Stanford, CA: Stanford University Press.
Shen, Shixing, ed. 1989. *Daming huidian* (Compendium of the great Ming). Reprint of 1587 edition. Yangzhou: Jiangsu guangling guji keyinshe.
Shen, Yuan. 1997. "'Aqina,' 'saisihei' kaoshi" (A study of the terms "Aqina" and "saisihei"). *Qingshi yanjiu* (Studies in Qing history), no. 1: 90–96.
Suerna, Yonggui, Wang Jihua, Cai Xin, Defu, and Suolin eds. 1995. "*Qinding xuezheng quanshu*" (Imperially endorsed compendium of educational administration). Reprint of 1774 edition. In *Xuxiu siku quanshu* (Extended books of the four imperial repositories), vol. 828. Shanghai: Shanghai guji chubanshe.
Wang, Chongxi, and Shu Maoguan, eds. 2003. "*Jiaqing xin'an xianzhi*" (The Jiaqing gazetteer of Xin'an). Reprint of 1819 edition. In *Zhongguo difangzhi jicheng guangdong fuxianzhi ji* (Comprehensive collection of Chinese gazetteers: Guangdong), vol. 18. Shanghai: Shanghai shudian; Chengdu: Bashu shudian; Nanjing: Jiangsu guji chubanshe.
Xie, Kaichong, ed. 1966. *Kangxi lianghuai yanfazhi* (The gazetteer of salt administration of Lianghuai during Kangxi's Reign). Reprint of 1694 edition. Taipei: Taiwan xuesheng shuju.
Xie, Zhaozhe, ed. 1995. *Lidai biji xiaoshuo jicheng mingdai biji xiaoshuo* (Comprehensive collections of notes and novels of various dynasties: Ming Dynasty), vol. 55. Shijiazhuang: Hebei jiaoyu chunbanshe.
Xu, Yuanchong, trans., Jiang, Shengzhang, ed. 1993. *Shijing* (The book of Odes). Changsha: Hunan chubanshe.
Zhao, Erxun, Ke Shaomin, Yu Shimei, Wang Shujian, Guo Zengxin, and Li Jiaju, eds. 1976. *Qingshigao* (The drafts of the Qing history). Beijing: Zhonghua shuju.
Zhu, Tingli. 1821. *Liangyaji* (The collected works of Liangya). Reprint of 1821 edition.

CHAPTER THREE

Banditry, Marginality, and Survival among the Laboring Poor in Late Imperial South China

ROBERT J. ANTONY

Introduction

In the early 1830s the provincial judge of Guangdong issued a proclamation concerning the problem of banditry in the province. In part his proclamation read:

> In Guangdong province, the law against bandits is very severe. In cases of a general pardon from the throne, those who have robbed in bands are not included. If a bandit has escaped three years, and plundered three times, he is executed immediately after conviction, and his head suspended in a cage. This is not the mode of treating banditti in any other province. Here the law is not only severe, but the exertions of the police to seize offenders are strenuous. (*Chinese Repository*, April 1836)

In the late imperial era Guangdong province had a much-deserved reputation for violence and banditry. Officials throughout the eighteenth and early nineteenth centuries repeatedly complained that banditry was greater in Guangdong than elsewhere in the empire, and therefore they constantly insisted that special laws were needed to control the unruliness in the province. In this chapter I want to address two important questions: who became bandits and how did officials respond to banditry. After a brief discussion of the sources used in this study, I examine the problem of banditry within the context of the socioeconomic changes over the eighteenth and early nineteenth centuries. Next, I briefly look at the Qing state's reaction to banditry, particularly the central government's promulgation of harsh new laws to control banditry in Guangdong.

Sources and Evidence

This study draws on a large body of both primary and secondary historical materials. The central core of evidence is based mostly on the criminal case records found in the Qing imperial archives, which today are housed in Beijing at the First Historical Archives and in Taibei at the National Palace Museum and at Academia Sinica. The main body of evidence used in this study is derived from approximately 550 palace memorials (*zouzhe*), 780 routine memorials (*tiben*), 200 imperial edicts (*shangyu*), and 250 miscellaneous archival legal records (Park and Antony, 1993: 93–137). These sources cover the years from 1760 to 1845 and focus on Guangdong province. Besides these archival sources I have consulted the relevant local gazetteers, the *Veritable Records*, the *Statutes and Precedents of the Qing Dynasty*, the *Conspectus of Penal Cases*, as well as other Qing legal treatises and various contemporary Western accounts found in journals and books. From these sources I have arranged a dataset of roughly 2,000 cases, which comprises vital information on convicted bandits.

For the study of crime and law enforcement in Qing dynasty Guangdong, the most important sources are the criminal case records contained in the palace and routine memorial collections. These memorials shed much new light on the conditions in local society and the daily lives of ordinary people. In particular, much of the information about the poor, the illiterate, and those labeled as misfits in society—exactly those individuals most likely to have become involved in banditry—cannot be gained elsewhere. As official reports these documents also detail government reactions to crime and lawlessness in Guangdong. In particular, the routine memorials, which include the summaries or sometimes complete depositions of suspects and witnesses, provide us not only with detailed descriptions of the actual crimes but also of the individuals and circumstances involved—the names and provenance of victims, the types and values of stolen property, reports of any injuries or deaths, as well as the names of arrested suspects, their age, sex, place of residence, occupations, and marital status. Such ethnographic information is invaluable to the social and legal historian (Antony, 1988: 15–22; Ownby, 1996: 22–24).

Useful as these archival records are, nonetheless, they are problematical. China's literate elite produced the bulk of written materials in the traditional era, and as formal writings the court records were written by and for the scholar-officials themselves. To say the least, these sources are biased. Adding to the problem, the judicial cases are prosecution records and have obvious limitations. One important problem is that crimes are legally defined and categorized by the state and reflect the concerns of officials at a particular time. Also, only a small fraction of the total number of crimes ever appeared in official court records, and there was always a presumably larger "dark figure" of unreported or undetected cases. These so-called dark figures make all criminal statistics, both today and in the past, a sample. Nonetheless, they do reveal important social relationships and attitudes, as well as trends in criminality when studied over a long period of time. This is exactly what is important in historical studies. For historians, according to Bronislaw Geremek (1987: 10), "it is more important, or more realistic, to reveal internal relationships, and to study changes in the frequency of different types of crime or in the severity of their repression, than to establish definitive figures." Although biased and problematical, nonetheless, the archival records are the most important materials for historians seeking to learn about society and crime in China's late imperial age.

The Problem of Banditry

The problem of banditry was in large measure the product of tensions and contradictions arising from the concomitant processes of commercial growth and population explosion over the eighteenth and early nineteenth centuries. I begin my study in the period called the High Qing—a time when many Chinese believed that they were living in the best of all possible worlds—and I end my study with China's defeat in the Opium War. This was a time of profound change, transformations, and contradictions. As China's population more than doubled from 150 million in the late seventeenth century to over 400 million by the mid-nineteenth century, demographic changes produced an age of great opportunities and great anxieties. Rather than creating a Malthusian crisis, the population explosion helped stimulate a commercial revolution. In fact, the conditions in China actually compared favorably to those in Western Europe at about the same time (Marks, 1998; Buoye, 2000; Lin 2006; Pomeranz, 2000; Wong, 1997).

Nevertheless, the material benefits of this "prosperous age," referring to the years from 1780 to 1810, were unevenly distributed. Despite a flourishing economy, for China's laboring poor population pressure intensified competition for jobs and kept wages low.[1] For them the rising standards of living meant higher costs of living. What may have been an age of prosperity for some people was for others an age of hardship and privation. Over this whole period many areas of China witnessed the weakening of the traditional family system, massive unemployment and especially underemployment, and the concomitant development of a huge floating population of itinerant wage laborers, porters, peddlers, and vagabonds. What began as an age of peace and prosperity gradually deteriorated into an age of intense competition, restlessness, and turmoil.

The situation progressively worsened over the course of the early nineteenth century. The population, in many areas, reached a saturation point and the economy entered a period of stagnation and then full-scale recession by the 1820s and 1830s. Naturally, those people at the lowest rungs of the social ladder—namely the working poor—were the most adversely affected by the demographic and economic changes. Several historians have pointed out that banditry swelled in South China as a result of the economic recession as well as an unusually large number of natural disasters beginning in the 1820s (Lin, 2006: 115–146). As early as 1816, the Qing scholar-official, Gong Zizhen, warned that the unequal distribution of wealth had developed to such an extent that the resulting social disorders threatened the very existence of the state (Lin, 2006: 212).

This chapter argues that banditry was a strategy of resistance and survival among Guangdong's laboring poor. The archival cases show four things: one, most of the individuals who were arrested for banditry were poor, underemployed laborers; two, they were highly mobile; three, they regularly alternated between crime and legitimate pursuits; and four, most incidents of banditry occurred in the densely populated and highly commercialized core area of the Canton Delta. These findings should not be surprising, for sociologists have long understood that areas with high population density, high degrees of poverty, and high amounts of transience are prone to violent crimes. These also are areas that are generally more permissive of criminal behavior.

In the late eighteenth and early nineteenth centuries Qing officials believed China was facing a rising crime wave. What they were most worried about were crimes against property, especially banditry. By 1800, if not earlier, it seemed to many people that the bonds holding society together were disintegrating and that society was in danger of being engulfed by crime and immorality. The situation appeared particularly troubling in South China, especially Guangdong. According to Governor Zhang Chengji, at the end of the eighteenth century, the people of Guangdong were "accustomed to ruthlessness and violence," and that despite the staunch efforts to eliminate banditry it continued to increase day by day (*Gongzhongdang*, case no.2066, JQ 2.2.24). The state condemned banditry, especially when committed by bands of armed men, not simply because it endangered the life and property of "good people," but also because it threatened the social order and thereby the position of the ruling elites themselves. Banditry, like rebellion and treason, challenged and threatened the dynasty's ability to rule. Ever since ancient times most officials believed that banditry was the central problem of law and order. It was particularly troublesome because it implied violence together with organization (Antony, 1995: 98–132).

In Guangdong there was a saying, "If by thirty you have not found a living, you just as well fall among the weeds," that is, become a bandit (He, 1925: 98). But who became bandits and why? The motivations for becoming a bandit were diverse and complex. Some people turned to crime with hopes of getting rich quick, while others found it necessary for survival. But whatever their individual motives, the case records clearly demonstrate that most bandits shared in common humble backgrounds—poverty, transience, and disappointments in life.

While the archival records reveal little about the psychology of criminals and criminality, they do shed important light on the identities and personal backgrounds of bandits. They reveal information on their ages, marital status, geographic mobility, and occupations, as well as the seasonal and geographical distributions of their criminal activities. All of the individuals in my dataset were males ranging in age from eleven to seventy *sui* (years of age). The mean age was 32.6, while 70 percent were between the ages of twenty-six and forty-five. Significantly, slightly over half of the convicted bandits were over thirty. Clearly banditry was not merely an occupation of younger men but also of older and mature adults (see table 3.1).

Although most of the convicted bandits were single males, nevertheless a significant percentage were married and had children. About

Table 3.1 Number of bandits by age

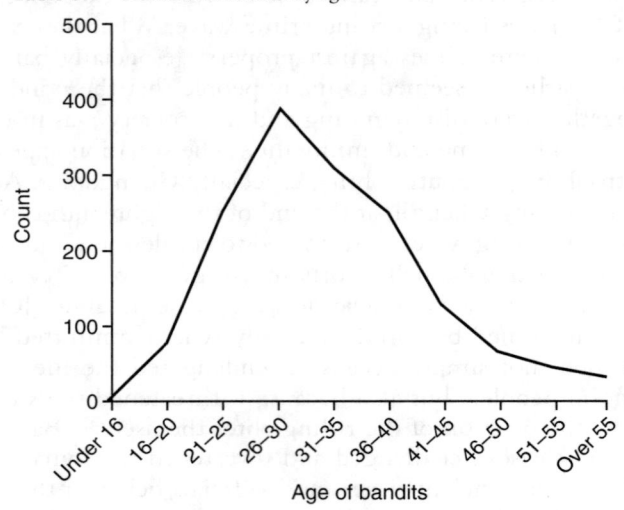

[Line chart showing count of bandits on y-axis (0-500) versus age groups on x-axis: Under 16, 16–20, 21–25, 26–30, 31–35, 36–40, 41–45, 46–50, 51–55, Over 55. The count peaks at age 26–30 at approximately 390.]

Source: Based on data found in the archival collections of imperial palace memorials (*gongzhongdang*) and imperial edicts (*shangyudang*) at the National Palace Museum in Taibei, Taiwan.

67 percent were bachelors and 33 percent were married. Among the unmarried men, 53.4 percent were under thirty years old. The individuals in this group, which the literature described as "bare sticks" (*guanggun*) or in the Canton area as "rotten youths" (*lanzai*), were usually characterized as wild and restless young men who bullied and terrorized villages and markets. They formed a major pool of recruits for bandit gangs, as well as for secret societies, local militia, crop-watching associations, martial arts clubs, and the like. They were classic examples of "marginal men"—impoverished, unmarried young men who moved about from place to place looking for work (Perry, 1980: 59–60).

Yet a large number of bandits appear to have been married with families. Among the married men, 58 percent had children. Married bandits also tended to be older. By a margin of roughly two to one, more bandits who were over forty were married than single. Marriage and having dependent children clearly did not prohibit individuals from becoming bandits. The fact that such a large number of convicted bandits were mature working family men suggests that they turned to crime in times of desperation or as a necessary supplement to honest work.

Information on the occupational backgrounds of convicted bandits is the most important evidence identifying their social and economic standing. This evidence clearly shows that the vast majority of bandits came from China's laboring poor, those people who lived on or near the fringes of respectable society earning only a subsistence living. They were poor not by choice but because of economic conditions beyond their control. They mainly worked at unskilled, menial jobs as hired workers, porters, coolies, peddlers, sailors, and watchmen, or at semiskilled jobs as itinerant barbers, carpenters, tailors, healers, singers, tinkers, and monks. The largest numbers of bandits, some 49 percent, were property-less, unskilled wage laborers.

Because labor was cheap and employment was irregular, workers had no job security. For most of them life was precarious and full of uncertainty. Unemployment and chronic underemployment forced many of them into a life of crime, where stealing became necessary for survival. It is no wonder that most of the convicted bandits claimed that they joined gangs because of poverty and the difficulties of holding down a steady job.

Banditry was often an integral part of the struggle for self-preservation among the poor and marginalized segments of society. Surely the ethical code of the poor was not the same as that held by their more comfortable and affluent neighbors. An old adage put it nicely: "The gold-thread plant is bitter, the licorice root is sweet; if you don't go against your conscience, how can you make money" (Arkush, 1990: 330). The poor had to devise their own rules and standards of conduct to survive. Many among the laboring poor regarded violence and crime, especially crimes against property, as a normal, perhaps even legitimate, means of maintaining the minimal standard of living or for improving upon their livelihoods. Thus we may speculate that the socialization process in a moral environment in which crime was not only condoned but also encouraged may have been conductive to violence and to a bandit tradition among the poor.

Besides poverty, mobility was also an important factor linked to banditry and violence. Most convicted bandits had at one time or another engaged in occupations that made them highly mobile. The poor were easily the most mobile sector of the population. Within the larger society they appeared a surplus population of vagabonds who wandered about seeking work wherever and whenever they could find any. Almost 70 percent of the convicted bandits worked in areas outside their native county. As a result, a significant portion of Guangdong's population was constantly in a state of transience and flux. Undoubtedly the regular movements of large numbers of people caused a great deal of dislocation in the province and severely hindered the efforts of the government, local communities, and households at tight supervision and control. This floating population of laboring poor was not only the most mobile segment of the population but also its most lawless and violent. Movement and violence went hand in hand—violence contributed to mobility just as mobility contributed to violence (Ownby, 1996: 13–17).

These members of China's laboring poor were all considered dangerous because they were highly mobile and therefore uncontrollable. What is more, they worked in lowly jobs considered to be dangerous. These were jobs that bred and perpetuated poverty as well as vagrancy. For many, too, work and crime went hand in hand. Work, begging, and crime were a continuum and crime was a common, daily occurrence. A laborer might engage in all three activities, even on the same day, simply because he had to in order to survive. As Geremek (1987: 11) has pointed out in his study of medieval Paris, "People on the margins did not only commit crimes, their very existence seemed to be a crime." The same appears to have been true as well in late imperial Guangdong. Mobility and poverty were characteristics of marginality; for the laboring poor nomadism was their natural condition.

It would be wrong to assume, however, that everyone facing economic difficulties and deprivation became bandits. Most people simply did not turn to crime. But among those who did, some became professional criminals and even more became occasional bandits. This latter group was comprised of part-time offenders who committed one or more crimes, but who were at other times law-abiding subjects. As amateurs they lacked any special criminal skills, but instead tended to rely on courage and violence in obtaining their objectives. They made crime an important, even essential, part of their overall survival strategy; but they differed from the professional bandit in that they did not make crime a career or rely on crime as their sole source of livelihood. Whether habitual or occasional in their criminality, they nonetheless engaged at least part of the time in legitimate occupations. They either committed crimes during periods of lawful employment as a supplement to honest wages, or went on temporary sprees of criminality during intervals between periods of legitimate labor.

Gangs, too, were not long lasting nor did they have fixed membership. Because they lacked steady or regular jobs, their lifestyles tended to alternate between legitimate pursuits and banditry. In fact, for many individuals banditry was a seasonal activity that closely followed the

Table 3.2 Number of robberies by Chinese lunar month

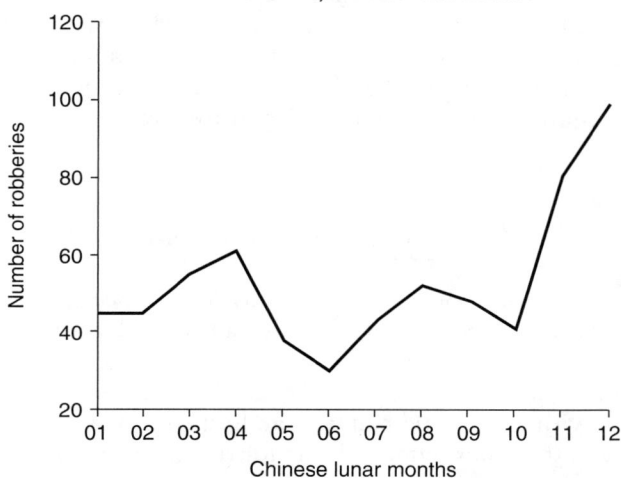

Source: Based on data found in the archival collections of imperial palace memorials (*gongzhongdang*) and imperial edicts (*shangyudang*) at the National Palace Museum in Taibei, Taiwan.

agricultural calendar, raging during the slow winter months and slacking off during the busy summer months. Banditry spiked upward during the winter months, especially during the lunar New Year (see table 3.2). This was not only a time when people needed to repay their debts, but also a time when large amounts of goods and money were moving along the rivers and roads. Then in the summer months—fifth through seventh lunar months—when men were needed for planting and harvesting, banditry declined. It appears that some men engaged in occasional banditry at times when other legitimate opportunities for earning a living were lacking.

In Guangdong bandits appeared everywhere: on land, in mountains, on rivers, along the coast. There was nowhere that they could not be found. Contrary to conventional wisdom, however, they concentrated in the thickly settled and economically advanced core Canton Delta as well as along major trade routes. As Governor-General Deng Tingzhen explained to the throne in 1837, the Canton Delta was not only the most densely populated area in Guangdong and the commercial hub of South China, but it was also the most crime ridden and bandit infested (*Gongzhongdang*, case no.621, DG 17.2.27). Here too was the seat of the provincial government and an area with the heaviest concentrations of government troops and degree-holding gentry. It also had the largest floating population of beggars and itinerant workers who had come to the area seeking work. Guangzhou prefecture, which included the capital of Canton and most of the Canton Delta, had roughly 50 percent of the total number of bandit incidents in the province between 1760 and 1845.

The Reaction of the State

Banditry was a common and continuous occurrence in local society that both ordinary people and officials had to deal with on a regular basis. The Qing state reacted to banditry in a number of ways. While large military campaigns may have been the most expedient method for dealing with large-scale banditry and rebellions, this was not necessarily the best or most effective way for the government to deal with the more common and routine small-scale forms of banditry. Military campaigns against bandit gangs also were less practical in densely populated core areas, such as the Canton Delta. In most cases officials used various policing and legal methods to deal with banditry, including the promulgation of new laws. In fact, during the late eighteenth and early nineteenth centuries, at a time when a number of officials perceived a serious rise in predacious crime, the state reacted by enacting a series of harsh laws, many of which dealt specifically with Guangdong province, which they viewed as a particularly troublesome area. This was especially true of violent crimes against property.

Increasingly concerned about the apparent rising crime wave, the Qing state responded by implementing more draconian measures against banditry. In fact, the archival records clearly show that beginning in the 1780s there was a more frequent use of capital punishment, particularly summary executions, in dealing with bandit cases. Furthermore, between 1780 and 1845, the existing laws (statutes *lü*) on robbery were continually being supplemented with harsher new substatutes (*li*). During that time, for instance, Guangdong alone had at least twelve new laws that aimed to curtail banditry in that single province.

These new laws, however, should be understood within the larger context of Qing efforts to protect private property. One of the first new laws appeared in 1780, when the state enacted a substatute dealing specifically with bandits and pirates in Guangdong province that operated in gangs of ten or more men. In 1803 there was a new law against gangs of robbers who plundered grain transport boats. Another law in 1811 dealt with Guangdong river bandits and sworn brotherhoods who operated in gangs of over forty men. Then in 1814 a new law was promulgated against robbers who stole public funds, and in 1816 there was a new law against bandits who climbed over city walls to rob the inhabitants. Between 1820 and 1824 Guangdong was again spotlighted with a series of new substatutes dealing with bandits who engaged in extortion and kidnapping. In 1836 a new law specifically singled out sailors aboard tribute grain boats who plundered and killed. In 1845 there was a new law against gangs of armed bandits in Shandong province, and also in that same year yet another new law dealing with robbers in Guangdong and Guangxi who plundered and kidnapped (Antony, 1990: 31–53).

The promulgation of these new laws, each of which dealt with specific problems of gangs of bandits, was clear indication of the growing concern among Qing officials over the unfolding forms of serious violent crimes against property. In each of these new laws the standard penalty of decapitation was supplemented with "exposure of the head," a practice normally reserved for the most serious crimes. And in three of the new laws—those of 1811, 1836, and the Guangdong-Guangxi law of 1845—sentences were to be carried out summarily, that is, without awaiting the required approval from the throne. Clearly the state believed that the standard punishments had been neither expedient nor harsh enough to deter the increasing number of serious bandit cases occurring throughout China, but especially in Guangdong, at the time.

Although Qing officials made concerted efforts at curbing banditry in Guangdong during these years, how effective were they, and did new, harsher laws really work? Although statistical evidence is inconclusive, other evidence strongly suggests that despite their efforts officials were ineffective in eliminating banditry in Guangdong. There were many reports in Western journals exclaiming "an alarming increase in crime" in recent years in the province (*Chinese Repository*, January 1836). Persistent sociopolitical problems prevented effective law enforcement. Despite increasing numbers of subcounty officials and functionaries in the province, they were never able to keep pace with demographic and commercial expansion (Antony, 2002: 27–59). Official corruption and negligence were rampant. Officials often concealed acts of banditry in order to escape censure, or they would report robbery cases as minor offenses. Often, too, soldiers and officials refused to pursue bandits beyond their own jurisdictions, thereby allowing them to completely escape the law (*Shangyudang*, JQ 12.10.26, and JQ 24.11.10; *Canton Register*, June 12, 1838). Even when officials were diligent in carrying out their duties, there still were no apparent decreases in the number of bandit cases. After 1836, banditry had gotten so out of hand in Guangdong that one official lamented that there was nothing that the government could do to curb brigandage and violence (*Canton Press*, December 5, 1835).

Conclusion

Banditry was an integral part of the struggle for self-preservation among the poor and marginalized segments of Chinese society. Most bandits were not professional robbers or killers, but rather they were amateurs who oscillated between crime and legitimate work. In the highly competitive and contentious world of late imperial South China aggression and violence were regular parts of life for the laboring poor. They literally had to fight to survive, not just against pernicious landlords and corrupt officials, but also with other members of their own class for scarce resources and jobs. Chronic underemployment forced many poor laborers into a vicious life cycle of work and crime in which banditry became not only a necessary part of their survival strategy but also an important tool for resistance against those in authority over them.

There was not only a steady increase in the number of bandit cases between 1760 and 1845, but also a high concentration of these cases in China's most prosperous and economically developed areas, particularly Guangdong. By the late eighteenth century, Guangdong's population was booming out of control. Although the population explosion helped to stimulate tremendous economic growth, the benefits were unevenly distributed. Rising prices, the relative scarcity of jobs and resources, and pressure on the land combined to produce a huge floating population of landless and highly mobile poor. It was precisely in these circumstances that the contrasts between rich and poor were most pronounced, and banditry was most rampant.

Contrary to conventional wisdom, which insists that banditry was weakest in highly developed core areas, in late imperial Guangdong my archival evidence clearly shows that banditry was actually strongest in the core Canton Delta, the area that was the most densely populated and most highly commercialized. Banditry was not only rampant in the area that was the richest but that also had the keenest competition for jobs. Therefore, banditry provided an important outlet for some people among the laboring poor to supplement their regular incomes and allow them to survive in an otherwise harsh social environment.

The chief response of the Qing state to the perceived rising crime wave in Guangdong was the promulgation of increasingly harsher laws. These new laws aimed not only to curb banditry but also at the same time to protect private property and extend state power deeper into local communities. The new legislation and expansion of state power, on the one hand, helped to align officials with local elites in their mutual efforts to control the unruly lower orders. On the other hand, these efforts only exacerbated the problem of banditry by criminalizing even larger segments of the laboring poor and thereby further alienating them from mainstream society.

Yet in the end, despite all the efforts, officials seemed helpless in curbing banditry in Guangdong. In fact, predacious crimes continued to increase over the next several decades before the tumultuous explosion of the Taiping Rebellion in the 1850s. Banditry was like the rumblings beneath the surface, an unpropitious warning of the more terrible disorders just ahead.

Note

1. In this study I do not use the term laboring poor in a Marxist sense, but rather simply in a descriptive sense to describe those individuals who were chronically poor although they continued to work for their livelihoods. These poor workers were also necessarily marginal people. Here I follow the suggestions of Bronislaw Geremek, who explained that individuals became marginalized in two senses: first, society excluded them because they were disorderly or engaged in shameful activities, and second, they cut themselves off from society by violating the standards of collective behavior by engaging in criminal or shameful activities (1987: 7–8).

Bibliography

Antony, Robert J. 1988. "Pirates, Bandits, and Brotherhoods: A Study of Crime and Law in Kwangtung Province, 1796–1839." Ph.D. diss., University of Hawai'i.

———. 1990. "The Problem of Banditry and Bandit Suppression in Kwangtung South China, 1780–1840." *Criminal Justice History* (Fall): 31–53.

———. 1995. "Scourges on the People: Perceptions of Robbery, Snatching and Theft in the Mid-Qing Period." *Late Imperial China* 16, no.2 (December): 98–132.

———. 2002. "Subcounty Officials, the State, and Local Communities in Guangdong Province, 1644–1860." In Robert J. Antony and Jane K. Leonard, eds., *Dragons, Tigers, and Dogs*, 27–59. Ithaca, NY: East Asia Program, Cornell University.

Arkush, David. 1990. "Orthodoxy and Heterodoxy in Twentieth-Century Chinese Peasant Proverbs." In K. C. Liu, ed. *Orthodoxy in Late Imperial China*. Berkeley, CA: University of California Press.

Buoye, Thomas. 2000. *Manslaughter, Markets, and Moral Economy: Violent Disputes over Property Rights in Eighteenth-Century China*. Cambridge: Cambridge University Press.

Canton Register. 1827–1843. Canton and Macau.

Canton Press. 1835–1844. Canton and Macau.

Chinese Repository. 1832–1851. Canton and Macau.

Geremek, Bronislaw. 1987. *The Margins of Society in Late Medieval Paris*. trans. by Jean Birrell. Cambridge: Cambridge University Press.

Gongzhongdang (Unpublished imperial palace memorials), National Palace Museum, Taibei.

He, Xiya. 1925. *Zhongguo daofei wenti zhi yanjiu* (A study of the bandit problem in China). Shanghai: Taidong tushuju.

Lin, Man-Houng. 2006. *China Upside Down: Currency, Society, and Ideologies, 1808–1856*. Cambridge, MA: Harvard University Press.

Marks, Robert. 1998. *Tigers, Rice, Silk, and Silt: Environment and Economy in Late Imperial South China*. Cambridge: Cambridge University Press.

Ownby, David. 1996. *Brotherhoods and Secret Societies in Early and Mid-Qing China: The Formation of a Tradition*. Stanford, CA: Stanford University Press.

Park, Nancy, and Robert J. Antony. 1993. "Archival Research in Qing Legal History." *Qingshi wenti* 14, no.1 (June): 93–137.

Perry, Elizabeth. 1980. *Rebels and Revolutionaries in North China, 1845–1945*. Stanford, CA: Stanford University Press.

Pomeranz, Kenneth. 2000. *The Great Divergence: Europe, China, and the Making of the Modern World Economy*. Princeton, NJ: Princeton University Press.

Shangyudang (Unpublished imperial edicts), National Palace Museum, Taibei.

Wong, R. Bin. 1997. *China Transformed: Historical Change and the Limits of European Experience*. Ithaca, NY: Cornell University Press.

CHAPTER FOUR

Politics of Faith: Christian Activism and the Maoist State in South China

JOSEPH TSE-HEI LEE

Introduction

The response of Chinese Christians to the socialist state after the Communist Revolution of 1949 reveals the complexity of church and state relations in Maoist China (1949–1976). This chapter looks at the experience of Christian communities in the Chaozhou-speaking region of northeastern Guangdong province. Because these communities constituted an integral part of the local political, social, and economic power structure before the Communist takeover of South China, they refused to be subject to the control of the Maoist state. They did not subscribe to the highly politicized anti-imperialist rhetoric of the state-controlled Three-Self Patriotic Movement (*sanzi aiguo yundong*): self-rule autonomous from foreign missionary and imperialist control, financial self-support without any foreign donations, and self-preaching independent of any missionary influences. As the overarching organization of the one-party state, the Three-Self Patriotic Movement sought to ensure that all Chinese Protestant congregations would submit to the socialist ideology.

By rejecting the Maoist vision of a socialist state, the Christians adhered to the principle of the locality of the church, proclaiming that each church should be an autonomous body, governing its affairs and remaining independent from state control. They also relied on existing lineage and village networks to create autonomous worshipping communities across the region. This pattern of Christian activism not only highlights the role of popular resistance against state-imposed modernity, but also reminds us of what James C. Scott (1985) calls "weapons of the weak" in popular protests by a subordinate group against the hegemonic power under the most oppressive circumstances. However, the Communist state perceived ideological identification as synonymous with absolute loyalty to the new socialist nation. Therefore, religious conversion was viewed as a challenge to Maoist ideology and a protest against the state.

The central issue for this study is to examine the place of religion within the context of the rise of the Maoist state. It focuses on the interactions between Christianity and state power, and the state's influence on the religious and political identities of Chinese Christians. In recent years, Anthony C. Yu (2003) has called for more attention to state control of religion in China. As Yu asserts, "there has never been a period in China's historical past in which the government of the state, in imperial and post-imperial form, has pursued a neutral policy toward religion, let alone encouraged, in terms dear to American idealism, its 'free exercise.' The impetus to engage religion, on the part of the central government, is for the purpose of regulation, control, and exploitation whenever it is deemed feasible and beneficial to the state" (2003: 4). The imperial dynasties of the past and the Republican and Communist regimes have continuously pursued a policy of engaging religions as long as these religions supported the states.

This study argues that the complexity of church-state relations can be better understood if one examines the involvement of Chinese Christians in negotiating with the state over sacred and secular matters. In twentieth-century China, the church and state constantly negotiated with each other over the control of religions, religious institutions, and rituals. When the state was strong, the church participated in the formation of state power. But as the state power declined, the church reverted to their original autonomy and crossed the boundaries between sacred and profane in order to claim political, social, and economic influences. In other words, the church and local Christians were not passive recipients of the ideological conformity that state authorities decreed and imposed on them. Therefore, the role of local agencies and the contest for religious and political power in Chaozhou lie at the heart of the discussion.

Throughout the turbulent period of Maoist China, how did the Communist authorities attempt to hijack religion to legitimize political rule and regulate religious activities at the grassroots level? How did Chinese Christians respond to the state's policy of political and ideological control? What were the incentives underlying Christians' responses to the Communist state? This chapter addresses these questions by employing a bottom-up social history approach to investigate the nature of religion and state power at the grassroots level. It presents case studies of the Baptist, Presbyterian, and Catholic communities in Chaozhou. These Christian groups were self-supporting, self-administrating, and self-propagating movements in twentieth-century China. They strongly believed that they were called out of this world to follow Jesus Christ, and that they could exist outside of politics yet coexist with the Communist government. These cases are chosen to illustrate how the Communist authorities exploited Christianity to claim legitimacy and establish ideological control over the Christian population, and how Christian communities, in turn, drew on their religious resources to strengthen themselves in the competitive arena of politics.

Beginning with an overview of Christianity in Chaozhou, this chapter discusses how the expansion of the one-party state marginalized Christian communities nationally and locally. This is followed by a critique of the state persecution of Christians during the Three-Self Patriotic Movement. In addition, this study examines a wide range of strategies that the Christians in Chaozhou employed for survival and empowerment throughout the Maoist era.

With respect to Communist religious policy, this research relies on unpublished Chinese archival materials, all of which were compiled by the Guangdong Provincial Bureau of Religious Affairs, the Shantou Municipal Bureau of Religious Affairs, and the Shantou Municipal Bureau of United Front during the 1950s. These official records are highly problematic. As Vivian Wagner (2002) points out, the Chinese archival system was an instrument of control used by the Maoist state against dissenters in all political purges. The official reports concerning the local Christians are no exception: they were compiled to provide Communist officials with information to control the church. They consist of controversial evidence about the "political crimes" of foreign missionaries and Chinese church leaders. The political nature of the reports presents two methodological problems for historians.

The first problem concerns the controversial nature of the materials. All the materials were written in the orthodox Maoist discourse and intended for Communist Party officials in charge of religious affairs. They often characterize the Chinese church leaders as "counterrevolutionaries," "reactionary forces," and "class enemies." These labels are not hollow slogans. They strongly accuse the church leaders of acting like "class enemies"—those who had been socially and politically dominant under the former Nationalist regime and were unwilling to surrender their privileges to the People's Government after 1949. Such accusations justify persecution by all available means, including state violence, against them (Wang, 2002: 27–59, 84–93).

The second problem concerns factual discrepancies in the reports. Throughout the 1950s onward, the Communist Party had recruited some church members as informants and collaborators. This was what Odoric Y. K. Wou (1994: 187–211) called a bottom-up strategy of coalition politics in the Communist revolutionary movement. Most accusations concern individual church leaders' connections with Nationalist government officials before and after the Communist Revolution. However, throughout the mid-twentieth century, China was in perpetual flux, and the views of local church leaders toward the Communist Party varied in time and place. Their views about the Communist Party recorded in the official reports—what was said in public—might differ considerably from opinions expressed in private. Instead of making generalizations about the local Christians and their interaction with the state, scholars should highlight the complexities of Communist religious policy and the diverse responses of Christians.

Nevertheless, these problems are not sufficient reasons for rejecting the reports completely. For one thing, the Communist state has not released all archival materials about the Three-Self Patriotic Movement and its impacts on the church. These materials give us valuable information about the Christians' survival tactics in Chaozhou after 1949, their organizational structures and social networks, as well as their responses to the Three-Self Patriotic Movement. All these details cannot be seen in any other sources, and it was these very features that aroused state suspicion toward this tiny fraction of the Christian population.

The Christian Expansion into Chaozhou

Chaozhou seems to be an isolated region in China (see map 4.1). Located on the South China coast, Chaozhou was far away from the central and provincial governments and notorious for its long history of rural violence. The Chaozhou dialect was the dominant language in the coastal areas, whereas the Hakka dialect was widely spoken in the poorer interior. Since the eighteenth century, large numbers of people from Chaozhou left their families to find work in Siam (now

Map 4.1 Chaozhou Prefecture
Source: Designed by the author and reproduced with permission

Thailand), planning to return to China upon retirement. While living abroad, they maintained close contacts with their home villages through strong kinship and native place ties, which provided an effective network of support. Beginning in the 1830s, American Baptist missionaries who preached among Overseas Chinese in Siam found in the process a way to reintroduce Christianity into the Chinese mainland (Christianity was banned as a heterodox religion in 1724). They encouraged Overseas Chinese converts to spread the Christian faith through native place networks abroad in Siam and, later, through kinship networks after they returned home. Because these networks were outside Chinese official control, they provided a stable and effective channel of religious transmission to facilitate Baptist expansion from Siam to China. This pattern of development highlights the importance of established Chinese maritime routes from Siam to Chaozhou in missionary efforts to bring Christianity to the Chinese mainland before the creation of the unequal treaty system. Christianity was thus not simply a foreign imposition but spread through specifically Chinese networks (Lee, 2007: 247–266).

The Beijing Convention of 1860 laid down the framework for Christian expansion throughout the late nineteenth century. After establishing themselves in the treaty port of Shantou, the American Baptist and English Presbyterian missionaries encountered much hostility from Chinese literati, government officials, and lineage elders in administrative cities. Faced with these antagonistic power holders, the Baptist and Presbyterian missions shifted the focus of evangelization toward the interior.

Overall, Christianity in Chaozhou grew as a grassroots movement, appealing to a large number of people in the remote areas. With more baptisms in the interior than on the coast, conversion in Chaozhou was predominantly a rural phenomenon. It was the countryside, not urban areas that became the center of Christian movement. The higher concentration of church members in the interior challenges Paul A. Cohen's argument that in late imperial China, people along the coast were more likely to subscribe to Christianity than people in the hinterlands (Cohen, 1974: 197–198). These rural Christians came from diverse social backgrounds: they were farmers, artisans, merchants, medical practitioners, beggars, and widows. Rather than living on the fringes of the society, they were deeply integrated into the political, social, economic, and cultural spheres of the local communities. They used their networks to convert relatives, neighbors, and friends; a pattern of church growth that not only fitted well with the missionary expectation of self-propagation through native agency but also marked the beginning of mass conversions in grassroots society.

Equally significant was a considerable overlap of Chinese kinship and Christian identities. Where the churches were erected outside the walled villages and surrounded by Christian households, they were often misunderstood by outsiders as independent Christian settlements. These Christian households, in fact, constituted an essential part of the local society, as they identified themselves with a particular denomination and their lineage (or village) factions. This overlap of religious, kinship, and territorial identities characterizes most Christian communities in Chaozhou (Lee, 2003).

As Christianity began to take roots in Chaozhou, the complexity of political issues involving foreign missionaries and Chinese converts were acute. The Christian expansion into Chaozhou was characterized by the intensity of resource conflicts between Christian and non-Christian communities. The rival factions in these conflicts searched for new sources of power to strengthen their hands. Missionaries' ability to intervene in local conflicts had to do with powerful backing from foreign powers in Shantou and beyond. Through their intervention, missionaries empowered the Christian communities and undermined the traditional power holders such as lineage leaders, temple managers, and local officials. In areas notorious for limited government control and a long history of collective violence, the church became "a protective society," whose members would help each other in disputes and litigations (Gibson, 1901: 184). The political dimension of Christianity had a far-reaching impact on the interactions between church and state in the twentieth century. This pattern of development is similar to the growth of popular religions and their interactions with political actors and local communities in North China (Duara, 1988; Dubois, 2005; Chau, 2006).

Maoism and the Church–State Relations

As with the imperial states of the past, the Communist state continuously pursued a "united front" policy of engaging China's Protestant communities. The purpose was to sever their ties with foreign missionary enterprises, to place the diverse Protestant denominations under the control of a Leninist mass organization, and to purge reactionary forces and class enemies from the church. Underlying the Communist religious policy was the ideological conflict between state and religion. C. K. Yang argues that Maoist ideology was a nontheistic "faith" that manifested distinctly religious characteristics. Two aspirations of the Chinese nation express the essences of its idealistic nation: nationalism and materialistic progress. All reforms, revolutions, and radical movements in the nineteenth and early twentieth centuries sought to promote materialistic progress and establish a strong nation. The Maoist state made the same claim, but demanded from its people the unconditional subordination of all personal concerns. This appeal by the state was based on the premise that Maoist ideology offered the only guide to China's ultimate destiny, the only means to national independence and modernization (Yang, 1967: 381–387). Determined to emancipate the common people from religion and "superstition," the Communist state propagated a secular, scientific, and rationalistic worldview (Smith, 2006). It denounced religion as "the opiate of the people" and an obstacle toward the socialist revolution. Its effort to control Catholics and Protestants led to a coercive assimilation of all Christian institutions into the Maoist state.

Against this backdrop, the Three-Self Patriotic Movement is to be discussed. The term "Three-Self" was originally coined by Rufus Anderson of the American Board of Commissioners for Foreign Mission and Henry Venn of the Church Missionary Society in the nineteenth century. "Three-Self" describes a mission policy that organized native Christians in Africa and Asia into self-supporting, self-governing, and self-propagating churches. After the Communist Revolution, the Chinese government replaced the "Three-Self" slogan with "Three-Self Patriotic Movement" in order to legitimatize the state's takeover of the Protestant church. Politically, the Three-Self Patriotic Movement was a mass organization along the lines of the Communist Party's united front policy. It was launched by the one-party state to politicize the religious sphere and control the Protestant communities. On June 28, 1949, Wu Yuzong, general secretary for Publications of the National Committee of the Young Men's Christian Association (YMCA) in China, acted as a middleman between the Communist Party and the National Christian Council. He urged church leaders to support the Communists. Many leaders of the YMCA and Young Women's Christian Association (YWCA) assisted Wu Yuzong in pursuing a pro-Communist agenda among Protestant circles. The collaboration between the Communist Party, YMCA, and YWCA dates back to the revolutionary movement between the 1920s and 1940s. Zhou Enlai, later the premier of the People's Republic of China, and his comrades used the YMCA in Tianjin as a base for their revolutionary activities in North China. The YMCA in Shanghai provided a safe haven for Communist underground activists in the Lower Yangtze Region. Those YMCA and YWCA leaders who were dissatisfied with the Nationalist government and sympathetic to the Communist cause had been recruited as party members. Wu Yuzong was said to have become an underground party member, planted into the Protestant church after he first met with Zhou Enlai in 1943 (Gu, 1984: 31–32). Deng Zhaoming points out that Wu Yuzong was the only Protestant among pro-Communist intellectuals invited to have consultation with the Communist leaders in September 1949 shortly after Beijing was captured by the People's Liberation Army. The Communist agents arranged for Wu to return to China from Hong Kong through North Korea (Deng, 1997: 8–9). Prior to its revolutionary victory, the Communist Party had co-opted some YMCA and YWCA leaders (Wickeri, 1988, 2007).

In July 1950, Wu Yuzong led a delegation of nineteen Protestant church leaders to meet with Premier Zhou Enlai and draft a statement known as "The Christian Manifesto," which expressed Chinese

Christians' loyalty to the Communist state. At that time, the Korean War broke out and anti-American sentiment ran high. The Manifesto called on Christians to fight imperialism, to make known the political stand of Christians in China, and to build a church under the management of Chinese themselves. It marked the beginning of the Three-Self Patriotic Movement. On the surface, the movement called for the indigenization and ecclesiastical autonomy of Chinese churches. But its fundamental goal was to force the Christians to sever their institutional ties with foreign missionary enterprises in particular and foreigners in general.

Change in global politics affected Christians in China. After the outbreak of the Korean War, the government expelled all foreign Catholic and Protestant missionaries. The expulsion was a nationalistic act and symbolized the end of foreign imperialism in modern China (Ling, 1999: 148–180). In the midst of the Korean War, the Preparatory Committee of the Oppose American and Aid Korea Three-Self Reform Movement of the Christian Church was founded to denounce Western missionaries. After a series of denunciation campaigns, the Preparatory Committee sponsored the first National Christian Conference, held in the summer of 1954, in which Wu Yuzong was elected chairman and was assigned to organize the Three-Self Patriotic Movement. The officials of the Bureau of Religious Affairs served as "advisors" to the Movement. According to Beatrice Leung (2005), the Bureau of Religious Affairs was initially established to handle religious affairs under the Bureau of National Minorities, and in 1951 it was transferred to the Educational and Cultural Section of the Home Affairs Department. In addition, the United Front Department of the Communist Party's Central Committee set up a Religious Section to implement Communist religious policy. The majority of religious cadres were Communist Party members, who kept an eye on religious activities. Within less than a decade, the Three-Self Patriotic Movement ended the missionary era in China and marked the beginning of the Communist takeover of churches (Wickeri, 1988: 117–153; Ling, 1999: 122–180). Clearly, the leaders of the Three-Self Patriotic Movement had served as mere agents of the state to reshape Christian churches according to the Communist Party's designs. Under tremendous pressure for absolute loyalty to the Maoist state, political neutrality was not an option and the churches could only exist in limited scope (Deng, 1997: 5–22; Kindopp and Hamrin, eds., 2004).

In Chaozhou, the Communist intervention into church affairs led to the takeover of church properties. In early 1950, the Shantou municipal government required all foreign missions and Chinese churches to register their properties with the authorities. This policy identified the locations and values of all foreign mission and Chinese church properties. During the Korean War, the Shantou municipal government confiscated all the American Baptist and English Presbyterian mission properties. These properties were registered in Shantou in the 1930s under the name of the foreign missionary enterprises. The government claimed to transfer the foreign missions' properties to the Chinese churches in order to gather support among local Christians against their missionary patrons. This tactic of divide and rule aimed at creating internal conflicts within the Baptist and Presbyterian institutions. It sought to weaken the Christian communities by cutting their economic and cultural ties with the West. This would eventually allow the government to put all denominational churches into the Three-Self Patriotic Movement, thereby making it easier to control and manipulate the Protestants. In Chaozhou as in other parts of China, the foreign missionary enterprises owned most church properties and supported many schools, hospitals, and clinics. The local Christians owned only the market and village churches and few city churches. When the state monopolized the educational and medical institutions in the 1950s, it deprived the church of an important source of income. Without financial support from the West, it was extremely difficult for the local church leaders to operate efficiently and to maintain their social and cultural prestige. In 1957, most local churches appealed to the Shantou municipal government to return foreign mission and Chinese church properties occupied by the state. But the municipal authorities ignored their requests (Archives of the Shantou Bureau of Religious Affairs, Call no.85-1-54).

After seizing the properties, the state created the Local Committee of the Three-Self Patriotic Movement to integrate all the local congregations into the state mechanism of religious control. During the Korean War, the Shantou Bureau of Religious Affairs mobilized the Christians to support the nationwide Three-Self Patriotic Movement. Ironically, the structure of the state-controlled Three-Self Patriotic Movement in Shantou revealed the strong Baptist and Presbyterian presence. Of the thirty-seven Three-Self committee members, eight were Baptists, sixteen Presbyterians, one Seventh-Day Adventist, four Little Flock members, two leaders of the New Chinese Christian Church, one representative of the True Jesus Church, one representative of the Chinese True Jesus Church, and four representatives with unclear denominational affiliations. The Three-Self Patriotic Movement proclaimed to indigenize the leadership structure of Chinese churches by involving native church leaders, but this was only a tactic to gather support for the socialist state (Archives of the Shantou Bureau of Religious Affairs, Call no.85-1-53).

The chief Presbyterian leader Zheng Shaohuai became the first chairman of the Three-Self Patriotic Movement in Shantou in July 1957. Cai Haizheng, a Presbyterian, and Hong Xirong, a Baptist, became the vice chairmen. These church leaders collaborated with the state provided that there was freedom of worship among the urban congregations. Keeping a low profile and avoiding confrontation with the state appeared to be the most sensible survival strategy. They believed that the Three-Self Patriotic Movement was more about expressing their loyalty to the Communist state rather than building a church run by and for the local Christians. In fact, the denominational churches and their village congregations in Chaozhou had long become a truly Three-Self Church in the late nineteenth century; almost all the rural congregations were created, managed, and supported by the worshippers since the time of their founding. The Christians only relied on the missionaries for running the extensive networks of educational and medical institutions.

These Three-Self Patriotic church leaders in Shantou were not mere agents of the state to control the local Christians. They played a dual role in church and state interactions: an implementer of the Communist Party's designs as well as a moderator against some antireligious policies. Politically they mediated between the Christian communities and Communist officials. They constantly appealed to the Shantou municipal government for the return of church properties. They subscribed to the Communist rhetoric of anti-imperialism and stressed that the Christians in Chaozhou were patriotic; therefore, they should be given financial assistance by the state in times of difficulty. During the land reform, they complained about the harsh anti-Christian policies in the countryside, and urged the municipal, district, and village authorities to reopen the market and village churches for worship. They had effectively used the Three-Self Patriotic Movement Committee in Shantou as an institutional umbrella to support evangelistic activities throughout the 1950s and early 1960s.

As the state sought to establish legitimacy among the Christian population, it avoided any controversial discussion about religious doctrines with the Christians. Instead it imposed a nationalist discourse of the Communist revolution and anti-imperialism on the local churches. Missing in this kind of nationalist narrative was the social history of

Chinese churches. There is no mention of the unique circumstances that had made Christianity more successful in Chaozhou than in other parts of China. Neither is there any discussion of the extensive Christian maritime networks across the South China Sea.

In addition, the state forced all church leaders to demonize the foreign missionaries whom they had known for many decades. This was a regular procedure throughout China. Those church leaders who refused to do so had to attend many political study sessions. While the state appeared to have co-opted the urban church leaders in the Three-Self Patriotic Movement, the socialist transformation of rural China threatened the Christian movement in the countryside. In 1950, the central government in Beijing had introduced the Agrarian Reform Law, which confiscated landowners' holdings for redistribution among landless peasants (Hsü, 2000: 652–653). Almost all the Christian villages in China failed to protect their landed properties during the land reform. In Chaozhou, all the rural congregations ceased to function after the land reform. By the mid-1950s, 121 of the 123 Baptist congregations no longer existed institutionally. The church buildings were converted into state schools, warehouses, village factories, and government offices. The Xiashan congregation in Chaoyang district and the Shen'ao congregation in Nan'ao Island were the only functioning churches outside Shantou (Archives of the Shantou Bureau of Religious Affairs, Call no.85-1-54). The land reform designed to break landlords' dominance had the added impact of undermining the socioeconomic basis of Christian villages.

After the land reform, the government followed up with a campaign of agricultural collectivization in 1953. It wanted to stop the reemergence of rich peasants, to achieve agricultural specialization, and to increase production. This campaign reorganized village communities into mutual aid teams where peasants worked as a collective unit (Hsü, 2000: 653). The redrawing of the village boundaries merged the Christian communities with their non-Christian neighbors. This, in turn, reduced the influence of the rural churches in local politics. On many occasions, the local authorities appointed non-Christian outsiders as officials in predominantly Catholic and Protestant villages in order to replace the existing Christian power structure with a socialist one.

Despite the state's attempt to subdue the Christian communities, there were many factors affecting the power relations between the Christians and Communist officials. One major factor had to do with the personality and administrative style of the officials. If the outside officials were hostile toward the Christians, there would be strong resistance from the latter. Instead many officials tended to avoid any conflict with the Christians. Moreover, the Christians often changed the officials' attitudes toward Christianity. In rural areas characterized by complex webs of social relationships, the Christians used the practice of gift exchange to win the officials to their side. As a result, the officials turned a blind eye to any religious activities as long as the Christians met the grain production quota. There were many reports of large-scale Christmas celebrations in Catholic and Protestant villages across Guangdong province in 1958 and 1959. Clearly the Christians and Communist officials were very pragmatic in dealing with each other. There was much room for church-state mediation at the grassroots level (Archives of the Shantou Bureau of the United Front, Call no.D007-42).

The most serious challenge facing the Christians was the continuous organization of mass campaigns by the government. The campaigns against "reactionaries" and "class enemies" purged church leaders with foreign connections. In particular, there was the Three Anti-campaign in 1951 to combat corruption, waste, and bureaucratism. In 1952, there was also the Five Anti-campaign against bribery, tax evasion, fraud, theft of government property, and leakage of state economic secrets; this campaign led to a nationwide attack against the churches (Hsü, 2000: 658; Kindopp and Hamrin, eds., 2004). In these campaigns, the state labeled the church leaders as political and social outcasts. This labeling affected how the church leaders and their family members were treated by the local work units. If the church leaders belonged to landholding and merchant families, they were labeled as landlords and capitalists, resulting in an uncertain future for them and their children. This explains why many young Christians escaped to Hong Kong during the 1950s and 1960s.

The most intense period of persecution took place during the 1960s. The Socialist Education Movement (1962–1965) put tremendous pressure on local church leaders. The campaign emphasized the theme of class struggle, this time identifying the class enemy as "people in positions of authority in the Party who take the capitalist road... There are some people in the communes, districts, counties, special districts, and even in the work of the provincial and Central Committee departments, who opposed socialism." The rhetoric revealed the irreconcilable differences between Chairman Mao and Liu Shaoqi, who criticized Mao's economic policies in the Great Leap Forward. But the Guangdong provincial and Shantou municipal authorities exploited the

Socialist Education Movement to attack the Catholics and Protestants in rural Chaozhou.

The Local Christians' Survival Strategies

What happened to the Christians in Chaozhou throughout the Maoist era? The following cases throw light on the survival strategies of the Catholics and Presbyterians in Mianhu market in Jiexi district (Archives of the Shantou Bureau of the United Front, Call no.D007/14). Mianhu market is located at the upper Rong River, which is a dividing line between the Hakka- and Chaozhou-speaking areas in Northeast Guangdong. In the late nineteenth century, the Catholic and Protestant missionaries had to reach Mianhu before traveling upstream to the Hakka territories. In 1972, there were 496 Catholics and Protestants in Mianhu, accounting for 2 percent of the local population. Adjacent to Mianhu were the Catholic communities in Houyang village and Lutianba. There were 15 Catholic families with 102 people in Houyang, making up 12 percent of the village population. Lutianba was a pure Catholic settlement with twenty-eight families consisting of 138 people. These Catholics were the third generation of converts and constituted the backbone of the church in that area.

Throughout the Maoist era, the Catholics and Protestants in Mianhu employed a wide range of survival tactics to respond to the politicization of Chinese society. The first strategy was to create a diffused network of support. Because Christianity was an integral part of the kinship and lineage structures, many Catholics and Protestants relied on the long-standing social networks to maintain internal unity among their church members and to pursue religious activities. Lutianba used to be the regional center of Catholicism in the upper Rong River before 1949, but it ceased to function during the land reform. Throughout the 1950s, local Catholic women like Zhou Wanxiao, Li Huiyang, and Chen Yue'e organized religious activities at homes. Twenty worshippers showed up every week and there were about a hundred attendants during the Christmas and Easter services. While the priests were put in jail, the laity played an important role in looking after the widely scattered Catholic villagers.

Another strategy was to shift the center of religious operation from urban to rural areas in order to avoid confrontation with the state. The former Catholic Bishop Su Bingqian returned to his native village in Huilai district for retirement in 1955. But upon his return he regularly received Catholic visitors and coordinated religious activities across Chaozhou. Throughout the late nineteenth century, the center of Christianity was the countryside. The success story of rural church implantation inspired the church leaders to return to their roots in the 1950s.

The third strategy consisted of recruitment of church members among victims of Mao's political campaigns—mainly landlords, capitalists, and officials of the Nationalist regime—because the Christians could easily appeal to them with a promise of salvation and an explanation for their suffering. To the new converts, the Christian message coincided with their desires for support in the midst of political and social upheavals. This phenomenon of Christian conversion solidified an ideological resistance to the Maoist state. Equally important was the strategy to educate the children of Christian families. Because the state monopolized the educational institutions and propagated its Communist ideology, the church leaders sought to counter the state's atheistic propaganda. Besides, the Communist state remained a closed system to the Christian youth. The strong political pressure on individual Christians made it difficult for them to assimilate into the socialist order.

What concerned the state most were the acts of Christian resistance against the officials. Huang Zhongren, a Baptist, pretended to uphold the thought of Chairman Mao in the political study sessions, but he often presented himself as the spokesperson of the local Protestants when dealing with the officials. In addition, many Baptist and Presbyterian doctors and nurses in Mianhu formed a united front to challenge the party officials in district hospitals and clinics. In villages with a strong Christian presence, the Catholics and Protestants won support and sympathy from non-Christians and local leaders. They even engaged the agents of the state in rural politics. In Lutianba, the Catholics seized power in the production teams and criticized the village cadres for not protecting their interests at the beginning of the Cultural Revolution. These Catholic villagers controlled their territories until 1972 when the Shantou municipal government sent officials to mediate between the Catholics and village cadres. The Catholics and Protestants never acted as passive victims when they encountered the Maoist state; whenever possible, they would take advantage of the political climate for empowerment.

The final strategy was to rely on the Overseas Chinese Christian networks for support. Remittances sent by the churches in Hong Kong and Southeast Asia proved beneficial to Christians in Chaozhou throughout the Maoist era. The local Catholics in Mianhu received remittances from Peng Jiangyuan, a wealthy merchant in Singapore and Li Yinmin, a priest who left Shantou for Hong Kong in the early 1950s. The Baptists in Chaozhou received support from Lu Mingcai, known as Lui Ming Choi in Cantonese, a very successful Chaozhou merchant who had founded many Baptist elementary and secondary schools in Hong Kong. This South China Sea maritime network was a key to understanding the dynamics of the Christian movements in the post-1949 era because it created an invisible maritime highway that channeled resources from Overseas Chinese Christians into their Chaozhou homelands.

Conclusion

The story of Christian activism in Chaozhou during the Maoist era is insightful at both factual and conceptual levels. Shortly after the Communist Revolution, the Maoist state launched the Three-Self Patriotic Movement to integrate the Christian communities into the socialist order. But when the state co-opted these communities, it did not see the need for cooperation with the church. The church, unwillingly, found itself in opposition to the state. Rather than maintaining a policy of accommodation, the state deliberately acted against the church in order to control the religious sphere. Therefore, the art of managing tensions between religion and politics was an integral part of the state-building process. But the anti-Christian propaganda and policies failed to mould the Christians into rational, atheistic, and Communist people during Mao's reign. Both the Catholics and Protestants refused to accept the subservient role that the state had assigned them. They used their limited resources to organize religious activities in a socialist state. Faced with political pressures, many Christians used the word *chiku*, literally translated as "tasted bitterness," to refer to their experience of persecution. One Catholic clergyman recalled, "When we were bombarded with the anti-Christian propaganda, we tasted the bitterness. But we did not swallow it. We survived." When the state forced the Christians into a suffering mode, it transformed persecution into a unique opportunity to gain heavenly rewards (Carbonneau, 2006).

The Christians in Chaozhou followed a pattern of religious activism common to many independent Chinese Protestants and pro-Vatican Catholics throughout the Maoist era. They ignored what they could not change, while making use of the situation to preserve their strength. They organized cell groups and home meetings at the grassroots level, which later sowed the seeds of religious revival during the reform period (Chan and Hunter, 1991; Aikman, 2003). If a single lesson emerges from this religious development, it is that these Christians had successfully established highly autonomous and diffused worshipping communities according to their needs, despite persistent interference and systematic control from the state.

These stories of church-state interactions suggest that Christian conversion was a challenge to Maoism. In an authoritarian society where the state equated religious identification with political and ideological loyalty, the act of conversion was a resistance against the state. The Maoist state was very hostile toward any ideology and effective organization outside the control of the government. The church was viewed as a threat to the socialist state because of its religious doctrine, its emphasis on the autonomy of the church, and its effective organization and widespread network (Madsen, 2004). Given the impetus to place religious communities under state control in the past, tension and conflict always remain an integral part of church-state relations in contemporary China.

Bibliography

Aikman, David. 2003. *Jesus in Beijing: How Christianity is Transforming China and Changing the Global Balance of Power*. Washington, DC: Regnery.

Carbonneau, Robert E. 2006. "Resurrecting the Dead: Memorial Gravesites and Faith Stories of Twentieth-Century Catholic Missionaries and Laity in Western Hunan, China." *U.S. Catholic Historian* 24 (Summer): 19–37.

Chan, Kim-Kwong, and Alan Hunter. 1991. *Prayers and Thought of Chinese Christians*. Boston, MA: Cowley.

Chau, Adam Yuet. 2006. *Miraculous Response: Doing Popular Religion in Contemporary China*. Stanford, CA: Stanford University Press.

Cohen, Paul A. 1974. "Littoral and Hinterland in Nineteenth Century China: The Christian Reformers." In John King Fairbank, ed. *The Missionary Enterprise in China and America*, 197–225. Cambridge, MA: Harvard University Press.

Deng, Zhaoming. 1997. *The Vicissitudes of the Three-Self Patriotic Movement in the 1950s and its Predicament Today*. Hong Kong: Christian Study Centre on Chinese Religion and Culture.

———. 2001. "Indigenous Chinese Pentecostal Denominations." *China Study Journal* 16, no.3 (December): 5–22.

Duara, Prasenjit. 1988. *Culture, Power, and the State: Rural North China, 1900–1942*. Stanford, CA: Stanford University Press.

Dubois, Thomas David. 2005. *The Sacred Village: Social Change and Religious Life in Rural North China*. Honolulu, HI: University of Hawai'i Press.

Gibson, John Campbell. 1901. *Mission Problems and Mission Methods in South China*. Edinburgh and London: Oliphant, Anderson and Ferrier.

Gu, Changsheng. 1984. *Yesu kuliao: Gu changsheng huiyilu, 1945–1984* (Jesus wept: Memoir of Gu Changsheng, 1945–1984). Yale Divinity School Library, China Records Project Miscellaneous Personal Papers Collections, Record Group Number 8, Box 244.

Hsü, Immanuel C. Y. 2000. *The Rise of Modern China*. Oxford: Oxford University Press.

Kindopp, Jason, and Carol Lee Hamrin, eds. 2004. *God and Caesar in China: Policy Implications of Church-State Tensions*. Washington, DC: Brookings.

Lee, Joseph Tse-Hei. 2003. *The Bible and the Gun: Christianity in South China, 1860–1900*. New York: Routledge.

———. 2007. "Christianity and Chinese Diaspora in the Nineteenth Century." In Leo Suryadinata, ed. *Chinese Diaspora since Admiral Zheng He: With Special Reference to Maritime Asia*, 247–266. Singapore: Chinese Heritage Centre.

Leung, Beatrice. 2005. "China's Religious Freedom Policy: The Art of Managing Religious Activity." *China Quarterly* 184 (December): 894–913.

Ling, Oi-Ki. 1999. *The Changing Role of the British Protestant Missionaries in China*. London: Associated University Presses.

Madsen, Richard. 2004. "Catholic Conflict and Cooperation in the People's Republic of China." In Kindopp and Hamrin, eds. *God and Caesar in China*, 77–106.

Scott, James C. 1985. *Weapons of the Weak: Everyday Forms of Ideological Struggle*. New Haven, CT: Yale University Press.

Shantou Municipal Archive. 1957. Archives of the Shantou Bureau of Religious Affairs and Archives of the Shantou Bureau of the United Front.

Smith, Steve A. 2006. "Talking Toads and Chinless Ghosts: The Politics of 'Superstitious' Rumors in the People's Republic of China, 1961–1965." *American Historical Review* 111, no.2 (April): 405–427.

Wagner, Vivian. 2002. "Class Struggle and Commerce: Utilizing the Archival Heritage of the PRC." Paper presented at the XIV European Association of Chinese Studies Conference in Moscow, Russia (August 26–28).

Wang, Cheng-Chih. 2002. *Words Kill: Calling for the Destruction of "Class Enemies" in China, 1949–1953*. New York: Routledge.

Wickeri, Philip L. 1988. *Seeking the Common Ground: Protestant Christianity, the Three-Self Movement and China's United Front*. Maryknoll, NY: Orbis Books.

———. 2007. *Reconstructing Christianity in China: K. H. Ting and the Chinese Church*. Maryknoll, NY: Orbis Books.

Wou, Odoric Y. K. 1994. *Mobilizing the Masses: Building Revolution in Henan*. Stanford, CA: Stanford University Press.

Yang, C. K. 1967. *Religion in Chinese Society: A Study of Contemporary Social Functions of Religion and Some of Their Historical Factors*. Berkeley, CA: University of California Press.

Yu, Anthony C. 2003. "On State and Religion in China: A Brief Historical Reflection." *Religion East and West* 3: 1–20.

CHAPTER FIVE

The Transnational Redress Campaign for Chinese Survivors of Wartime Sexual Violence in Shanxi Province

YUKI TERAZAWA

Introduction

Since the subject of former military sex slaves, the so-called "comfort women" of the Japanese Imperial Army during the Asia-Pacific War, became widely known in the early 1990s, many groups and individuals in Asia and around the world have keenly watched the evolution of efforts to obtain redress for these women. Following Kim Haksoon of South Korea, who came forward in August 1991, women from South Korea, the Philippines, Taiwan, and the Netherlands have provided testimony about their ordeals and brought court cases against the Japanese government.[1] The investigation of wartime sexual violence and slavery on mainland China began later. Although a few Chinese victims in Shanxi province had been identified in the early 1990s, it was not until the mid-1990s that activists and scholars began to seriously research and publicize the experiences of these Chinese women. Eventually three court cases involving a total of sixteen survivors of wartime rape in Shanxi province were brought before the Japanese court,[2] along with a case on behalf of eight survivors from Hainan Island.[3]

This chapter discusses the cases of wartime rape involving women in rural Shanxi, and the movement the survivors and their supporters have created to obtain redress. Even after the women came forward, the struggle to obtain redress has been very difficult to pursue, largely owing to the indifference and opposition of the Japanese people and its government. Recent publicity in China about the issue helped gain genuine and often strong sympathy from many Chinese people but has not led to an organized and sustained effort either by the Chinese government or the general public to support the survivors. In this unfavorable environment, the transnational coalition supporting the claims of the Shanxi women played a critical role for helping them make progress toward redress. The coalition has consisted of the survivors, local Chinese sympathizers, and lawyers and activists based in Japan. This example of coalition building provides a unique model for reaching out to aged survivors isolated in the countryside in a nation where the government aggressively censors grassroots citizens' movements.[4]

The redress movement for Chinese survivors of wartime sexual violence is highly political as with other comfort women redress campaigns in general. Although the women themselves are not at all political, except for Wan Aihua, who used to be a local communist leader, the redress movement has been shaped by the dynamics of political forces, including nationalist sentiments at the grassroots level that see the survivors' predicament as originating in the oppression of the Chinese people by the Japanese. In other words, the campaign has political consequences that go far beyond obtaining redress for individual survivors to include the political agenda of many of the participants. The redress movement is not unique in this regard; indeed, it is likely that the political topography of the contemporary world makes all redress campaigns possible and inevitably has a hand in shaping them. What is unique about the activism pursued by the support group I focus on (Akirakani Suru Kai) is that it took extensive precautions not to embroil the survivors in political and journalistic intrigue or exploitation: the group attempted to protect the survivors from being taken advantage of by various groups or the state, and avoid situations where the plight of the victims became secondary to the interests of the groups representing them. This strategy demonstrated the group's cautious approach to media coverage as well as involvement in overtly political campaigns (e.g., working closely with politicians). This decision has limited the size and influence of the movement, but it certainly has helped sustain a victim-centered movement that places utmost importance on acting according to the survivors' own wishes and caring for their well-being.

The Japanese Occupation of Shanxi and Wartime Sexual Violence

Shanxi province was one of the major battlefields for Japan's invasion of China in the late 1930s. It held particular strategic importance for the Japanese Army, the Chinese Communists, and other forces resisting the Japanese invasion and occupation. The Japanese Army initially marched into Shanxi in November 1937, the same year it began a full-fledged invasion of Chinese territory lying outside the Japanese puppet state of Manchuguo located in the northeast. In the next three years, the Japanese Army in Shanxi could not subdue the Chinese forces, especially the Communist Army based in the southern mountainous areas of the province. In August 1940, the Communists launched a large-scale campaign that caused humiliating losses to the Japanese Army. In response, Japanese troops started a fierce counterattack—a genocidal war—involving the total destruction of villages they considered to be under the Communist influence. It was during this counteroffensive that many of the worst cases of sexual violence occurred (Ishida and Uchida, eds., 2004: 126–185).

These sexual assaults can be divided into several categories. First, when the Japanese Army marched into local villages, soldiers randomly raped and abducted women, some of whom were detained for several months to over a year as sex slaves. Second, Japanese occupiers also procured women through village "self-rule" organizations they set up. They would demand that local Chinese provide a certain number of women for sexual services to the Japanese military. Chinese village leaders sought to lessen the impact on their communities by selecting women with lower social standing and protecting women with more prestige. In this way, village leaders attempted both to appease the Japanese and to reduce the extent to which village women would be raped and their properties looted. Third, Japanese soldiers raped and tortured women who were active in the resistance movement not only to crush their will to fight against the Japanese but also to obtain information about subversive Communist activities. A good example is Wan Aihua, who was an underground Communist leader (Ishida and Ômori, 2000: 21–78; Ishida and Uchida, eds., 2004: 74–75, 93–110).

Another factor that contributed to the high number of rapes in Shanxi was the isolation of Japanese troops. Ishida Yoneko points out that the Japanese military was dispersed thinly to secure the vast territories of Shanxi province. This dispersion made it difficult to supervise troops in peripheral areas and kept the stress level of Japanese soldiers very high. This partly explains the high incidence of violent acts committed against Chinese civilians and troops. Furthermore, Japanese troops stationed in peripheral areas oftentimes were not led by officers trained in Japanese military academies but by senior soldiers, who lacked proper education and knowledge of the regulations governing the conduct of armed forces. Thus, Japanese troops in the periphery had plenty of opportunities to engage in criminal activities without the knowledge of higher-ranking officers (Ishida and Ômori, 2000: 57–66).

It is also true that rank and file Japanese soldiers in general did not receive an adequate education on wartime criminal activities. In fact, rape was codified as a criminal activity in Japanese military regulations of the time. But lack of knowledge about this military code prevented soldiers from realizing that rape constituted a serious war crime, and only a very small number of Japanese soldiers who raped Chinese civilians were punished (Tanaka, 2003: 28–29). In addition, deep-seated racism dehumanized the Chinese in the eyes of Japanese soldiers, and left little feeling of guilt and remorse for acts that would be considered both immoral and criminal at home (Ishida and Uchida, eds., 2004: 126–185; Kondô, 2002).

Historians have also examined the complicated relations between rape and the establishment of a system of comfort stations. Ironically, it was the notorious "Rape of Nanjing"—the massacre of large numbers of civilians in the Chinese capital accompanied by extremely brutal rapes—that prompted the Japanese military to set up the comfort stations.[5] The Japanese leadership reasoned that creating a facility where soldiers could receive sexual services would calm down agitated soldiers. Yoshimi Yoshiaki points out that behind the establishment of comfort stations was an anxiety on the part of Japanese military commanders about the possibility that low-ranking soldiers would express their discontent and frustration in the form of violence against their superiors along with brutality against local Chinese civilians (Yoshimi, 2000). The Japanese military leaders believed that the use of comfort women would also prevent the spread of venereal diseases and the infiltration of spies disguised as prostitutes.

Some feminist historians refer to the rape cases in Shanxi province as having the characteristics of both individual random rape and the comfort women system. Soldiers raped local women in Shanxi during army offensives, but they also detained them for many months for the sole purpose of providing sexual services. The fact that Japanese military leaders requested local Chinese village heads to supply women to be used as sex slaves indicates a sense of entitlement on the part of Japanese troops to receive sexual services, commonly offered at comfort stations. There is also the example of Nan Erpu from Yu district of Shanxi, who was designated for exclusive service to a leading serviceman. This closely resembles the comfort station system, which provided officers with a special club or brothel staffed by Japanese sex workers or Korean women who were considered highly qualified.

According to currently available sources, the system started with the establishment of a comfort station in Shanghai in 1932. The idea proliferated rapidly and became institutionalized after the Rape of Nanjing in December 1937. Sexual services, in fact, became an integral part of Japanese military life. The troops stationed in Yu district were not provided with military brothels, so they established a system resembling comfort stations by abducting and detaining local women. Researchers who have worked on wartime sexual violence by the Japanese Army during the Asia-Pacific War assert that, contrary to the expectation of the high-ranking Japanese military leaders, the comfort women system did not reduce rape incidents but rather promoted them. In fact, the presence of comfort stations made both sexual slavery and random rape seem like acceptable activities in the eyes of Japanese servicemen (Ishida and Uchida, eds., 2004: 238–271).

The Survivors' Stories

Like many survivors of rape, victims of the Japanese fell prey to the prejudices of their local villages, and sometimes their own families, once the Japanese left. After the war, rape victims were discriminated against economically and ostracized socially. For over fifty years, Chinese rape victims kept silent about their experiences. Although other villagers discreetly gossiped about what had happened and often mistreated them, open discussion of their predicament was taboo. Villagers' harassment and segregation of rape survivors occurred in silence—without an open acknowledgment of how these incidents presumably reflected on the survivors' families, village communities, and the nation.

The experience of Nan Erpu, uncovered by Japanese researchers' interviews with her brother, Nan Shuancheng, her adopted daughter, Yang Xiulian, and former village leaders Yang Shitong and Yang Baogui, demonstrates how agonizing the experiences of sexual slavery and postwar discrimination were (Ishida and Uchida, eds., 2004: 49–76). Born and raised in Nantou village in Yu district, Nan Erpu was married at the age of seventeen to a man twenty years older than herself. Because she did not get along with her husband, she returned to her natal home. When the Japanese Army marched into her village in 1942, she was about twenty years old and still lived with her natal family. Led by a low-ranking officer, a group of six Japanese soldiers raided her house. Her father was out working in the field. Her mother hid Nan Erpu in an underground storage space, but the Japanese soldiers found her. The officer chased the mother out of the house and raped Nan Erpu. She was taken away to a house in a fortress, where she was detained and raped by the officer every day. At one point she became pregnant and delivered a male child, which later died of a cold.

It should be noted that the Japanese Army used women like Nan Erpu not only for receiving sexual services, but also for obtaining money in the form of abduction rackets. Indeed, Nan Erpu's father sold a large portion of his land and gave the money to the Japanese Army, but was still unable to win his daughter's freedom. She was finally released eighteen months after her abduction because the officer she serviced was transferred to another location. Unfortunately, her release was only temporary. A Japanese soldier came to her house and brought her to Hedong village, where the Japanese military base was located. During the days, she stayed in a house in the village; at night she was taken to a fortress on the hill, where she was raped by soldiers. After two months, she escaped to her sister's house in a neighboring village and she eventually fled to adjacent Yangqu district. The soldier who had captured Nan Erpu at her parents' house tried to find out from her brother, who was ten years old at the time, where she had gone. Because the brother would not reveal his sister's whereabouts, the soldier bound his hands to a horse's saddle and had the horse run, dragging him behind. The brother's belly was badly injured and bled profusely. The head of the village's self-rule organization, which was collaborating with the Japanese, begged the soldier to free the boy. The boy was released, but still infuriated, the Japanese soldier burned the house of Nan Erpu's family. Having lost a large portion of their land and their house, the family became impoverished, and Nan Erpu's uncles and cousins had no choice but to work as live-in farm laborers at other villagers' farms.

Nan Erpu continued to suffer during the postwar period. During the 1950s she received a three-year prison sentence for "historically antirevolutionary" activities—being together with Japanese soldiers for too long and having a child. After serving two years in jail, she was released. Although she was out of prison, she was still treated as a collaborator of the Japanese (*tongdi fengzi*) and therefore historically antirevolutionary. During the Cultural Revolution (1966–1976), she was repeatedly humiliated in public. As part of her punishment she was forced to do overtime work and was often the last person allowed to go home. Other rape survivors in Shanxi experienced a similar predicament, if not as extreme as the one from which Nan Erpu suffered. This is why some survivors have a strong aversion to being called former comfort women, which connotes they collaborated with the Japanese, instead of being rape victims.

Nan Erpu's second husband married her knowing what happened to her during the war. Because he tried to protect her, he was also subject to persecution by the village community. The couple adopted a baby girl in 1964, and Nan Erpu cherished the child. However, the combination of harsh persecution during the Cultural Revolution combined with serious pain from various medical problems finally led her to commit suicide in 1967. Her adopted daughter is now pursuing the court case on behalf of her mother.

Other women also went through terrible sufferings. In the aftermath of the Japanese occupation, many of them had no choice but to get married to undesirable marriage partners (lacking in wealth and status), leaving them at the bottom of the village hierarchy. Often their own relatives, and even their own children, treated them with condescension and contempt. There were many instances where family members were open about their desire to avoid the survivors or their unwillingness to take care of the women in their old age (Katô, 2004).

One of the reasons that young men rejected rape survivors as their marriage partners was because they feared that these women would be infertile owing to the injuries resulting from incessant rape while they were captives of the Japanese Army. Most women got married because marriage was often the only means for women's economic survival, especially in isolated farming villages in rural Shanxi. However, once their husbands and their family discovered the women were barren or they had sexual difficulties because of either psychological trauma or recurring physical ailments, they divorced them.[6] This was evident in the cases of Zhao Runmei and Gao Yin'e. After divorce, the survivors and their natal families commonly sought other marriage partners. Some women went through a painful process of repeated marriage and divorce two and even three times (Ishida and Uchida, eds., 2004: 76–83).

Coming Forward

It required a series of fortunate coincidences to bring these humble farmers' wives and widows from a remote corner of rural China to the international hearings and courthouses in Tokyo. Zhang Shuangbing, a local elementary school teacher in Yu district, played an important role in encouraging the rape survivors to come forward. It was his sustained interest and kind deeds carried on for over ten years that finally persuaded rape survivors to come forward.

Zhang Shuangbing first encountered one of the survivors, named Hou Dong'e, in the fall of 1982 when he returned from a school fieldtrip to the mountains with his students. He noticed a field where millet crops had not been harvested, while all the surrounding fields had already been finished. In this field, Zhang saw an old woman with bound feet kneeling down and cutting millet plants one by one. This scene indicated her social ostracism and lack of support. When he asked local villagers who she was, he was told that she was one of the women who had been brought to the Japanese fortress during the war. Zhang was both curious and sympathetic. He wanted to know the details of her abduction and detention at the Japanese fortress, but she was reluctant to reveal anything more than that she was indeed brought to the Japanese fort. Deeply moved by her difficult circumstances, he wondered if he could help her to receive government assistance (Ishida and Uchida, eds., 2004: 196–197; Kawami, 2004; Zhang, 2002).

Ten years passed, and the redress movement by former comfort women in other Asian nations had begun. In 1992 Zhang Shuangbing read a newspaper article by the writer Tong Zeng stating that many Chinese women were sexually assaulted by Japanese troops, but not a single victim had come forward to testify publicly. The implication of Tong's article was that these Chinese rape survivors along with survivors from other nations could demand redress from the Japanese government. This prompted Zhang Shuangbing to persuade Hou Dong'e to talk about her experience. She was reluctant to do so initially, but finally she opened up when Zhang Shuangbing brought his wife and left them to talk by themselves. Eventually Hou Dong'e's testimony was sent in written form to the Japanese government with a request for an apology and reparation. She never received a response. Hou Dong'e planned to attend an international public hearing on comfort women issues scheduled to be held in December 1992 in Tokyo. Unfortunately, she became ill on her way to Tokyo and could not attend the hearing (Ishida and Uchida, eds., 2004: 196–197; Kawami, 2004). The presentation of the testimony at this hearing was left to another survivor.

This survivor was Wan Aihua whom Zhang Shuangbing discovered when he was conducting research on survivors of wartime rape by the Japanese military, including Hou Dong'e, in Yangquan village in Yu district. By the early 1990s Wan Aihua was living in the provincial capital, Taiyuan. With the help of Li Guiming, her adopted sister's grandson and a farmer, Wan Aihua traveled to Yangquan village to meet Zhang Shuangbing. Having confirmed that Wan Aihua was willing to give her testimony, Zhang Shuangbing worked with Tong Zeng and Lin Boyao, the leader of an activist group for expatriate Chinese in Japan, to enable Wan Aihua to travel to Tokyo. It was still early in the period during which China was slowly shifting its policy restricting ordinary Chinese citizens from traveling abroad. In addition to the problem of obtaining a travel permit, the sensitive nature of her trip made it imperative to solicit the cooperation of Chinese officials and to deal with cumbersome bureaucratic procedures. In the end Wan Aihua was able to obtain a travel permit, and she traveled with two Chinese officials from the provincial government of Shanxi to Tokyo (Kawami, 2004). In this way, she became the first Chinese woman to provide public testimony on sexual assaults committed by the Japanese military in wartime China. Wan Aihua's meeting with Japanese activists on this occasion led to the forming of the redress movement for Shanxi women.

Support Groups

Eventually, two different groups were formed to support the rape survivors in Shanxi. The first group, the Association to Support the Lawsuits of Chinese Comfort Women, known in Japanese as "Chûgokujin 'Ianfu' Saiban Wo Shien Suru Kai" or "Shien Suru Kai," led by the attorney Ômori Noriko, was constituted by various peace activists and progressive Japanese citizens, some of whom worked with the Japanese Communist Party. The group also solicited support from a Chinese lawyer, Kang Jian, and from a Japanese organization called the Association to Support the Claims of the Chinese War Victims, which has supported lawsuits against the Japanese government and corporations concerning Japan's war atrocities in China ranging from cases of slave labor to the victims of biological weapons.

In 1995 Ômori worked with several other lawyers to file two separate lawsuits against the Japanese government involving cases of sexual violence. The six plaintiffs were victims first identified by Zhang Shuangbing, who continued to support them throughout their legal fight. The Tokyo District Court dismissed both cases in 2001, followed by the Tokyo High Court's rejections of the plaintiffs' claims in 2004 and

2005. The attorneys appealed but in March 2007 the Japanese Supreme Court upheld the rulings of the lower courts to end the legal process. The main basis of the High Court's argument to dismiss the first case was that the Japanese government is not legally responsible for damages inflicted upon the plaintiffs owing to the rule of state immunity effective under Japan's prewar constitution, and the Supreme Court supported this reasoning. To dismiss the second case, the Supreme Court referred to a 1972 Joint Communiqué between China and Japan. By signing this document, the Chinese government relinquished its pursuit of war-related compensation, and as the judges argue, individual Chinese have lost their rights to claim compensation from the Japanese government through legal means. Ōmori and other attorneys who represented the survivors disagree with the Court's arguments and stress that the Court cannot deny the survivors the right—even if it is not technically legal—to receive redress and reparations from the Japanese government. They intend to continue their support for redress, urging the Japanese government to take administrative action to respond to the survivors' claims (*Bengodan Seimei*, 2007).

The second support group, which supports ten other victims, including Wan Aihua, also filed a lawsuit in 1998. This group, comprising over three hundred supporters, is led by historian Ishida Yoneko and is called the Association for Uncovering the Reality of Sexual Violence Committed by the Japanese Military in China and Supporting the Legal Cases for Redress, which activists usually refer to in Japanese as "Akirakani Suru Kai."[7] Many of its members, including Ishida, have been working since the late 1980s for the redress of Chinese slave laborers for the Kajima Company in the Hanaoka mine in northeastern Japan during the war. Prompted by the testimony of Wan Aihua, who desired to pursue a legal case against the Japanese government, activists and lawyers began to make research trips to Shanxi in 1996.

When she went back to Shanxi from her first visit to Tokyo, Wan Aihua took the initiative to discover other surviving victims. She asked Li Guiming to help find other rape survivors who would be willing to provide testimony and to fight the court case against the Japanese government. It was not difficult for Li Guiming to identify other survivors because, as we saw earlier, the identity of the survivors was usually an open secret. However, he confronted a huge obstacle convincing the women to come forward. To overcome this silence, he resorted to an approach similar to the one that Zhang Shuangbing used to overcome Hou Dong'e's reticence: Li Guiming visited them again and again, helped them with farm work, and eventually gained their trust. In the case of Yin Yulin, it took three years of visits before she finally shared her testimony, and she acceded only when her sister and brother-in-law helped Li Guiming to persuade her to speak out (Ishida and Uchida, eds., 2004: 186–187; Kawami, 2004). Eventually Wan Aihua, Li Guiming, and members of the Akirakani Suru Kai who visited Yu district began to work with nine other survivors who came forward.

The Transnational Movement

The support groups for Shanxi survivors differ from other transnational groups working with former comfort women from Korea, Taiwan, and the Philippines because China has made it very difficult to form local support groups for the survivors. Activists and lawyers located in Japan knew well that the national government in Beijing would be concerned about the forming of a private and independent nongovernmental organization that could potentially challenge the government, and that an attempt to form such a group would invite sanctions from the government. Even if the government would have relented and allowed the formation of a local support group in Shanxi, Ishida's group has so far been unable to assemble a sufficient number of local Chinese to provide sustained assistance to the survivors in rural Shanxi. The fact that they live in isolated farming villages is one of the important reasons that makes it difficult for Chinese sympathizers (except those who live in the same village) to keep providing their help, or even to keep in touch with the survivors. This situation led the Japan-based group to take on a significant portion of the work toward redress, including research, publicizing the cases, and raising funds for travel and medical expenses for the survivors.

During the early and mid-1990s the Chinese government was unsupportive, if not explicitly obstructive, of the survivors' individual initiatives to gain apologies and compensation from Japanese companies and the Japanese government. It is true that by this time the Chinese government had shifted its interpretation of the war; it discussed the war within a nationalistic framework rather than adhering to the logic of class struggle. That is, it presented the damages incurred by the war as the victimization of the Chinese people by the imperialist powers—Japan in particular—rather than the sufferings of the proletariat, including Japanese workers and peasants, caused by wars between capitalist states that a privileged few controlled (He, 2007a: 2, 2007b). However, it seems the Chinese government was walking a fine line between nationalistic rhetoric to win the popular support of the Chinese people and the necessity of maintaining a reasonably amiable diplomatic relationship with Japan, which was a crucial trade partner and source of economic and technological assistance.

In these circumstances, Ishida and other members of the Akirakani Suru Kai were not sure if individual Chinese survivors could bring their cases to the Japanese court without inviting sanctions from the Chinese government (Fukuda, 2004; Ikeda, 2004; Kawami, 2004; Tamaki, 2004). Unsupportive of the redress movement and suspicious of the Japanese activists' motivations, the Chinese government did not easily allow the Japanese activists into Yu district, a region that was still supposed to be closed to foreign visitors for military reasons. Thus, when Ishida's group attempted in 1996 to go and meet the survivors in Yu district for the first time, its members had to rely on resourceful mediators to gain access. Respectable nongovernmental organizations and individuals (such as the aforementioned Lin Boyao) who had long worked to develop friendly relations between China and Japan, along with influential Japanese scholars specializing in Chinese studies, helped negotiate with Chinese government officials. Permission was granted under the condition that the Shanxi provincial officials accompany Japanese activists traveling to Yu district, and that these foreign visitors not stay in villages overnight. The latter rule has created great inconvenience for visitors from Japan. They had to take a road trip several hours one-way to visit the survivors and then return the same day. Since 1996, however, activists have not been prohibited from visiting women or interviewing them.

As it turned out, China's central government did not object to the Japanese activist group working with the survivors or to their lawsuit against the Japanese government. At the same time, it has not given substantial support to the survivors with the court cases. The farthest Chinese officials have gone is to criticize the dismissal of one of the Shanxi sexual violence cases at the Tokyo Higher Court in 2004 during a press conference attended by a Ministry of Foreign Affairs spokesman (*Xinhua General News Service*, 2004; *Agence France Presse*, 2004). In April 2007, the same month the Japanese Supreme Court struck down two cases involving wartime sexual slavery in Shanxi, Chinese Premier Wen Jiabao reverted to a conciliatory stance on Japan's wartime responsibility (Sato, 2007). The current administration led by President Hu Jintao was able to consolidate power by early 2007, and perhaps this is why the Chinese Foreign Ministry no longer needs to bend to grassroots activism that is critical of Japan. Moreover, China has been repeatedly accused of its own human rights violations by the international community, and far-reaching publicity of Japanese war crimes might bring attention uncomfortably close to human rights violations within contemporary China. This may have to do with the fact Chinese political leaders have never attempted to discuss with Japanese political leaders—or even to mention—the issue of wartime rape.

The lack of support from the Chinese government did not hinder activists from conducting extensive research on wartime rape in Shanxi. Realizing the advantage of drawing on the expertise of professional historians specializing in Chinese and Japanese history and feminist scholars studying wartime sexual violence, Ishida formed a study group in 1999 known as the "Seibôryoku No Shiten Kara Mita Nicchû Sensô No Rekishiteki Seikaku Kenkyûkai," whose members engaged in archival work, scrutinized source materials, and assembled the often fragmentary statements of the survivors into an intelligible narrative. Both independent and academic historians contributed significantly to this collaborative effort. Some independent historians who joined the group had been active for over ten years through such groups as the Tokyo-based Association for No More Nanjings (No Moa Nankin No Kai) searching for evidence of atrocities by the Japanese military in China. Their growing knowledge of Japan's offensive war in China during the 1930s and 1940s as well as their skills of archival research were fundamental in producing solid, fact-based reports about rape incidents in Shanxi.

Working with the survivors in this fact-finding research was difficult. The researchers faced huge problems communicating with the survivors. The women spoke a local dialect of Yu district, and thus, contrary to the initial expectations of researchers, native Chinese speakers from other areas could not understand the women's speech. The research team had to locate capable translators who would accompany their research trips to the women's villages and also to find Chinese students or former students from Shanxi residing in Japan in order to transcribe the audiotapes of oral interviews. Moreover, the survivors' lack of schooling made it difficult to identify the precise spelling of their names, the exact year of their birth or an event, or the exact size of relevant objects or distances between places. This type of information, which could not be verified through oral interviews with the women, had to be uncovered in other witnesses' statements and visits to the places where relevant incidents took place.

The extreme trauma the women suffered was one of the major reasons for their fragmentary speech. Occasionally the survivors passed out before or in the middle of their description of the most traumatic events. When this happened, researchers had to provide a more comfortable environment for the survivors to relate their stories. Indeed, Wan Aihua fainted in the middle of her talk both at the 1992 international hearing and at the 2000 NGO-led international war crimes tribunal in Tokyo, and could not provide a full account of her experiences. However, she presented a cohesive and detailed account for a smaller, more informal meeting that was also held during her 1992 visit (Tasaki, 2004). At other times, the survivors suffered temporary amnesia. For example, Gao Yin'e insisted that her current husband is her second husband while he claimed that he was her third. Attorney Kawaguchi Kazuko believes that the heartbreak of two divorces because of her infertility caused her to suppress the memory of her second divorce. Another survivor, Zhang Xiantu, testified that she was gang raped by seven or eight Japanese soldiers in Hedong village before she was taken to a Japanese military base on the hilltop. But when she gave her testimony in the court, she could not remember this scene even though the rest of her testimony corresponded to the story she had given in Shanxi. Kawaguchi suggests that this temporary amnesia is a symptom of posttraumatic stress disorder, the psychological problem from which Zhang Xiantu suffers.

It should also be noted that the narratives the Akirakani Suru Kai published in their reports certainly do not cover everything that happened during and after the rape incidents. Although the researchers conducted exhaustive oral interview research, there sometimes were minor related events that were not told. The following anecdote is a good example. During the early stages of their research, when both the researchers and survivors had not yet identified and worked out problems with mutual understanding, one of the survivors underreported the number of rape incidents that took place. This survivor was reluctant to reveal to Japanese people what she considered extremely shameful experiences for herself and her family. It was only after the researchers gained more of her trust and she came to better understand the significance of her testimony that she told them that the number of rape incidents was much greater than that she initially recounted.

Also, there are certain facts that the survivors and other witnesses related to trusted researchers but that have not been discussed in publications. The researchers made deliberate judgments to omit select details, such as hostile attitudes of the women's family members towards the survivors during and after the war, which would have had detrimental repercussions on the lives of the survivors, their families, and others in village communities. Ishida states that her research team did not manipulate the information that they gathered from the victims and other witnesses for the sake of court hearings: they made it a priority to maintain their academic integrity and to leave a legitimate historical documentation for the generations to come. They decided not to write down certain information, mostly secondary, only in cases where publication would have detrimental effects on the lives of the survivors, their families, and other villagers, and would obstruct their ongoing research and activist work by inviting resentment from the victims and other witnesses (Ishida, 2004; Katô, 2004).

Considering the challenges the research team faced, it is obvious that the group could not pursue this research without the exceptional good will, interest, and courage local Chinese supporters demonstrated. These supporters include He Qing, the retired official of the foreign affairs division of the Shanxi provincial government, who offered extensive support to facilitate the trip to Yu district. Also, faculty such as Zhao Qingui and Li Shuxia, who specialize in Japanese studies at Shanxi University and other schools, served a critical role as liaisons and translators, filling in the cultural and sociological background of village life in Shanxi as well. Japanese activists have also relied on personal friends, who helped them obtain cheap airplane tickets, find adequate means of transportation from Taiyuan to Yu district, and find accommodation and restaurants. Thus, in addition to Zhang Shuangbing, Li Guiming, and the family members of the survivors who strongly supported the court case, these local supporters have constituted a crucial component of the transnational coalition for the redress of the Shanxi women.

The research team also drew on the support of Kondô Hajime, a former Japanese soldier who agreed to testify in court that he had joined in a gang rape of a Chinese woman (unidentified) in Shanxi and visited a comfort station in the city of Taiyuan in Shanxi several times during the war (Ishida, Katô, and Utsumi, eds., 2005; Terazawa, 2006). His testimony helped convince presiding judges about the truthfulness of the survivors' accounts. Kondô constitutes another uniquely important element of the transnational redress movement.

When the Akirakani Suru Kai engaged in research and publicity of the survivors' cases, two of the greatest challenges it faced were to avoid patronizing or controlling the survivors, and to prevent other groups or individuals, such as journalists, from taking advantage of the women's testimonies. Keeping in mind this general concern, the group seriously deliberated how to support the survivors in economic terms. Needless to say, economic disparity between activists in Japan and the survivors and their supporters in rural Shanxi is vast. The women survivors and their families were sometimes in dire need of material support. Activists based in Japan, whether they mean to or not, can manipulate and dominate the survivors and their local supporters by giving them money and gifts. For example, before Ishida's group began to carry out research in China there were cases in which Japanese journalists paid former comfort women in other Asian countries for their accounts of wartime experiences. Not only does this type of payment relegate the survivors to a dependent position with respect to the researcher, but also the survivors could have adapted their stories to fit the perceived wishes of the interviewer. The Akirakani Suru Kai has been cautious to avoid this pitfall. As a pro bono case, lawyers pay for all the legal and travel expenses from their own pockets. Activists pay for their own trips to Shanxi. The Akirakani Suru Kai also raises funds to cover travel expenses to invite Chinese survivors and other witnesses for court hearings. Except for paying travel expenses and bringing small gifts when visiting the survivors, however, the only financial support that the activist group has provided to the women is coverage of a portion of their medical bills. The activists deemed this arrangement reasonable given that like many rural residents in China the aged survivors often could not afford medical treatment and would be left to die at home if they suffered from serious illness. Resisting the temptation to give other types of assistance has not always been easy for Japanese activists. The economic needs of the survivors and their families sometimes seem dire, and the amount of money required to alleviate their problems looks modest when converted into Japanese currency (Fukuda, 2003; Katô, 2004). Succumbing to this temptation, however, could make the women targets of jealousy or turn them into tools by family members looking for economic gain. It could also create a relationship of domination and subservience between the Japanese supporters and Chinese rape survivors. This possibility is especially horrifying since it echoes the system of domination that was established between the Japanese aggressors and Chinese local residents during the war.

The issue of redress for victims of wartime rape in Shanxi, which initially enjoyed very limited publicity in Chinese press, began to gain more and more attention and sympathy from Chinese journalists and people in general. One probable reason for this is that after it became clear that the Chinese government would not interfere with the redress movement, the Chinese press and citizens felt more freedom to express their interest and support for the court cases. There was also momentum created by other cases. Following the filing of a lawsuit by the

Chinese survivors of forced labor and torture who worked for Kajima Company in 1995 (the Kajima-Hanaoka case), over a dozen forced labor cases involving Chinese victims, the Japanese government, and Japanese corporations that used Chinese slave labor, along with the four cases concerning sexual slavery, have been filed in Japanese courts. Although these legal fights have been very challenging to pursue after such a long lapse of time and have often resulted in defeat on the part of the plaintiffs, the revelation of egregious human rights abuses has led to several victories for the plaintiffs, including the historic court-mediated settlement of the Kajima-Hanaoka case. News about these court cases has been reported in China through newspapers, television, and the Internet. The fact the government has increasingly refrained from censoring the circulation of news from overseas could have been helpful for widely publicizing news about the redress movements for the survivors of Japan's war atrocities. However, it is important to remember that the growing interest nationwide in China about the victimization of Chinese people by the Japanese military and corporations during the war has not led in the case of the rape survivors in Shanxi to a reliable and sustained support either by Chinese private individuals or groups.

This is evident in the following example. In 2004 a journalist based in Taiyuan published a series of articles in a local newspaper, *Shanxi Commercial Daily* (*Shanxi Shangbao*). Moved by the story of the women's sufferings during the war, the various hardships that they had to endure after the war, and their courageous fights in Japanese courts, a group of taxi drivers formed a group called Home of Customers, and, along with other individual donors, raised a significant sum to help ease the survivors' economic hardship. In June 2004, the group drove a caravan of over a dozen taxies several hours on rough roads to present gifts to the survivors (Dong, 2004). Unfortunately, the visits of survivors by taxi drivers lasted no more than a few years (Ishida, 2006a: 5–6). This case points to the limits and danger of relying on the news media, which tend to have a short attention span, and local, private groups without a solid foundation that are unable to sustain their support for an extended period.

Defeat in Japanese Courts and New Directions

Attorneys representing Wan Aihua and other women have not necessarily been optimistic about winning their cases. In fact, they have been quite open about the extreme difficulty of succeeding, and made sure that the plaintiffs wanted to pursue the lawsuit despite the challenges. Members of Ishida's group have been relieved that their pursuit of the court case has generally helped the women victims make progress with their psychological problems, and has made some of them even healthier. There had been some worry that the anxiety and stress of the ongoing legal fight would harm their health (Ikeda, 2004; Kawaguchi, 2004a, 2004b). Even though they were aware of the difficulties, the dismissals of their cases by the Japanese Supreme Court between 2005 and 2007 devastated the survivors and resulted in detrimental effects to their mental and physical health (*Japan Economic Newswire*, 2005b; *New York Times*, 2007).[8]

During a visit to Yu district in March 2006 by the Akirakani Suru Kai members after the deliverance of the Supreme Court decision, the two Japanese lawyers had a very hard time explaining the loss of their case to the plaintiffs. For example, they could not easily dispel Wan Aihua's confusion as she kept asking why they lost the case when the court wholeheartedly acknowledged the truthfulness of their testimonies (Ishida, 2006b: 8–9). The Akirakani Suru Kai members subsequently saw deterioration of some survivors' health conditions. Rather than expressing their anger in words, they internalized the pain and suffered quietly, with posttraumatic stress disorder recurring for some survivors. The news of the court decision was particularly hard on one survivor, Zhao Runmei. She began to suffer from insomnia, lack of appetite, acute weight loss, amnesia, and late night pacing (Tamaki, 2006: 8). The weakening of her health led to her death in January 2008.

Upon visiting the survivors and their families in the aftermath of the Supreme Court ruling, not only were the activists from Japan concerned about the worsening of survivors' health but also about reviving the sense of shame shared by the family members of the plaintiffs, if not by the survivors themselves. When they visited the women's villages in August 2006, the activists were flabbergasted to discover that not only were villagers uninformed about the court's decision, but many villagers lacked knowledge about who the visitors from Japan had been and exactly why they had been regularly visiting the survivors. Since they knew the women were rape victims of Japanese soldiers and most visiting activists were Japanese (there were also a few expatriated Chinese and Koreans residing in Japan), some villagers vaguely thought these visitors were bringing money as compensation to the survivors either as private individuals or agents of the Japanese government. This discovery prompted the supporters from Japan to suggest holding an informational town meeting and building a memorial for the rape survivors in their villages. In this way, they wanted to commemorate the survivors' ordeal and to educate local residents about the courageous fight the survivors took on. While the surviving women tended to support the idea of a memorial, their families were clearly unwilling either to hold a town meeting or to create a memorial. For them, doing so was to expose the shame inflicted upon the women and their families (Ishida, 2006b).

To overcome these problems, the Japan-based activists came up with the idea of holding an exhibition both in Japan and China to publicize the issue of wartime rape and violence. With a few exceptions, the survivors and families were supportive. Several groups in addition to the Akirakani Suru Kai, including the Shien Suru Kai, the Hainan Net, and the Osaka Executive Committee for Commemorating the Sixtieth Anniversary of the Nanjing Massacre, decided to work with the Women's Active Museum on War and Peace (WAM)—a small, privately funded museum established in 2005 in Tokyo—to organize an exhibition to be held starting in June 2008 (Ikeda, 2007).

Given the lukewarm support of the Chinese government, activists from Japan did not expect they could easily find a Chinese institution that would readily hold an exhibition of rape survivors. Responding to requests from the activists, the provincial government of Shanxi suggested the Eighth Route Army Taihang Memorial Museum, which commemorates the Communists' resistance against the Japanese Army, as a possible site for the exhibition. To the surprise of the Japanese, the director and staff at the museum were quite enthusiastic about organizing the exhibition (Ikeda, 2007). The speedy negotiation process, starting in the spring of 2007, resulted in an agreement to hold the exhibition beginning in the fall of 2008 concurrent with the exhibition at WAM (Terazawa, 2008). Japanese supporters hope that the concurrent exhibitions will help the survivors to eventually obtain some form of redress and to reclaim their dignity by helping to dispel the sense of shame that still hovers over their families and village communities.

Japanese Nationalism and the Comfort Women Issue

In contrast to growing awareness in China and support from the international community on the issue of sexual violence and slavery in China and elsewhere in Asia, the vast majority of Japanese remain ignorant, uninterested, or hostile in this and other redress movements for the survivors of Japan's wartime atrocities. The comfort women issue attracted fairly high-level attention from the media, citizens' groups, various politicians, the Foreign Ministry, public intellectuals, and human rights lawyers in Japan from 1991, when Kim Haksoon and other former Korean survivors of military sexual slavery first publicized their experiences, until the mid-1990s. Since then, however, media coverage of the issue has generally declined while conservative politicians and intellectuals began to portray rape survivors as paid prostitutes who willingly offered sexual services. The media's loss of interest since the mid-1990s has been paralleled by a series of defeats in comfort women legal cases and the Japanese government's adamant refusal to provide anything more than token handouts to the survivors from a private funding agency called the Asian Women's Fund.[9] This lack of interest was evident at the symbolic war crimes tribunal organized by human rights and feminist groups in 2000 in Tokyo, during which the Japanese government was put on trial for establishing sexual slavery as a military institution during the Asia-Pacific War. The organizers invited survivors from various Asian and European nations and solicited legal specialists from all over the world to act as judges. The event led to extensive coverage in the Asian and Western media, but the international community was appalled that a number of important Japanese media outlets simply ignored the event.

Within this general atmosphere of apathy and hostility, Japanese activists and lawyers from various ideological persuasions have sustained support groups for the survivors of wartime sexual violence, including the two groups supporting the survivors in Shanxi. Feminist and women's rights activists and lawyers constitute the core of these groups, but the range of political views represented is fairly wide, encompassing radical and left-leaning feminists, such as the late Matsui Yayoi, several Christian groups that adhere to a more moderate version of feminism and peace activism, and resident Korean women who have formed one of the most dynamic components of the coalition of comfort women activist groups.[10] Besides feminists, the redress movement for former comfort women has attracted activists from human rights groups, labor unions, peace activist groups, leftist organizations and parties, religious groups, circles of concerned academics and intellectuals, and ordinary Japanese people without an affiliation to any of these groups. In addition to their support of the comfort women movement, this diverse group helps others damaged by Japan's actions during and after the Asia-Pacific War, including legal cases against the Japanese government and individual corporations. The survivors the activists support include Chinese victims of germ warfare and of chemical munitions;

Korean and Taiwanese former BC class criminals (who claim they suffered unfair penalties); former POWs of the Japanese Army from the United States, the Netherlands, and Great Britain; and Japanese former POWs who were detained as slave laborers in Siberia under the rule of the Soviet Union.

The motivations of the various types of activists for getting involved in redress campaigns vary. Some, like Kondô Hajime, are ex-soldiers who committed rapes and killings of civilians themselves. A few are veteran activists attempting to build a friendly relationship between Japan and Communist China, an effort they pursued even when China was ostracized by the Western world and Japan had no diplomatic relationship with it.[11] Conversations I have had with activists since 1996, when I was first introduced to many of these groups, indicate that many have joined the campaign based on their strong desire to prevent Japan from building another authoritarian government with a large military force that could be used to invade surrounding countries. They believe that making the Japanese government take responsibility for the Japanese Army's wartime atrocities and teaching young people about this issue are crucial for this cause. Although they are constantly attacked by right-wing activists and intellectuals for having a pernicious influence on the Japanese people and nation, these progressive groups often present arguments that are steeped in their unique version of nationalism in postwar Japan. A common argument is that it is a good idea for Japan to resolve the postwar redress issues including that of comfort women, in order to ensure a democratic and prosperous Japanese nation in the future and to keep amicable relations with other Asian nations.

These liberal Japanese activists have been working to counter a new wave of political activism on the part of the conservatives. From the mid- to late-1990s, conservative, nationalist politicians, intellectuals, and ordinary citizens skillfully organized groups with generous funding to pursue their conservative agenda. These groups include the Nippon Conference (Nihon Kaigi), the Association of Younger Diet Members to Reconsider Japan's Future (Nihon No Zento To Rekishi Kyôiku Wo Kangaeru Wakate Giin No Kai, led by former Prime Minister Abe Shinzo), and the Japanese Society for History Textbook Reform (Atarashii Kyôkasho Wo Tsukuru Kai). All these groups were reorganized or newly established in 1997, underscoring the dynamic regeneration of the conservative movement during this period.[12] An important factor that contributed to the rightward shift of Japanese politics, however, was the weakening of left-leaning social movements between the late 1970s and the early 1990s. In particular, the liberalization of Japan's economy, the loss of many manufacturing jobs, and the accelerating privatization of publicly owned businesses (e.g., the National Railroad) undermined the bargaining power of labor unions, which had constituted an important base for progressive political parties. The sluggish economy since the early 1990s has upset many Japanese people's lives and has given rise to a sense of insecurity among the public. This economic anxiety may have made more appealing the nationalistic rhetoric and the assertive posture of the conservatives, who could easily blame "irritating" foreign nations such as China, North and South Korea and demonize those left-leaning, progressive, "unpatriotic" intellectuals and citizens.[13]

The cartoonist Kobayashi Yoshinori and other conservatives were disturbed by the progressive activists' campaign for publicizing sexual violence and other atrocities committed by Japanese soldiers as they believe that Japanese people must protect their "grandfathers" by any means, even if they had committed such offenses in the war (Kobayashi, 1996–2000, 1998–2003). Like Kobayashi, many people were eventually drawn to the movement to present Japanese history in a way that makes the students proud of their nation. The conservatives seem to have felt quite uneasy when they were exposed to the comfort women issue for the first time (Oguma and Ueno, 2003). The newly uncovered history of the comfort women was too upsetting for them to accept. This led them to listen to conservative intellectuals who presented the comfort women issue as a leftist-feminist campaign to undermine Japan's national pride and interest. In other words, many Japanese people were already seeking an excuse to ignore the issue. Embracing the notion that the comfort women issue was an anti-Japanese plot hatched by Japanese leftists and neighboring countries in East Asia was an effective way to divert attention away from the facts about the atrocities. The campaigns by well-organized conservative groups and the nationalistic sentiments shared by many ordinary citizens make it immensely difficult to draw support from the Japanese general public for the redress movement for the survivors of wartime sexual violence by the Japanese military.

Conclusion

A useful metaphor for describing how activists could organize a coalition drawing groups and individuals positioned differently in terms of class, gender, race, nationality, or sexual orientation is that of a web or network. The existing transnational coalition for the old women survivors in Shanxi demonstrates how groups and individuals of different political persuasions and interests situated quite differently within the web of political forces could form temporary strategic alliances to work on a single issue. Although maintaining such a coalition would often be difficult and accompanied by significant risk, the redress movement could not have gone as far as it has, nor will it be able to move forward in the future, without such tactical and oftentimes odd associations across national borders.

By continuing to network across borders, both national and identity-based, the survivors of wartime rape by Japanese troops and their supporters in Japan and in the women's home countries have been successful in obtaining significant support from the United Nations and the International Labor Organization. Also, various Asian American groups have become powerful allies leveraging their own transnational ties with South Korea, China, and Japan. The grassroots organizing of more than 200 Asian American groups and persistent petitioning by the Coalition 121, led by the Korean American activist Annabel Park, contributed significantly to the successful passage of a resolution on the comfort women issue by the United States House of Representatives in July 2007 (Tokudome, 2007). The European Parliament also adopted a similar resolution in December of the same year. Both bodies urged the Japanese government to acknowledge the facts of wartime rape and sexual slavery for which the Japanese Army was responsible, issue an official apology, and take administrative actions to offer reparations.[14]

The Chinese survivors in Shanxi that the Shien Suru Kai and the Akirakani Suru Kai have supported died one by one over the past ten years. Only seven of the sixteen women are still alive today. Supporters of the survivors in Japan and around the world ask whether Japanese people and their government would want to leave this issue of wartime rape and slavery unresolved, letting the survivors die without offering acceptable apology and redress. Not only does this leave a terrible problem for the later generations of Japanese, but ignoring the survivors' claims undermines the human rights of their own people. Would Japanese people wish to write off as a tolerable act rape, kidnapping and forced relocation of ordinary Japanese citizens carried out by foreign troops and governments? It may not be easy to convince many Japanese people and politicians to take the rape survivors' claims seriously, but to memorialize the survivors' experiences and to work toward their redress are important for those survivors who had come forward and for all the other war victims in Japan, China, and elsewhere.

Notes

1. All the Korean, Chinese, and Japanese names are written with the family name first, followed by the first name.
2. Zhang Shuangbing has interviewed about sixty victims since 1992 in Yu district in Shanxi province alone. Except for the few women who joined in suing the Japanese government, the rest of the victims refused to come forward (Zhang, 2002). It is most likely that many victims had died before Zhang conducted his research and many chose to keep their silence. The cases that Zhang and Japan-based researchers unearthed should be viewed as a tip of the iceberg.
3. Besides the Shanxi rape cases mentioned in this chapter, Chinese scholars have done in-depth research on cases of wartime rape by the Japanese Army in Nanjing, Shanghai, and elsewhere.
4. Hayakawa Noriyo first introduced the subject of wartime rape and redress campaign involving the survivors in Shanxi province in her paper presented at the Conference of the International Federation for Research in Women's History in Belfast, Northern Ireland in August 2003.
5. The total number of victims of atrocities in Nanjing beginning in December 1937 has become a controversial issue. Because the so-called Nanjing Massacre is an amalgam of numerous incidents on different scales involving a gamut of physical attacks, killings, and rapes, it is extremely difficult to count the number of victims accurately. Such an attempt would entail time-consuming and painstaking research of primary source materials and oral history records. Kasahara Tokushi, an authority on this subject, defines the period of the atrocities as between December 4, 1937 and March 28, 1938, and estimates the total number of victims (including Chinese soldiers, prisoners of wars, and civilians) as "over 150,000 to 160,000, or close to 200,000, or even over 200,000" (Kasahara, 1997: 223–228). For an insightful discussion of the conflicting memories of the atrocities in Nanjing, see Fogel (2000).
6. The women were repeatedly raped day and night during their detention. Zhao Runmei, one of the survivors, remarked, "Every night, more than ten soldiers raped me, while during the day three to four soldiers did so.... Because of this gang rape ... my genitals swelled and my lower abdomen ached. My hips and thighs were chafed, and my inner thighs were bloody" (Ishida and Uchida, eds., 2004: 80–81; Terazawa, 2006: 135–136).
7. This group was formerly called in Japanese "Chûgoku Ni Okeru Nihongun Seibôryoku No Jittai Wo Akirakanishi, Baishô Seikyû Saiban Wo Shien Suru Kai." After their lawsuit ended in 2005, activists modified its official name, deleting the latter half as the group no longer helped the survivors with their lawsuit.
8. The Akirakani Suru Kai members were not surprised by the dismissal of their case in November 2005. But what made them dumbfounded were the extraordinarily expeditious deliberations of their case at the Supreme Court. The Japanese justice system is notorious for its slow decision-making processes.
9. Many survivors refused to receive compensation from this fund because they regarded this form of compensation as Japan's attempt to avoid an official acknowledgment of its war responsibility. It should be noted that survivors in China and North Korea as individuals were not eligible for receiving compensation from this program. The Japanese government has argued that it cannot provide compensation to individual victims in China and North Korea because there are no support groups to supervise the distribution of the funds within these countries. While the Japanese government often contends that it has already offered compensation to former comfort women through the Asian Women's Fund, it has taken no action to deal with the survivors in China and North Korea.
10. For the views of resident Korean feminist activists, see the dialogue between resident Korean scholar Kim Puja and the leading Japanese feminist scholar Ueno Chizuko (Nihon no Sensô Sekinin Shiryô Sentâ, 1998).
11. For various types of peace activism in postwar Japan, see Franziska Seraphim (2006, 2007).
12. These groups have successfully pushed their conservative agendas, resulting in the official visits of prime ministers and other Diet members to Yasukuni Shrine, which has deified the

deceased servicemen of the Japanese Army. These groups have also pushed the publication of a "new" history textbook that suppresses Japan's war atrocities in Asia. They have worked to revise Japan's postwar constitution in order to enable Japan to convert its self-defense force into a regular army. It should be noted that many right-wing nationalists are sympathetic toward the families of those Japanese citizens abducted by North Korean agents in the 1970s and 1980s, and that some nationalists have been actively engaged in the movement to retrieve the abductees from North Korea.

13. For an overview of the right-wing visions and sentiments, see *Atarashii kyôkasho wo tsukurukai ga tou nihon no bijon* (Fujioka, 2003) and *Netto uyokutte donna yatsu?* (Kobayashi, 2008). For a critical study of younger nationalists who expressed their ideas via the Internet, see *Netto uyoku to sabakaru minshu shugi* (Kondô and Tanizaki, eds., 2007). For a left-wing critique of the rise of Japanese nationalism, see "Nihon ni okeru 'shûkyô uyoku' no taitô to 'tsukurukai' 'nihon kaigi.'" (Uesugi, 2003)

14. In Japan, various groups that support the former sex slaves of the Japanese Army have attempted to strengthen their activism by forming an umbrella group known as "Ianfu" Mondai Kaiketu Ôru Rentai Nettowâku (or Ôru Rentai, "The All Solidarity Network to Resolve the 'Comfort Women' Issue") in November 2007.

Bibliography

Agence France Presse. 2004. "China Tells Japan to Properly Handle Court Case by Chinese Sex Slaves." December 16.

Bengodan seimei (The statement of the legal counsels). 2007. Chûgokujin "ianfu" jiken bengodan and chûgokujin sensô higai baishô seikyû jiken bengodan (The Chinese "comfort women" lawsuit legal counsel and the legal counsel for Chinese war victims' compensation lawsuits). April 27. Retrieved on May 28, 2008 from http://www.suopei.org/saiban/ianfu/seimei-bengodan.html

Dong, Mao. 2004. "Aixin boche Xiyangzhen" (Love pours in Xiyangzhen). *Shanxi Shangbao* (Shanxi Commercial Daily). June 11.

Fogel, Joshua A. 2000. *The Nanjing Massacre in History and Historiography*. Berkeley, CA: University of California Press.

Fujioka, Nobukatsu. 2003. *Atarashii kyôkasho wo tsukurukai ga tou nihon no bijon* (The vision for Japan that the group to write a new textbook explores). Tokyo: Fusôsha.

Fukuda, Akinori. 2003. Interviewed by author (August). Tokyo, Japan.

He, Yinan. 2007a. "History, Chinese Nationalism and the Emerging Sino-Japanese Conflict." *Journal of Contemporary China* 16, no.50 (February): 1–24.

———. 2007b. "Remembering and Forgetting the War: Elite Mythmaking, Mass Reaction, and Sino-Japanese Relations, 1950–2006." *History and Memory* 19, no.2 (Fall/Winter): 43–74.

Ikeda, Eriko. 2004. Interviewed by author (August). Tokyo, Japan.

———. 2007. "Bukyô no hachirogun taikô kinenkan wo tazunete" (Our visit to the Eighth Route Army Taihang Memorial Museum in Wuxiang). *Chukouqi* (The Newsletter of the Sanseishô, Akirakani Suru Kai), no.43 (October 27): 2–4.

Ishida, Yoneko. 2004. Interviewed by author (August). Taiyuan, China.

———. 2005. "Shinobiyoru saigetsu: Dakarakoso" (Time passes by and that's why). *Chukouqi*, no.35 (May 9): 7–9.

———. 2006a. "Ima watashitachiga yarerukoto, mosaku shite irukoto" (What we can do for them and what we are considering doing). *Chukouqi*, no.41 (December 20): 2–6.

———. 2006b. "Konomamadewa owarenai" (We cannot end our fight as we have been left). *Chukouqi*, no.40 (June 30): 6–12.

Ishida, Yoneko, Nobuhiro Katô, and Aiko Utsumi, eds. 2005. *Aru nihonhei no futatsu no senjô* (The two battlefields in the experience of a soldier). Tokyo: Shakai Hyôron Sha.

Ishida, Yoneko, and Ômori Noriko. 2000. "Chûgoku Sanseishô ni okeru nihongun seibôryoku no jittai" (The facts of sexual violence committed by the Japanese Army in Shanxi province, China). In Nishino Rumiko and Hayashi Hirofumi, eds. *"Ianfu" senji seibôryoku no jittai,* (The facts of wartime sexual violence involving "comfort women"), vol. 2, 21–78. Tokyo: Ryokufû Shuppan.

Ishida, Yoneko, and Tomoyuki Uchida, eds. 2004. *Kôdo no Mura no Seibôryoku* (Sexual violence in villages of yellow earth). Tokyo: Sôdo Sha.

Japan Economic Newswire. 2005a. "High Court Rejects Chinese Women's Suit over Wartime Rapes." March 31.

———. 2005b. "Top Court Rejects Chinese Women's Suit over Wartime Rapes." November 19.

Kasahara, Tokushi. 1997. *Nankin Jiken* (The Nanjing incident). Tokyo: Iwanami Shoten.

Katô, Nobuhiro. 2004. Interviewed by author (August). Tokyo, Japan.

Kawaguchi, Kazuko. 2004a. Interviewed by author (July and August). Tokyo, Japan.

———. 2004b. "Kawaguchi Bengoshi no Shôgen" (The testimony of Attorney Kawaguchi). *Chukouqi*, no.33 (December 10): 2–7.

Kawami, Kimiko. 2004. Interviewed by author (August). Tokyo, Japan and Beijing, China.

Kim, Puja, and Son Yonok, eds. 2000. *"Ianfu" senji seibôryoku no jittai* (The facts of wartime sexual violence involving "comfort women"), vol. 1. Tokyo: Ryokufû Shuppan.

Kobayashi, Daisuke, ed. 2008. *Netto uyokutte donna yatsu?* (What kinds of people are the Internet rightists?). Tokyo: Takarajimasha.

Kobayashi, Yoshinori. 1996–2000. *Shin gômanisuto sengen* (New haughtiness manifesto), vol. 18. Tokyo: Shôgakuka.

———. 1998–2003. *Shin gômanisuto sengen supesharu* (New haughtiness manifesto special), vols. 1–3. Tokyo: Gentôsha.

Kondô, Hajime. 2002. "Senjô de watashiga taiken shitakoto" (What I experienced in the battlefields). In *No moa nankin no kai*, ed. *Nankin daigyakusatsu 64 ka nen, 2001 Tokyo shûkai hôkokushû* (The report on the Tokyo meeting to commemorate the 64th Nanjing massacre anniversary), 49–60. Tokyo: No moa nankin no ka.

Kondô, Ruman, and Tanizaki Akira, eds. 2007. *Netto uyoku to sabukaru minshu shugi* (The rights of internet activists and the subculture of democracy). Tokyo: San'ichi Shobô.

The New York Times. 2007. "Japan Court Rules against Sex Slaves and Laborers." April 28.

Nihon no Sensô Sekinin Shiryô Sentâ, ed. 1998. *Shinpojium: Nashonarizumu to "ianfu" mondai* (Symposium: Nationalism and "Comfort Women" Issues). Tokyo: Aoki Shoten.

Nômoa Nankin no Kai, ed. 2002. *Kurikaesuna sensô to gyakusatsu* (Never repeat wars and massacres). Tokyo: Nômoa Nankin no Kai.

Oguma, Eiji, and Ueno Yôko. 2003. *Iyashi no nashonarizumu* (Nationalism of healing). Tokyo: Keiiôgijuku Daigaku Shuppankai.

Sato, Shigemi. 2007. "Japan Ruling Denies Chinese Right to War Damages." *Agence France Presse*. April 27.

Seraphim, Franziska. 2006. *War Memory and Social Politics in Japan, 1945–2005*. Cambridge, MA: Harvard University Asia Center.

———. 2007. "People's Diplomacy: The Japan-China Friendship Association and Critical War Memory in the 1950s." *Japan Focus: An Asia Pacific e-journal* (August 18). Retrieved on July 10, 2008 from http://japanfocus.org/_Franziska_Seraphim-People_s_Diplomacy____The_Japan_China_Friendship_Association_and_Critical_War_Memory_in_the_1950s

Tamaki, Keiko. 2004. Interviewed by author. August. Tokyo, Japan.

———. 2006. "Hachigatsu hôchû hôkoku" (Report on our August visit). *Chukouqi*, no.41 (December 20): 7–10.

Tanaka, Yuki. 2003. *Japan's Comfort Women: Sexual Slavery and Prostitution during World War II and the US Occupation.* New York: Routledge.

Tasaki, Toshitaka. 2004. Interviewed by author (August). Tokyo, Japan.

Terazawa, Yuki. 2006. "The Transnational Campaign for Redress for Wartime Rape by the Japanese Military: Cases for Survivors in Shanxi Province." *NWSA (National Women's Studies Association) Journal* 18, no.3 (Fall): 226–233.

———. 2008. Field observations by author. Wuxiang, Shanxi province, China.

Tokudome, Kinue. 2007. "Passage of H. Res. 121 on 'Comfort Women,' the US Congress and Historical Memory in Japan." *Japan Focus: An Asia Pacific e-journal* (August 30). Retrieved on July 10, 2008 from http://www.japanfocus.org/products/details/2510

Uesugi, Satoshi. 2003. "Nihon ni okeru 'shûkyô uyoku' no taitô to 'tsukurukai' 'nihon kaigi'" (The emergence of the "religious right" in Japan, "the group to write a new textbook" and the "Japan Conference"). *Senso sekinin kenkyû* (The Report on Japan's War Responsibility), no.39, 44–56.

Xinhua General News Service. 2004. "FM Spokesman: Japan Should Properly Handle 'Sex Slave' Issue." December 16. Retrieved on May 28, 2008 from http://english.people.com.cn/200412/17/eng20041217_167651.html

Yoshimi, Yoshiaki. 2000. "'Jûgun ianfu' seisaku ni okeru nihon kokka no shiki meirei keitô" (The Japanese government's command structure for the "military comfort women" policy). In Kim Puja and Son Yonok, eds. *"Ianfu" senji seibôryoku no jittai* (The facts of wartime sexual violence involving "comfort women"), vol. 1, 42–64. Tokyo: Ryokufû Shuppan.

Zhang, Shuangbing. 2002. "Interview by the Presiding Judge." *Court Document, Tokyo Higher Court, Case Number (Ne) 2621* (June 2). Transcriber, Kutsuzawa Miyuki.

CHAPTER SIX

The Chinese Underclass and Organized Crime as a Stepladder of Social Ascent

MING XIA

Introduction

Barrington Moore Jr. declares, "No middle class, no democracy." This statement can be supported from two perspectives. First, the middle class has instrumental value for democracy. As the organizer of wealth production, the middle class must tame the professionals of violence management, namely, the state and its functionaries, in order to safeguard the distribution of wealth and to serve the need of wealth expansion (Bates, 2001). Second, the middle class has constitutive value for democracy. It forms the backbone of a civil society and sustains the functioning and maintenance of a democracy. Once it puts on a "golden straitjacket" (the "defining politico-economic garment" being today's liberal democracy), a state has to behave within certain parameters. Free people are guaranteed what is known in academic circles as the "Wilsonian Triad": the opportunity to empower themselves through democracy, enrich themselves through free market capitalism, and ensure themselves through civil society (Mandelbaum, 2002; Friedman, 2000).

Unfortunately, in this free and democratic nirvana, there is no seat for the underclass people, the poor, and marginal who are expanding rapidly all over the developing world. This "one-size-fits-all golden straitjacket" is too luxurious and elusive for them. Instead, the Chinese experience, historically as well as currently, demonstrates that the underclass devise an ingenious strategy for securing all three middle-class deserts. The Chinese underclass has found, literally speaking, their "triad." As black markets for illicit goods become an essential part of the economic institution under capitalism, the subaltern class can have new frontiers on which to thrive. In other words, the resource-deprived people can exploit the criminal underworld—featuring mafia-style capitalism and gangland rule—as a practical superhighway to achieve power, wealth, and brotherhood, three important goods that law-abiding citizens pursue under the Wilsonian triad. In his seminal article, "Crime as an American Way of Life: A Queer Ladder of Social Mobility," Daniel Bell (1962: 127–150) put it this way: In early American eras as well as modern times, "organized illegality became a stepladder of social ascent." Where there is an expanding underclass, there will always be plenty of entrepreneurial individuals who come close to the fringes of crime and who seek opportunity from vice-related industries and racketeering (Naylor, 2002; Naím, 2005).

The underclass and organized crime go hand in glove. Both in the West and China, history shows the causal linkages between the underclass and organized crime. Such linkages are demonstrated in Robert J. Antony's chapter on banditry in late imperial South China. In U.S. gang studies, scholars have pointed out that the factor of the underclass figures "prominently in explaining the onset and persistence of gangs" (Knox, 2000: 79). In an examination of the evolution of hoodlums in contemporary China, one historian delineated a continuous development from "refugees" and "vagrants" to "hooligans" and "hooliganism" and then to the criminal underworld (Wanyan, 1993). Parodying Moore we can also declare: "No underclass, no criminal underworld."

This chapter first analyzes how a huge population has been increasingly locked into the underclass status in tandem with the making of the bourgeoisie from among dominant groups now that China has been transforming itself into an economic powerhouse. Then it shows how this underclass has engaged in organized crime in order to subsist and to change their status. This study concludes with a discussion of the challenges that the underclass has created for the Chinese state as members seek benign neglect and positive recognition from the latter.

Defining and Estimating the Underclass

Various labels apply to the subaltern section of society that moves in and out of crime and vice. In *The Manifesto of the Communist Party*, Karl

Marx and Friedrich Engels (Tucker, 1978: 482) called such people "the social scum" and "the dangerous class"—that "passively rotting mass thrown off by the lowest layers of old society." In the document's original German version, the term that Marx and Engels used is *lumpen*-proletariat. "Proletariat" itself indicates the outsider status of this group of people: they may be "in" a society, but not "of" it. *Lumpen* (rogue) further indicates their doomed and desperate situation. Kellow Chesney (1970: 32) elaborates on the dangerous class as follows:

> When respectable people spoke of the *dangerous classes*—a phrase enjoying a good deal of currency—they were not talking about the laboring population as a whole, nor the growing industrial proletariat. Neither were they referring to that minority of politically conscious, mostly "superior" radical workingmen on whom any sustained working-class political movement ultimately depended. They meant certain classes of people whose very manner of living seemed a challenge to ordered society and the tissue of laws, moralities and taboos holding it together. These "unprincipled," "ruffianly," "degraded" elements seemed ready to exploit any breakdown in the established order. (Italics in the original)

In *The Origins of Totalitarianism*, Hannah Arendt (1979: 10, 107–108) uses another term, "[t]he modern mob—that is, of the *déclassés* of all classes," for those excluded from society and political representation and engaged in crime and vice. "The mob is primarily a group in which the residue of all classes are represented." It "hates society from which it is excluded."

In U.S. scholarship, the term "underclass" has a wider currency. Underclass means the distinct population that is marginalized or excluded from the mainstream society (especially the labor market), entrenched in poverty and welfare dependency, and often engaged in street crimes and other aberrant behavior (Katz, ed., 1993: 3–4). Knox (2000: 88) refers to its members as those "men and women permanently excluded from participation in mainstream occupations." To a large degree, the body of China's underclass (overlapping with *lumpen*-proletariat, or the dangerous class in Marxist terminology) consists of a vast floating population dislocated from the countryside, and the unemployed and destitute among urban residents.

In the Chinese context, "ruffians" or "rogues" (*liumang wulai*) are close to the *lumpen*-proletariat. In terms of ruffians as a social status in the class structure, a Chinese historian characterizes it with three features: (1) they are excluded from productive activities and have no legitimate occupation; (2) they are drifting about doing nothing socially constructive; and (3) they deviate from established order, values, and moralities and challenge the social order (Wanyan, 1993: 2–4). The underclass first and foremost is an economic concept: it indicates that this group of people has been thrown out of the production process. Then, it becomes political: the underclass is not represented in the system, but is often victimized. Finally, it is a social status. Due to its economic and political disadvantages, this group is further marginalized and stigmatized to the lowest status of the society.

In Chinese history, ruffians and hooligans were persistent pests in the society. In 1949, however, when the Communist regime was established, radical change to both social structure and public policy was introduced: ruffians as a social stratum were eradicated. Since the Chinese communist movement mobilized the lower classes and relied on their support for its ultimate victory, the new regime empowered the lower strata of Chinese society, even though it did not wipe out poverty as promised. As deprivation under the old regime turned into a credential for political trustworthiness and empowerment, the working class and the peasantry were elevated into the ruling class. "The people as masters" denoted their sacrosanct political status in China. Along with this achievement, the *lumpen* elements of the populace were assimilated into the political space under the newly established socialist structure. Between the ruling structure and the most ordinary people, the high adhesiveness rendered it impossible or unnecessary for the existence of a *lumpen*-proletariat during the initial decade of the communist regime (Lieberthal, 1973). Since the late 1970s when the Communist Party started abandoning its populist policy and shifting its power base toward the more affluent, the gap between the ruling structure and the ordinary people, however, began to widen. For the past quarter-century, especially entering the 1990s, a sizable underclass has been systematically created in the process of China's transition to a new political economy. In the entire history of the People's Republic of China, this is an unusual social process, which has been undoing the social achievements under Mao Zedong's egalitarian socialism.

Comparing recent developments with historical patterns, the ongoing great structural transformation of Chinese society caused the population of the underclass to bloat. For thirty years under Communist rule, Chinese society had a simple social structure: two classes (workers and peasants) and one stratum (cadres), collectively called "the people." Outside of this category, other elements associated with the old regime were called "citizens." They were politically deprived and did not enjoy the same political standing as the people. From the "people" and "citizens," someone might drop out and form a category of the "enemies," under the constant attack and suppression of the people's dictatorship. This artificially simplified structure was tightly controlled, and survived, to a large extent, because the three institutions fulfilled the function of political, economic, and social control. Work-units put residents in the urban areas under their thumb; the people's communes tied peasants to the land in the countryside; and the household registration system (*hukou*) strictly controlled the migration of people from countryside to cities.

Since economic reforms were introduced in the early 1980s, the communes were the first to collapse, along with their functions of economic production, administrative management, and social control (Xia, 1999). Then the work-units began to disintegrate as the market economy was introduced. Many state-owned enterprises went bankrupt or became privatized. The remaining state-owned enterprises shed their welfare and social control functions. Although the residential registration system has not been abolished yet, several strong social and economic forces have made it impossible to stay the same. Looking from the countryside, we can see strong push factors: increasing surplus population, shrinking farmlands (due to urban expansion, real estate development, and economic development), predatory local state officials, and deepening impoverishment. These have forced peasants to leave their land and seek opportunities in the urban regions. In the urban areas, construction booms, formation of the labor market, economic expansion, and urban residents' reluctance to take dirty jobs have created a tremendous need for new labor, pulling waves of migrants into cities and shaking up the old, rigid society.

Under these social and economic pressures, the Chinese social structure added two new categories: the urban unemployed and the migrant laborers. According to official statistics, in 1978 and 1980 China faced a high unemployment rate—around 5 percent with a total number of more than 5 million in the urban areas. Early reforms in the cities, especially the policy to encourage self-employed small business, alleviated somewhat the pressure of this unemployment. In 1984–1985, the army of urban unemployed was slashed by half and dropped to a little more than 2 million. However, this number climbed during the 1990s, from 3.77 million to 4.76 million in 1994 and 5.19 million in 1995 (Zhu et al., 1997: 180). In 2001, it reached 6.81 million (*Lianhe Zaobao*, March 8, 2002). Until 2003, the Chinese government did not include laid-off workers (*xiagang zhigong*) in the unemployed population. If we add this number of 5 million in 2001, the jobless urban residents reached almost 12 million. Meanwhile, rural laborers numbering 350 million constituted the largest social stratum in Chinese society. Chinese scholars estimated that about 200 million were surplus population in the countryside. Half of them became migrant workers—leaving their residential homes and working in cities and townships. The most authoritative estimate from the Chinese Ministry of Public Security (*Gong'an bu*) indicates that the population of migrants increased from 60 million in 1989 to 80 million in 1995, and to 100 million in 2000 (Wang et al., 2002: 19).

Grouping the urban jobless and rural migrants together, China is facing the most serious unemployment challenge in its modern history. These 300 million people—one-third each for urban unemployed, migrant laborers, and idlers in the countryside—constitute a huge lower class. Since the 1990s, a subaltern social stratum has been created in China. Even worse, this population is bloating. Alienation and exclusion from the emerging power-centric but market-driven social order have torn apart the traditional low-differentiated structure (Sun, 2004). This is an unprecedented event in the history of Communist rule.

Out of this huge lower class, within merely one decade, an underclass has formed and has constituted the backbone of crime and vice—often simultaneously participants and victims. Two diehard groups have been identified by Chinese law enforcement agencies as the most criminogenic: the elements released from the penal system, including jails and *laogai* camps (i.e., reform or reeducation through labor), and the blind floaters (*mangliu*) who lack proper ID card, temporary residential registration, and verifiable employment, the so-called three-withouts people (*sanwu renyuan*). Since the size of the latter is much bigger than the former and many former criminals often have joined in the floating population, He Qinglian (1998: 264; 2003: 250), almost a decade ago, pinpointed the "blind floaters as the foundation for the existence of the criminal underworld societies."

It is not easy to gauge the size of these two groups, because they often overlap and lie beyond the government's radar screen. In addition, the government carefully guards statistics on the jailed population in China. However, the Supreme People's Court reported that from 1983 to 1985, 1,395,000 criminals were sentenced, and the volume increased annually by a six-digit figure in the 1990s. According to statistics released by Chinese researchers, the number of criminals in jail (excluding prisoners in *laogai* camps) was 1,226,000 in 1986, 1,251,000 in 1990, and 1,417,000 in 1996, respectively; and 300,000 were released every year (Zhao, ed., 2003: 204, 228). In the late 1990s, the number of released inmates increased to at least a quarter-million every year; from 1998 to 2002, adding up to a total of 1.5 million (*Zhongguo sifa*, 1998–2003). As for the blind floaters, the low-end estimate ranged from 1 percent to 5 percent of the total migrants in the mid-1990s (Solinger, 1999: 137; Zhao, 1998: 51). Then, the national census indicated a total of 670,000 beggars (82 percent were professional beggars) nationwide (Wu and Xu, 1997: 450). Entering the twenty-first century, researchers have found that about 10 percent of the migrants belong to the blind floaters (Gransow and Li, 2001: 150–151). For example, the city of Shenzhen had a population of 7 million (including 5 million migrants) in 2000, in which 300,000 to 600,000 were blind floaters, about 50,000 of them were criminals, gang members, and thieves (Liu, 2003: 62). It is safe to believe that the blind floaters should count by the millions. The upshot is that an underclass, with a size close to 10 million, has become a fertile ground to foment vice, deviance, pilferage, and other crimes in China.

Roving over the Rivers and Lakes (*Chuang jianghu*)

Basically every society has three kinds of people in regard to their relationship to law: some are above the law, some within the law, and some below the reach of the law. The privileged few are the first group, having power and other resources to manipulate and twist the law for their favor. Law-abiding citizens form the second group. Usually in modern society, the middle-class people have the most to lose if they come too close to the law; therefore, they tend to have strong self-control and self-discipline. The third group includes those who have nothing to lose and therefore nothing to fear. For them, financial penalty has no meaning, since they have no property and credit; social shame does not work since they do not live in a moral community. The law often fails to reach this group. A healthy society should be able to press both the privileged and the desperate into the framework of law, making them stakeholders.

Unfortunately, the global trend—including China—is that globalization is accompanied by the fragmentation of society. Massive accumulation of capital by a market-dominant, select few is accompanied by deprivation and marginalization across an increasingly large population (Kaplan, 2000; Chua, 2004; Galeano, 2000). In China, under the bureaucratic authoritarian capitalism inspired by Milton Friedman's neoliberal thinking, ordinary Chinese are deprived of authentic voting rights. They have even less leverage to resist or cushion the formidable market force. As in any society, China's dislocated migrant laborers and juveniles represent two conventionally marginalized groups. If we add the gender factor, young female migrants are a uniquely powerless, marginalized group. Without regulatory oversight or welfare state, their marginalization has been quick and thorough.

Relying on cases from a research project funded by the Ford Foundation, I will apply sociological and anthropological methods to depict the structural choice-set in order to understand how the lower class people formulate their rational response to marginalization. In collaboration with Denise Hare of Reed College, Zhao Shukai (1998), from the Center for Development Studies affiliated with the State Council of the Chinese Central Government in Beijing, conducted multiyear surveys on migrant workers in forty districts from 1994 to 1997. Among the fifty-six interview reports and twelve notes published by the research group, the majority of interviewees touched upon their contact with hooligan groups or organized crime, as victims, informants, or participants.

In the following case, a young female migrant worker, who was second-in-command after the ringleader, described her experience upon joining a huge gang in Jiangsu province:

> The sworn brotherhood/sisterhood was popular in Northern Jiangsu. At age seventeen or eighteen, youngsters start to become sworn brothers. The society is now unsafe, how could we not band up? The ritual for sworn brotherhood is simple. When I was eighteen years old, I became sworn sisters with two other girls. We chose the right time at the right place to kowtow to each other. The important thing was not the ritual but that from then on we would weather adversity together and lend support to each other as we were in the same boat.
>
> When I joined the gang that I am affiliated with now, we did not have as many people as we do today. Our gang has a total of more than 200 members. Everyone has a certificate; by showing it, we all know each other and our respective ranks and ID numbers. Our gang keeps growing; members have spread all over the country. Only a few gangs are bigger than ours. For example, my older cousin leads another gang. He can amass at least 300 to 400 members for a small matter, and 500 to 600 for a big event.

My older cousin also has two handguns that can fire two bullets. He hides one and carries one with him, making him look more authoritative. My cousin has a good relationship with my gang. We always share information and help each other. We never make trouble with other gangs for no reason, just like the water in a well does not invade the water in a river. The local public security bureau has knowledge about our gang, but they do not bother us. They took away several brothers of ours in one feud and we taught them a lesson. Since then, they have always kept one eye open and another closed when they see us.

Now our members are in Tonghua, Wuxi, Nanjing, Suzhou, Changzhou, Shanghai, and faraway Heilongjiang. We are far from home, so the members of our gang have to keep their heads low. But unbelievably, through fights we came to make friends with many local snakes in Nanjing and Shanghai—more than 100 in the former and around 200 in the latter.

Gang affiliation indeed saves me from many troubles. For example, back in my hometown, as I was riding my bike to a neighboring village, three men with no good intention rode on their bikes to surround me and crashed into my bike. I had to speak some argots, so they dared not touch me. I told them to see me at a specific place and time and left my bike behind. The rule in the underworld is that you have to show up; if not, once they see you, you can only be taken back dead. The next day I went to meet them with five brothers of mine. Seven or eight of them were waiting. When they saw our faces and gestures, they were all dumbstruck. I asked: "As for the bike, do you want to fix it and send it back to me, or buy a new one?" They kept answering with their heads nodding, "Buy a new one! Buy a new one!" (Zhao, 1998: 325–328)

This narrative is revealing and representative of several common patterns that we can relate to other migrant laborers. First, law and public order have been in decay in many localities—particularly in the countryside. In response, young people have resorted to and revitalized the tradition of forming secret societies—sworn brotherhoods/sisterhoods serving as the foundation for a mutual aid and self-defense community (Xia, 2006). As another migrant recounted, "In the countryside, public security was chaotic. Even someone who killed a person could spend money to have his own life spared. Public order was lousy and law enforcement was lax" (Zhao, 1998: 272). Yet another corroborated this problem, "For the recent past, every year there was a murder in our village. So far not one has been solved. The year before last, a young girl was killed in the cornfield and another case happened again this year. The villagers—male and female, old and young—dared not step into the field after four o'clock in the afternoon" (278). For migrant workers who are vulnerable in a faraway, strange place, getting organized is one way to be secure. One migrant remarked, "Young women working outside like us often become sworn sisters to protect each other from being bullied. Seven new girls in our factory did this. I have also heard that the male laborers become sworn brothers. The migrant workers from Guichi, Guizhou also formed a society among fellow townsmen" (301).

Second, the widespread corruption of local officials, which has been most rampant at the village/township level, has bred the political-criminal nexus and further eroded the legitimacy of local states (Xia, 2004). As one migrant worker put it, "There were plenty of venal officials and law-breakers. Small domestic animals raised by farmers for food were not safe from being stolen. The farmers near my home would possibly not see meat in their food often for a month. When they ate noodles, they just add wild vegetables into their food. The officials often went to restaurants to eat big fish and delicious meat. They were dining on and drinking the blood and sweat of the peasants" (Zhao, 1998: 272). Another migrant worker talked about his impression of the local security force, "Now the joint patrol team is filled with local tyrants, hooligans, and people with dubious character. They steal at night and beat up people during the daytime" (278). Even having been victimized, migrants hesitated to seek help from the public security officials. As someone said, "We dared not report anything to the public security station. Anyway it is useless, too. If you do not provide money, the public security station did not bother. They would just say that they couldn't find anyone. Even if they got caught, they were soon released and immediately came for revenge" (287).

Third, for many migrants, leaving home means "step[ping] into the rivers and lakes," a phrase indicating that one leaves family and friends behind to live in the margin and defend oneself in a world of strangers. One often abandons some traditional values and behavioral norms and follows the more aggressive code of the underworld. Organized violence dominates. Either you become the victim or the master of it. The following example comes from one migrant worker: "There are roughly 1,500 villagers in our village. 80 percent of the young people above eighteen years old have left. Many are in Shanghai.

They do whatever they can name: peddling, working in construction sites, pocket-picking, selling flesh. Some got rich through stealing and have built big houses back home" (Zhao, 1998: 286). Another migrant worker shared with us his experiences:

> I have worked here for more than five years and have met people of all trades including an elder brother of the criminal underworld. I got to know him as I did interior improvement for his house. At that time, a friend of mine asked me to do him a favor and to work in home improvement. Before we finished, my friend told me that we were working for a big brother of the local underworld. Once I knew this, I did not ask for the labor fee. My friend also lost his 40,000 yuan on material costs. Later I came to know this big brother and he told me that I could always count on him if I have anything to settle in Changzhou.
>
> Migrant workers like us often would not get paid after we had done a job. I have been here for a longer time and have more friends. If my villagers would not get their pay, they would often come to me. I would drive there with my friends. Once we were there, the people who did not want to pay immediately did so. Of course we did not do it for nothing. Those whom we helped get money had to pay us. This is called "money dispels disaster." (316–317)

Rich data are available to illustrate that migrant laborers have a much higher likelihood of being perpetrators of crime. In the 3.63 million criminal cases filed in 2000, migrants who constituted roughly 7 percent of the entire population were responsible for 32 percent of total crime (i.e., 1.16 million criminal cases). The national crime rate was 29.1 per 10,000 people; but among the migrants, the crime rate reached 133.33 per 10,000; the differential is 104.23 per 10,000 (Wang et al., 2002: 49). Such a disproportionately high percentage of crime committed by migrants is particularly conspicuous in the coastal areas and metropolises. For example, in 2000, migrants accounted for more than 49.19 percent of criminal suspects in Shanghai, 55.57 percent in Chengdu, 62 percent (in 1996) in Beijing, 86.66 percent in Guangzhou, and 97 percent in Shenzhen (33–34; Zhao, 2003: 285). Also unsurprisingly, the blind floaters have been the hardcore of criminals among migrants. According to statistical information from Wuxi district in Jiangsu province for 1994, migrants were responsible for 82 percent of the suspects/cases; among the migrant suspects/cases, the blind floaters (5 percent of migrants) were responsible for 70 percent (Zhao, 1998: 6, 50).

Fourth, organized violence or crime becomes a route to respect and the first step toward accumulating primitive capital. This is how a migrant worker expressed his admiration for the tremendous wealth accumulated by a gang leader: "I have been to the house of this big brother. It was decorated as beautifully and luxuriously as a royal palace. He got around with a car. He was just around 30 years old. I once saw him hit other people. He was tough. I was told that he was once arrested in the 1983 Stern Blow campaign. His buddies were all executed, but he used money to redeem his life" (Zhao, 1998: 316–317). A migrant thief recalled his experiences and expressed his view of the world:

> I am nineteen years old and have no girl friend, but I have messed around with many girls. My home is in a village where the township site is located. Since my childhood, I have mixed with hoodlums in the streets, enjoying dancing, playing pool, dining in restaurants, and stirring up trouble in society. I stopped attending school after the primary years; my parents could do nothing about it. I had four sworn brothers. During the daytime we went to nearby villages to steal chickens; at night we stole fruits and vegetables from the farmers. We brothers loved to fight, and ordinary people dared not get in our way. The middle school kids were especially scared of us, because we would drag them out of the classroom and beat them up. Our hometown is economically backward, no decent work to do. People like us who idle about command respect. As we grew older, we became more audacious to venture out. In 1992 some of our villagers went to Hebei province, where, we were told, money could be easily made and the black gangs were rampant. Along with a group of my buddies I went to find a job in a brick factory. We were young and not good at backbreaking labor, so we tried to get it easy. Meantime, we also engaged in petty thefts and took liberties with girls. I do not see any wrongdoing or irresponsibility on my part, since there is no fairness and justice in this society. (Zhao, 1998: 330–331)

Another migrant laborer, a vendor, discussed some migrants from another province:

> Some people from Anhui province did nothing but earn a living by fist fighting. They are big bullies. Every month they

came to "borrow" money from our supplier, every time 2,000 to 3,000 yuan. Once they spoke, you had to give. But they never return with what they "borrowed." The supplier dared not disobey. If not satisfied, they either pulled out a knife to kill the supplier or smash the stand. So every time, the supplier gave them money to buy safety. Those people from Anhui are cruel and they always band together. (Zhao, 1998: 287)

Judging from these remarks, a spontaneous process has been occurring among migrant laborers to organize themselves into gangs and criminal groups. In 2001, the Ministry of Public Security, along with several provincial police bureaus, conducted a survey among 15,000 migrant criminal suspects in their detention facilities from 8 cities in 7 provinces. They discovered that gang crimes accounted for 57 percent of all their crimes versus 43 percent committed by loner criminals. Among all criminal gangs, 51.3 percent had three–five members, 34.5 percent had a two-member partnership, and 14.1 percent had more than five members. Within these groups, 42.4 percent of members shared the same hometown/village; 29.9 percent shared the same identity as migrant laborers; 5 percent were family relatives; and 0.9 percent were former inmates. Clearly, the primordial relationship was the most important social capital on which they relied. At this early stage of organized crime in China, most gangs are hoodlum groups (Wang et al., 2003: 248–251). But their evolution into more sophisticated crime enterprises has been ongoing. On the one hand, ever more migrant laborers participate in vice industries such as prostitution, drug trafficking, and the smuggling of women and children. On the other hand, after gangsters first muscle in on reprehensible rackets, they often try to become more respectable by capturing political power for their own use. The venal nature of the Chinese Communist Party and the jungle-like quality of the Chinese transitional economy open up many doors for China's robber barons—whom they call "Roguish Entrepreneurs from the Grassroots" (*Caomang qiyejia*).

Organized Crime as a Business Transaction and Enterprise

Criminals are often opportunists. Although criminal behavior challenges the established social, economic, and political order, rational and sophisticated criminals still try to take advantage of the current order, adapt to it, and identify niches for survival and thriving. Accustomed to the hierarchical control of the state, family, and clan, traditional peasants structured their secret societies and criminal organizations by emulating the state or family power. Leaders preferred to be called the "big king," "dragon head," or "big brother." Today, many violent cliques maintain traditional hierarchical structures for their members and impose predatory and terrorist conditions upon the population. For example, in Sanmenxia in Henan province, a vagrant peasant named Peng Miaoji organized a twelve-member, tightly knit clique in the mid-1990s. During a period of just four years, the clique killed seventy-six people (including entire families) and wounded thirty-two (*Yangcheng Wanbao*, November 27–28, 1999; December 5, 1999). Clearly they were engaged in irrational, antisocial, inhumane, and the rudest kind of crime.

Even as the market created ubiquitous and efficient institutions for social and economic transactions, criminals adopted the contractual relationship to manage their activities and created cunning manipulations to get deals done. Several recent high-profile cases show this type of transition (Xia, 2008). For example, the Zhang Jun clique (uncovered in 2001) based in Changde, Hunan province, was first created around a vagrant hooligan from the countryside. Like the bandit rituals in late imperial South China described by Robert J. Antony in chapter 3, Zhang Jun drank rooster blood liquor to form a sworn brotherhood with his followers. But the modern market economy made a deep imprint upon the Zhang Jun clique. Its chief Zhang Jun called himself "the CEO," and his protégés were all given titles such as "managers," "silversmiths," and "millionaires." After several bank robberies, Zhang gave money to his many mistresses and recruited a "regiment of pink cheeks" as his camouflage. Registered under the names of his mistresses, he set up a restaurant and a hair salon as his business front, and purchased an apartment as his hideout (*Zuomuniao*, 2002).

With markets proliferating, violent criminals are learning to use business strategy to manage their businesses. One sees boorish gangsters transforming themselves into professional criminals; predatory crime is evolving into enterprise crime. The criminologist Carlo Morselli (2005: 124) has argued, "Traditional understandings of achievement in crime lead us to believe that criminal entrepreneurs use criminal means to gain criminal achievement. This is not the case: criminal entrepreneurs use conventional means to gain criminal achievement, but they do so in criminal trades." In China, many criminals have plunged into the markets for profit. A study in 1996 estimated that the hidden economy was equivalent to 20 percent of the Chinese GNP (Huang, 1997: 333). Economic activities controlled by the criminal underworld, or the so-called black economy, constituted a big chunk, in addition to the "gray" economy of bribes and embezzlements. Two so-called victimless crimes, sex industry and drug trafficking, provided enormous, illicit markets for organized crime groups.

Prostitution, as the oldest profession, met its biggest setback under Mao Zedong's Communist rule. Today its fortune has been reversed. Prostitution was first revitalized in the cities along China's southeast coast to serve the businessmen and tourists mainly from Hong Kong, Taiwan, and abroad. Initially, most prostitutes were unemployed urban residents who came from the surrounding rural areas. For example, in Guangzhou, among 483 prostitutes detained in 1981, 391 (81 percent) were locals from the surrounding districts. Quickly, more women realized that prostitution provided a highway to economic improvement, and young women from northern and western China descended upon the coastal cities. The two movements were respectively called "The peahens fly to the southeast" and "Wild geese fly to the south." By 1985, migrant sex workers from other provinces and municipalities began to dominate the sex market of Guangzhou. Among those detained by the authorities in reformatories for women, 70 percent were migrants, and this number increased to 92.6 percent in 1988. Guangdong province became the capital of sex trade in China; as one popular saying went, "Counting East, West, South, North, and the center, Guangdong is the moneymaker." Reports were in circulation that many rural women left their villages with tattered pants and returned with golden rings and cash to build houses (Shan, 1995).

Researchers have found that as entrants into prostitution tended to be from the lower class, and because of the great demand, prostitutes on average became a high-income group. According to an authoritative report in the mid-1990s, 35 percent of the sex workers surveyed nationwide enjoyed a monthly income of 1,000–3,000 yuan (US$130–US$400), 55 percent 3,000–5,000 yuan (US$400–US$670), and 10 percent earned more than 5,000 yuan (US$670) (Shan, 1995: 533). Meanwhile, the average household income per capita was 3,179 yuan in the urban areas and 1,221 yuan in the countryside (Song, 1995: 15). For many women who lack power, capital, and education, prostitution becomes their means to participate in the new market economy. The idea that prostitution promotes prosperity (a different kind of PPP from purchasing power parity) has appealed to many individuals. It is estimated that China had at least 4 million prostitutes in 1992 and 5 million in 1996 (Qiu, 2001: 236–237). In the category of "escort girls," known as *sanpeinü* (companion girls for three activities: drinking, singing, and dancing), more than 60 percent of them also provide sexual service. There were 6–8 million *sanpeinü* at the turn of the century (Bai, 2002: 51–55). In a World Health Organization report in 2004, the Chinese government reported that the number of prostitutes was about 6 million. The number from the nongovernmental sources, however, has ranged upward of 30 million (Huang, 1997: 48; Sohu News, October 4, 2000; BBC News, February 2, 2004). One economist estimates that a total of 20 million sex workers in China control 500 billion yuan of income (about 6 percent of the GDP) and bring along 1,000 billion yuan of related spending and consumption (Liu and Tian, eds., 2001: 20; Boxun News, December 22, 2005).

For many local governments, this is a huge source of revenue that should be carefully kept within their jurisdiction. It has also been an open secret that local governments seriously believe prostitution promotes prosperity. For example, officials in Shenyang started to tax the "misses" or prostitutes, an indirect way to legalize prostitution. Ma Xiangdong, deputy mayor of Shenyang, said at the Standing Committee Meeting of the Municipal Government, "Shenyang has neither mountain nor water. If the environment for investment is not improved, and no 'misses' are available for people to play with, who will come to invest?" (Liu and Tian, eds., 2001: 56). In Anhui province, Vice Governor Wang Huaizhong commented on a case where a foreign businessman was caught patronizing a prostitute: "Foreign businessmen come to our city of Fuyang to invest. They have brought with them projects, capital, and profits, but not wives and female secretaries. They live in our guesthouses for a long time; it is quite understandable if they need someone for companionship" (Liu, 2007: 197). In 1998, the "sweeping out the sex industry" campaign (*shaohuang*) in Shenzhen drove out thousands of prostitutes and bar girls, and with them, within days, at least 10 billion yuan of savings deposits evaporated from local financial institutions. Prostitution created an economic boon in surrounding cities that forced Shenzhen municipal authorities to sharply reduce the antisex industry campaign (Bai, 2002: 140; Liu and Tian, eds., 2001: 44; Author's interview). Thus prostitution typically receives benign neglect and protection from local authorities. Occasional campaigns against vice are intended as show pieces of morality as well as a convenient way to squeeze the prostitutes to prop up the government budget. The relaxation of both internal inhibitors and external control mechanisms has given a green light to participation in the flesh market, and China's young, huge population is providing an unlimited supply.

In China, an illicit market in drugs has also emerged during the past two decades. According to statistics provided by the government, in 2002 there were 1.05 million registered drug addicts. Based on a widely accepted ratio of 1:4 between registered and unidentified drug users, the Chinese government estimated that at least 5 million active drug addicts existed in China. Using minimum consumption patterns and market price, the government agencies and researchers affiliated with the Ministry of Public Security believe that the total value of drugs consumed by addicts was anywhere from 100 to 140 billion yuan (Cui, ed., 1999: 10, 239). China lies between the Golden Triangle (Myanmar) and the Golden Crescent (Afghanistan)—two of the three biggest drug production areas in the world; 80 percent of heroin from the Golden Triangle, with an annual production volume of seventy–eighty tons, passes through the China corridor, and half of it goes on to the global market (Zhao and Zhang, 2004: 2–3; Cui, ed., 1999: 9). This creates a door of opportunity for Chinese to make profits. By cultivating poppy domestically and smuggling heroin and other drugs from foreign countries, the Chinese underclass participates in the drug trade far and wide (see table 6.1).

Although drug-related crimes (mostly drug trafficking) have involved people from all walks of life in China, most often they have involved peasants and the unemployed. For example, among 145 cases with 241 defendants tried in the courts of Inner Mongolia in 1990, 212 (88 percent) defendants were from the countryside. From 1989 to 1990, the courts in Baoshan, Yunnan province, sentenced 220 drug-related criminals, among them, 171 (77.7 percent) were peasants and 33 (15 percent) were unemployed or self-employed people (Zhao and Yu, 2002: 37). Police in Gansu province arrested 2,794 drug makers and traffickers in 1996; 2,066 (74.4 percent) of them were peasants or unemployed. In Panzhihua, a transshipment city for the Sichuan corridor, 78.4 percent of drug criminals were peasants (Zhongguo Jingcha, 1998: 295). Among the six most active drug trafficking provinces, with the exception of Guangdong all five—Yunnan, Sichuan, Guizhou, Guangxi, and Gansu—are poor provinces located in China's Far West (Wang et al., 2003: 386). The three national distribution centers for drugs in the 1990s are all in the poorest areas notorious for "barren mountains, unruly rivers, and roguish people." In Sanjiaji township, Linxia prefecture, Gansu province, unique social mores were reportedly formed: "Some drug traffickers returned home with huge wealth and

Table 6.1 Drug-related criminals and registered drug addicts

Year	Captured Criminals	Registered Drug Addicts
1991	18,479	148,000
1992	28,292	250,000
1993	40,834	NA
1994	50,964	380,000
1995	73,734	520,000
1996	NA	NA
1997	244,000	540,000
1998	231,900	596,000
1999	NA	681,000
2000	69,000	860,000
2001	NA	901,000
2002	90,000	1,000,000
2003	NA	1,050,000
2004	NA	1,140,400

Source: Based on statistics given in Cui, Min (ed.) *Dupin Fanzui* (Crimes of drugs) (Beijing: Jingguan jiaoyu, 1999), 7; Yang, Lijun, *Zhongguo dangdai xidu wenti* (Drug problems in contemporary China) (Beijing: Qunzhong, 2003), 66; Chen, Beidi, *Zhongguo Xidu diaocha* (Investigating drug abuse in China) (Beijing: Xinhua, 2006), 3; *Zhongguo Gong'an Nianjian* (The yearbook of public security in China, 2000) (Beijing: Qunzhong, 2001), 347; Zhonghua Jieduwang (China's Anti-Drug Net), "Zhongguo dupin wenti dangqian sida tedian" (Four features of the current drug problems in China), October 24, 2005.

held banquets to treat their friends. They turned into 'local heroes' and inspired countless peasants to follow suit, creating a vicious cycle. A limerick was circulated in Linxia: 'Rush to Yunnan as to the front, every year you can make hundreds of thousands; it is a good deal even risking the loss of heads.' Many ran drug trafficking as a family business involving all family members: 'If a father was executed, the son took over; if a husband was executed, the wife stepped in'" (Chen, 2006: 129). In Tongxin, Ningxia Hui Autonomous Region, a Chinese reporter gave the following observation:

> Exorbitant profits from drugs are the immediate temptation for drug-related crimes, which transformed some honest and kind people into desperate drug-traffickers. There, most rural residents depend on the weather for their livelihoods and subsist in poverty. For some of them, drug trafficking becomes an efficient and effective shortcut to freedom from want. Consequently, some avaricious peddlers and self-employed entrepreneurs switched to

the drug business; some peasants with dreams of wealth left hoes behind; brothers, fathers and sons; husbands and wives; fathers and daughters; mothers-in-law and their daughters-in-law joined hand-in-hand for the gamble and went by train or bus to the "front" defiant of life and death... Several jailed drug traffickers confessed frankly without regret, "Drug trafficking is to gamble with one's life. But one adventure can bring in hundreds and thousands of yuan. Even with a risk of losing one's head, it is a lucrative business... Getting into trouble for a short while, enjoying life forever; sacrificing one person, being blessed for several generations." (Chen, 2006: 131)

In Linquan district, Anhui province, peasants were enchanted by drugs and their profits en mass. Sixty-five drug traffickers from Linquan were arrested in Yunnan from January to October 1998; within four days in March 1999, twenty-nine traffickers from two townships in Linquan were arrested. In a small township with 3,000 residents, more than 100 were executed or sentenced to life in prison for drug trafficking offenses (Chen, 2006: 134). In addition to drug trafficking, farmers in poor mountain areas, especially from Sichuan, Anhui, Heilongjiang, Inner Mongolia, and Xinjiang provinces, have revitalized poppy cultivation on their lands, enabling them to reap profits dozens of times higher than planting agricultural crops (Cui, ed., 1999: 246–273). In 1990, 36 million poppy plants in areas of 3,000 *mu* (about 500 acres) were destroyed nationwide; the following year another 3.29 million poppy plants in areas of 300 *mu* (60 acres) were destroyed. In Sichuan province alone, 1,207,000 plants were destroyed in 1991; 1,050,000 in 1992; 721,000 in 1993, and 1,123,500 in 1994 (243). Despite the government's continuous efforts, the perseverance of poppy farmers was obvious.

Popular participation in these two vice markets, prostitution and drugs, has not remained at the mere level of hookers standing on street corners or hawkers running errands in the neighborhood. Participants in both the sex and drug markets have become increasingly well organized (He, 2003: 332–336). Since the 1980s, prostitution has evolved from an individual business into professionalized group-managed enterprises. Brothel owners, procurers, protectors, and prostitutes have formed a division of labor. Based upon information from Guangdong province, by the early 1990s, 80 percent of prostitutes were controlled by pimps or brothel owners (Shan, 1995: 384). Nationwide in 1994, 45.5 percent of prostitutes were affiliated with groups; 4,547 prostitution groups with 23,000 members were uncovered (Huang, 1997: 48). As for drug trafficking, the chain-structure network of connections with global criminal syndicates has become a dominant organizational form. According to statistics from some regions in China, joint crime (committed by partners and criminal groups) has accounted for 60 percent of drug-related crimes (Zhao and Yu, 2003: 37).

Organized, enterprise crime has clearly scooped up opportunities made possible by an opening and globalizing market. Mafia-style capitalism in China attests to the dynamics and ordering of spontaneous marketization. Under the double pressure of a corrupt party-state and an equally corrupt society, a strong jungle-like quality features heavily. The poorly and arbitrarily regulated environment has created ample opportunities for criminal entrepreneurs to rise up. As a notorious underworld axiom goes, "Once you are in the rivers and lakes, life runs beyond your control." Legitimate businesspeople have had to adapt to the uncertainty and brutality of the market through a process of blackening, namely, assimilating scrupulous and cunning stratagems in business warfare. The meteoric rise and fall of many Chinese robber barons illustrates how this jungle-like capitalism has elevated some to quick wealth but others to the deep abyss. One Chinese researcher observed, "In terms of their upbringings, most private entrepreneurs during the early period of China's market economy had no privileged background. Many of them were peasants who just cleaned up their muddy feet in the field, or the 'marginal elements' out of the system in cities. In the public perception, the absolute majority of businesspeople and shipowners in the private sector were people who had been released from prison after having served their full terms" (Fan, 2005: 4).

Chinese robber barons have often used three basic schemes. The first is to make quick money from Satanic purses (Naylor, 2002: 287). Drugs and prostitution are two deep Satanic purses, while a third deep purse is piracy. The Chinese pirates can produce anything: poisonous baby powder milk, fake cigarettes, pirated CDs and movies, adulterated liquor, counterfeit jeeps, and even counterfeit currency (Chen, 2006). An economist of China's hidden economy estimated that in 1990, 20 percent of the products on the market were either below quality standards or counterfeits of legitimate brands (Luo et al., 1998; Long, 2003; Huang, 1997: 4). The city of Lufeng, Guangdong province, has been the capital of counterfeiting: 80 percent of the confiscated counterfeit banknotes nationwide were printed here. In 2000, a twelve-person criminal group was prosecuted in Lufeng for having printed counterfeit currency with a face value of 773 million yuan (China

News Agency, September 15, 2000; *People's Daily*, December 5, 2000). The Dabie Mountain region, including parts of Anhui, Henan, and Hubei provinces, is another center for counterfeit currency and other fake products. All of these places share one thing in common: poverty. As the popular saying goes, "Wickedness comes from the poverty of people" (He, 1997; Ye et al., 2004: 243–249).

The second scheme involves using violence and crime to accumulate primitive capital and to obtain more resources from state-controlled industries and financial institutions. Three high-profile cases exemplify this: the Zheng Weihuo group in Chang'an, Shaanxi province; the Zhang Wei organized crime group in Wenling, Zhejiang province; and the Lai Changxin's "Yuanhua" group in Xiamen, Fujian province. Zheng Weihuo, Zhang Wei, and Lai Changxin were ruffians in the countryside and scuffled with the law in their youth. Violence and illicit business made them rich; then, wealth introduced them to the people in power. All three spent money lavishly on government officials and tried to satisfy their every need from brand-name clothes to foreign wines, jewelry, cars, houses, beautiful women, and even tuition for their children's education in the United States. Eventually they all became masters in surfing both the criminal underworld and the officialdom. Ultimately, Zheng Weihuo collected at least 5,000 yuan daily from his civil engineering firm, dance hall, fish farm, and quarry. By borrowing money from state-owned banks, Zhang Wei and his group swindled more than 500 million yuan. As for Lai Changxin, his group smuggled goods and raw materials valued at 53 billion yuan and evaded tariffs totaling 30 billion yuan (Zuomuniao, 2002: 316–377; Zhu, 2002; Liu, 2004; Zhang et al., 2001; Sheng, 2001).

The third scheme is to play the so-called karate game (a game with empty hands) in the financial sector. Wealth is accumulated first by registering empty business entities and seeking official endorsement to borrow huge bank loans, and then disappearing either by hiding somewhere or migrating to a foreign country. Beginning in 1999, *Forbes* magazine has annually ranked the richest people in mainland China. But many of these multimillionaires quickly ended up getting arrested (Zhou Zhengyi, Mu Qizhong, Yang Bing, and Liu Xiaoqing), disappearing mysteriously (Liu Bo, Lu Liang, Wu Zhijian, and Lu Junxiong), or seeking protection from foreign governments (Lai Changxin in Canada and Yang Rong in the United States). Most of these "problem moguls" came from modest or blemished backgrounds, but they capitalized on their social contacts and connections with people in power to get privileges to develop land and construction projects, and then, took out huge amounts of money from state banks, the stock market, and ordinary buyers. This strategy was called "using an empty hand to ensnare a white wolf." By swindling and taking advantage of loopholes in the financial system, many such villains indeed became rich (Ouyang, 2003).

Conclusion

Deng Xiaoping's reforms sounded the death knell for Maoist egalitarianism and threw Chinese society into a rapid process of stratification. Idealistic camaraderie quickly gave away to a callous cash nexus (Xia, 1999: 345–358). The working-class people and peasants, who formed the sacrosanct category of "the people" and enjoyed the privilege to discriminate against and dehumanize other "bad elements" of society such as intellectuals, former capitalists, landlords, and their children, now have seen the reversal of their fortune. As a state-guided capitalism with many social-Darwinist qualities is fully manifest in China, the social and economic gap between the rich and the poor has reached its most dangerous level, even compared to China's past standards. Because of the state's procrastination in reforming the residential registration system in cities and in privatizing land ownership in the countryside, and due to its systematic failure in allocating resources to primary education, job retraining, and micro-loans for the jobless and family businesses, a huge lower class has emerged since the 1980s, swelling rapidly during the 1990s. Within the Chinese Communist state a massive population of the poor has been created. Even more disturbing, the Chinese Communist Party has politically abandoned the fundamental interests of the disadvantaged. For the past three decades, the Chinese regime has increasingly revealed a right-wing capitalist bureaucratic authoritarian orientation, which evolved to its uttermost under Jiang Zemin and consequently prompted Hu Jintao and Wen Jiabao to pull the reins on the process. As a result, a huge part of the lower class has been condemned to the powerless and hopeless category of underclass.

In the race to get rich quick, the underclass has been systematically discriminated against by the current legitimate structure and public policy. The Chinese poor lack the financial capital, human capital, and social capital to get ahead in a sophisticated and globalized market economy. Deprived of the vote and thus political power, the poor and the underclass cannot force politicians to address their desperate needs.

Their destitution will only worsen as long as the oligarchic and authoritarian regime exists, for under these circumstances they have been forced to sell the only resource remaining to them: their bodies. The commercialization of women's bodies has provided an opportunity for female members of the lower class to participate in the capitalist economy. As their sisters, wives, daughters, and fellow villagers move into the sex trade, young and uneducated men leave the village and end up in segregated shantytowns in major cities. Under the domination of a patriarchal power structure, men in positions of power want to get their hands on poor women for sexploitation and want to keep their male compatriots as far away from power as possible. Brawny men, if they are not brainy, suffer the most and get hurt the deepest under a male-dominant elitist global capitalism (Sassen, 2001; Ehrenreich and Hochschild, eds., 2004).

Nevertheless, circumstances created by the changing political economy have made crime for the underclass a cost-effective means to subsist and even to advance socially. As political science teaches, power is the ability to make others do or not to do something, even against their will. Financial capital, human capital, and social networks can supply power. But violence and coercion are the supreme sources of power. Violence and the fear that violence invokes have opened a window for many, transforming disadvantaged people from a vulnerable population group to an underclass—a "dangerous population group" (*People's Daily*, January 20, 2006). By appropriating the sworn brotherhood tradition and the organizational form of secret society, the Chinese underclass has revolutionized its violence and amplified its terror. To use a brilliant term coined by the historian Wu Si (2004: 451), today's China has spawned a "life-risking group" (*bomin jituan*).

The meta-rule of Chinese societies, past and present, has been revealed through the research of Wu Si (2004): "Who commands the most violence decides." Now that productive force is correlated with profits, destructive force can be correlated with "bloody payment" (*xuechou*). When everyone was poor as in China under Mao Zedong, the price of life was too low for someone to extort bloody payment. Now that some in China are rich, the price of life is high enough for anyone to risk the law to change their place on the socioeconomic stepladder. This huge differential between the price of one life and another fuels a "blood-as-capital business" (*xueben jingying*) to seek bloody payment. Members of violent groups are willing to bet their lives upon other peoples' lives. The case of Zhang Jun is very illustrative here. In a TV series (2004) based upon his story, the protagonist instructed his followers about the nature of his "business," "What do we invest in our business? Our lives." As he was jailed, Zhang Jun reflected upon his life and said, "I stepped upon this pathway; the main cause was my poverty. Now when I look back, many things were wrongdoings. But I had no choice, because I had to survive. Money was not the only aim in my mind. I wanted power, the power that enables me to do whatever I desire, to do anything or kill anyone in China or Southeast Asia" (*People's Daily*, May 22, 2001; *Nanfang Duishi Bao*, April 17, 2001).

Even criminals eventually want to distance themselves from violence, shift money into legitimate businesses, polish up their manners, and seek recognition and respect from the community and mainstream society (Bell, 1962: 147–148). Despite symbioses between business and criminal worlds and between political and criminal nexuses (Xia, 2004), there is no consistent mode of relationship that has developed between the state and the underworld. The inclusion of criminal elements into mainstream society has been very selective, based primarily on the patron-client relationship between some officials and key criminal figures. As criminal underworld members have attempted to get a legitimate footing in the economy and some kind of recognition from the state, the Chinese government has failed to formulate flexible and constructive policies to respond to the strong desire of the underworld population for social ascent. Under the current regime, it is easy to lose innocence; once you have lost innocence, the system makes it extremely difficult to wash away the stigma and redeem yourself in a new way of life.

Bibliography

Arendt, Hannah. 1979. *The Origins of Totalitarianism*. New York: Harcourt Brace.
Bai, Xue. 2002. *Toushi sanpeinü* (Looking into escort girls). Beijing: Zhongguo wenlian.
Bates, Robert H. 2001. *Prosperity and Violence: The Political Economy of Development*. New York: W. W. Norton.
Bell, Daniel. 1962. *The End of Ideology: On the Exhaustion of Political Ideas in the Fifties*. New York: Free Press.
Chen, Beidi. 2006. *Zhongguo Xidu diaocha* (Investigating drug abuse in China). Beijing: Xinhua.
Chen, Chuanyi. 2006. *Tiandi renxin* (Heaven, earth and heart). Beijing: Zuojia.
Chesney, Kellow. 1970. *The Victorian Underworld*. New York: Penguin Books.
Chua, Amy. 2004. *World on Fire: How Exporting Free Market Democracy Breeds Ethnic Hatred and Global Instability*. New York: Anchor Books.
Cui, Min, ed. 1999. *Dupin fanzui* (Crimes of drugs). Beijing: Jingguan jiaoyu.
Ehrenreich, Barbara and Arlie Russell Hochschild, eds. 2004. *Global Women: Nannies, Maids and Sex Workers in the New Economy*. New York: Owls Books.

Fan, Weifeng. 2005. *Heihua: Caomang jingji shiqi* (Blackening: The era of roguish economy). Nanchang: Jiangxi jiaoyu.
Friedman, Thomas L. 2000. *The Lexus and the Olive Tree: Understanding Globalization.* New York: Anchor Books.
Galeano, Eduardo. 2000. *Upside Down.* New York: Picador.
Gransow, Bettina, and Li Hanlin. 2001. *Dushi li de cunmin* (Villagers in the city). Beijing: Zhongyang bianyi.
He, Qinglian. 1998. *Xiandaihua de xianjing* (The pitfalls of modernization). Beijing: Jinri zhongguo.
———. 2003. *Zhongguo xiandaihua de xianjing* (China's descent into a quagmire). Hong Kong: Broad Press.
He, Tieguang. 1997. *Zui'e de heidong* (The evil black hole). Beijing: Zhongguo shehui.
Huang, Weiting. 1997. *Zhongguo de yinxin jingji: 1996* (China's Hidden Economy: 1996). Beijing: Zhongguo shangye chubanshe.
Kaplan, Robert D. 2000. *The Coming Anarchy: Shattering the Dreams of the Post-Cold War.* New York: Vintage Books.
Katz, Michael B., ed. 1993. *The "Underclass" Debate: Views from History.* Princeton, NJ: Princeton University Press.
Knox, George W. 2000. *An Introduction to Gangs.* Peotone, IL: New Chicago School Press.
Lieberthal, Kenneth. 1973. "The Suppression of Secret Societies in Post-Liberation Tientsin." *China Quarterly* 54, 242–266.
Liu, Kaiming. 2003. *Bianyuanren* (The marginal people). Beijing: Xinhua.
Liu, Ning, and Tian Huiming, eds. 2001. *Heise youhuan* (The black fear). Beijing: Wenhua Yishu.
Liu, Wenyan. 2007. *Zui yu fa* (Crime and punishment). Beijing: Zhongguo funü.
Liu, Yan. 2004. *Xiamen teda zousi xilie'an* (Serious smuggling cases in Xiamen). Beijing: Renmin fayuan.
Long, Shiyun. 2003. *Zhongguo jiahuo* (Peril of "the fake" in China). Wuhan: Hubei renmin.
Luo, Hancheng, Wu Fang, and Li Yong, eds. 1998. *Gongheguo zai dajia* (The Republic is fighting against fake products). Beijing: Zhongguo jiliang.
Mandelbaum, Michael. 2002. *The Ideas That Conquered the World: Peace, Democracy, and Free Market in the Twenty-First Century.* New York: Public Affairs.
Morselli, Carlo. 2005. *Contacts, Opportunities, and Criminal Enterprise.* Toronto, Canada: University of Toronto Press.
Naím, Moisés. 2005. *Illicit.* New York: Anchor Books.
Naylor, R. T. 2002. *Wages of Crime: Black Markets, Illegal Finance, and the Underworld Economy.* Ithaca, NY: Cornell University Press.
Ouyang, Yifei. 2003. *Wenti fuhao* (Problem moguls). Beijing: Renmin ribao.
Qiu, Renzong. 2001. *Tamen zai hei'an zhong* (They are in darkness). Beijing: Zhongguo shehui kexue.
Sassen, Saskia. 2001. *The Global City: New York, London, Tokyo.* Princeton, NJ: Princeton University Press.
Shan, Guangnai. 1995. *Zhongguo changji: guoqu he xianzai* (Prostitution in China: Past and Present). Beijing: Falü chubanshe.
Sheng, Xue. 2001. *Yuanhua an heimu* (Unveiling the Yuanhua case). Hong Kong: Mirror Books.
Solinger, Dorothy. 1999. *Contesting Citizenship in China.* Berkeley, CA: University of California Press.
Song, Linfei. 1995. *Zhongguo jingji qiji weilai yu zhengce xuanzhe* (China's economic miracle: The future and policy options). Nanjing: Nanjing daxue.

Sun, Liping. 2004. "Ziyuan chongxin jijuxia de diceng shehui xincheng" (The formation of a subaltern society in the context of resource allocation). In Li Peiling, Li Qiang, and Sun Liping, eds. *Zhongguo shehui fenceng* (Social stratification in today's China), 339–357. Beijing: Shehui kexue wenxian.
Tucker, Robert C. 1978. *The Marx-Engels Reader.* New York: W. W. Norton.
TV series. 2004. *Tian bu changjian* (Under the heaven no hiding place for evil). Wuhan: Wuhan Yinxiang.
Wang, Zhimin, Ma Xi, Qin Mu, Xu Yinghao, Yuan Zhihang, Wu Sha et al. 2002. *Dangqian zhongguo liudong renkou fanzui yanjiu* (A study of the crimes among the migrant population in China today). Beijing: Zhongguo renmin gongan daxue.
Wanyan, Shaoyuan. 1993. *Liumang de bianqian* (Evolution of hooligans). Shanghai: Shanghai guji.
Wu, Junping, and Xu Ying. 1997. *Woshishui?* (Who am I?). Huhhot: Neimengu renmin.
Wu, Si. 2004. *Yinbie de lishi* (The hidden history). Haikou: Hainan.
Xia, Ming. 1999. "From Camaraderie to the Cash Nexus." *Journal of Contemporary China* 8, no.21: 345–358.
———. 2004. "The Criminal-Political Nexus in China: An Assessment." *Active Society in Formation, Woodrow Wilson International Center for Scholars, Asia Program Special Report* 124 (September): 12–18.
———. 2006. "Assessing and Explaining the Resurgence of China's Criminal Underworld." *Global Crime* 7, no.2 (May): 151–175.
———. 2008. "Organizational Formations of Organized Crime in China." *Journal of Contemporary China* 17, no.54 (February): 1–23.
Yang, Lijun. 2003. *Zhongguo dangdai xidu wenti* (Drug problems in contemporary China). Beijing: Qunzhong.
Yang, Shiguang, and Shen Hengyan, eds. 1995. *Xingman shifang renyuan huigui shehui wenti zhuanlun* (Special topics on the return of released persons into the society). Beijing: Shehui kexue.
Ye, Zhaoqing, Zhu Dayin, and Geng Changjun. 2004. *Laizi zhongguo shehui diceng de baogao* (Reports from the lower echelon of Chinese society). Wuhan: Changjiang wenyi.
Zhang, Xianhua, Zhuang Dongxian, Wen Jian, and Hong Yun. 2001. *Fengbao* (Storm). Beijing: Zuojia.
Zhao, Bingzhi, ed. 2003. *Zhongguo xingshi faxue* (Criminal law in China). Beijing: Zhongguo renmin gong'an daxue.
Zhao, Bingzhi, and Yu Zhigang. 2003. *Dupin fanzui* (Drug crimes). Beijing: Zhongguo renmin gongan daxue.
Zhao, Shukai. 1998. *Zongheng chengxiang* (Going between cities and the countryside). Beijing: Zhongguo nongye.
Zhao, Yanjie, and Zhang Tiejun. 2004. *Dupin de zhonglei he weihai* (Types of drug and their harms). Beijing: Zhongguo renmin gongan daxue.
Zhongguo Gong'an Nianjian (The yearbook of public security in China, 2000). 2001. Beijing: Qunzhong.
Zhongguo Jingcha xuehui (The China Police Association). 1998. *Dangqian zhongguo nongmin zhong de fanzui yanjiu lunwenxuan* (Selected papers on crimes among the peasants of contemporary China). Beijing: Zhongguo renmin gongan daxue.
Zhongguo sifa xingzheng nianjian (Yearbook of judicial administration). 1998–2003. Beijing: Falü.
Zhonghua Jieduwang (China's Anti-Drug Net). 2005. "Zhongguo dupin wenti dangqian sida tedian" (Four features of the current drug problems in China). (October 24). Retrieved on June 15, 2008 from www.5191.com/a12/jiedu/b04/20051024102500.htm

Zhu, Guanglei, Han Xiufa, Guo Daojiu, Zhou Zhenchao, Hou Po, Niu Litian et al. 1997. *Dangdai zhongguo ge jieceng fengxi* (An analysis of social strata in contemporary China). Tianjin: Tianjin renmin.
Zhu, Si'en. 2002. *"Juren" youxi* (Games for "giants"). Beijing: Qunzhong.
Zuomuniao (Woodpecker) Magazine. 2002. "Guaitai (Monster)." Beijing: Qunzhong.

CHAPTER SEVEN

Feminization, Recognition, and the Cosmological in Xishuangbanna

ANOUSKA KOMLOSY

Introduction

This chapter explores the feminization of Xishuangbanna (Sipsongpanna) and Dai (Tai) peoples in Yunnan province within the wider Chinese polity from the perspective of Dai cosmological understandings (see map 7.1 and map 7.2). Dai peoples in China are heavily promoted through the prism of feminization and often exploitation. This chapter looks at this process from the point of view of Dai peoples. It goes some way toward understanding how they read the abounding images of Dai women that pervade in Xishuangbanna (Banna) and constitute much non-Dai experience of them as a Chinese "minority nationality." In order to comprehend these issues from the Dai perspective, cosmological understandings of femininity, especially youthful femininity, must be taken into account. By focusing on these understandings we can better account for Dai pragmatic participation in some of these ongoing feminizing projects. Dai participation is not simply passive submission to Han fantasy but is rather part of the ongoing process of negotiation and accommodation that has a long and complex history in this border region.

The material presented in this chapter is the result of long-term fieldwork carried out in both Jinghong (Chiang Hung, the main city in Banna) and a Tai Lue village in Menghai district where interviews were carried out in Dai, Yunnan/Bannahua, and Mandarin languages.

This chapter addresses four interlinked issues. First, the feminization of Banna has contributed to its success as a tourist destination and to a view of both Dai peoples and the region as compliant and accommodating. Economic exploitation has led to the destruction of much of Banna's subtropical rainforest and the landscape has suffered terrible damage in recent decades. But the Chinese authorities hope that tourism will be the basis of future sustainable development. It is thought that local people will be encouraged to protect their environment (both "cultural" and "natural") in order to ensure its attractiveness for visitors and hence its profitability. Recent changes resulting from the "opening up" of the area have been of considerable financial benefit to many, including much of the Dai population. Second, the promotion of Dai women is a powerful tool in the perceived ongoing battle against the "Sinification" or "Hanification" of Banna.[1] The Dai feminine image is so unthreatening and appealing that it provides a highly visible and acceptable Dai presence in the wider, Han-dominated polity. Paradoxically representations of Dai women have given voice to an otherwise often muted and disregarded Dai presence. Third, Dai cosmological understandings of feminine potency do not view young women as weak or cowardly: but rather as liable to unleash dangerous and unpredictable forces. Fourth, within Theravada Buddhist moral understandings the maltreatment of any female necessarily binds the supposedly dominant male into an ongoing reciprocal, moral relationship. By enduring such a relationship the woman is expected to benefit, at least materially. Thus a feminized Banna, forced to play the role of a woman taken against her will, is entitled to material compensation from her overbearing and exploitative partner, in this case the Chinese polity.

Complex ontological and cosmological assumptions permeate the everyday lives of Dai peoples in Banna, informing all manner of decisions from house building to getting a tattoo to choosing where to hang the washing. Such knowledge does not, however, form a static body of "traditional" understanding. Rather, cosmological knowledge, its interpretation, and utility are always coming into being.[2] Dai inspirations—having shamanic, Buddhist, Chinese, Indian, Thai, and other sources—are heterogeneous, and the area has long been one of shifting identities and influences.[3] As C. Patterson Giersch reiterates throughout his 2006 historical study of the China-Burma borderlands, adaptation and change have been constants. This is still the case, though Dai priorities have changed due to the ongoing identity negotiations and renegotiations within Banna, a land that is no longer a frontier but rather a borderland under direct Chinese control. This chapter is about pragmatic accommodation to the current manifestations of Chinese state control in the region. These include the promotion of an ethnically distinct Dai within "multiethnic" China, the opening of Yunnan as the gateway to Southeast Asia, the Chinese Center's stress on societal harmony, and the need to promote sustainable development in an area that has an increasingly fragile environment.

Dai peoples speak (or are descended from speakers of) a Tai language/dialect, and in Banna there are speakers of several different Tai languages (Hansen, 1999; Giersch, 2006: 222; Komlosy, 2002). The largest language group is Daile (Tai Lue); they are Theravada Buddhists and labeled "Water Dai" (Shui Dai) in Chinese. Prior to the Communist Revolution of 1949 they were rulers who controlled the rich rice *paddi*. Today their "culture" has come to stand metonymically for that of Banna (through a slippage of ethnic to local representation) in a process

Map 7.1 Yunnan Province
Source: James M. Farrant

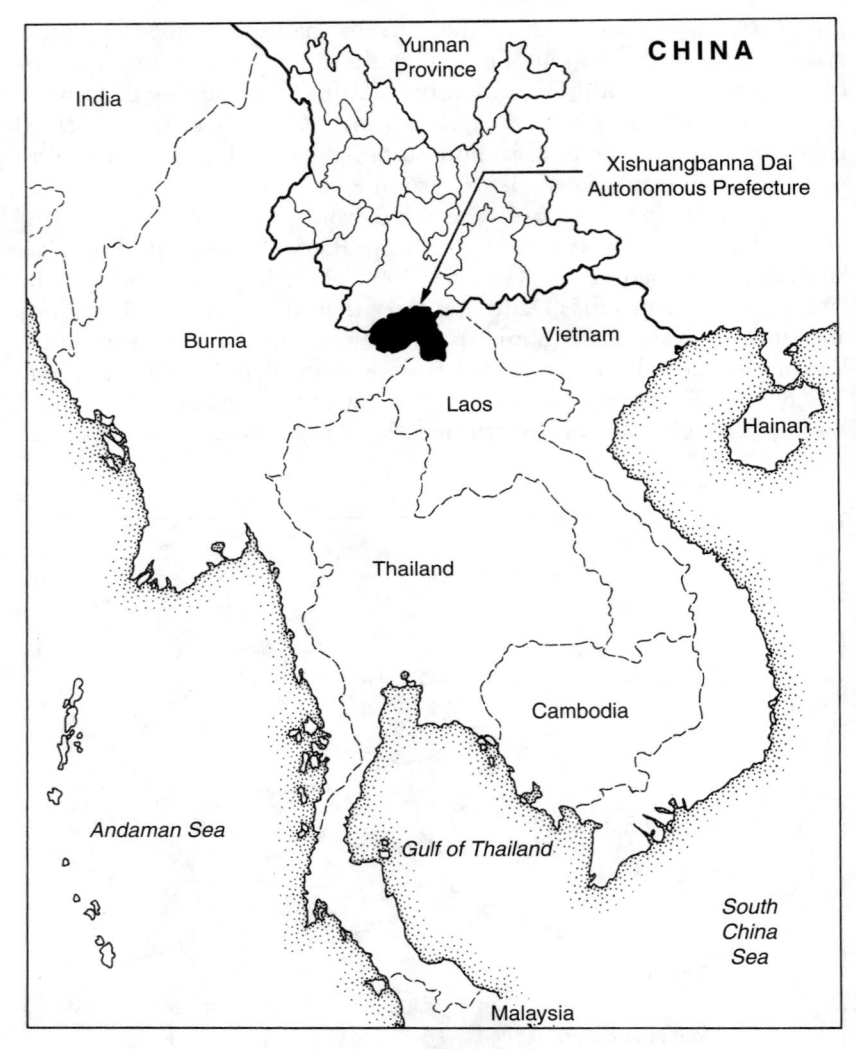

Map 7.2 Xishuangbanna Dai Autonomous Prefecture
Source: James M. Farrant

that can be seen as having foreclosed countless other ways of representing the area. This has caused some resentment among hill-dwelling peoples such as Ahka (Hani/Aini), Wa and non-Buddhist Tai (such as the Tai Ya and Pashee Tai). The category "Dai" is as complicated as all other ethnic labels.[4] Yet administratively "Dai" is used to refer to all

Tai speaking peoples, authorities (both Tai Lue and Han officials) give little consideration to diversity within this category, and it is a common assumption that all Dai people in Banna are Shui Dai (Tai Lue).

Local Identity, Accommodation, and Change

Since the eighteenth century the dominant picture in Banna has been one of accommodation, manifest in the exchange of ideas and ways of being, and intermarriage between different peoples. Yet since the Qing dynasty (1644–1911), there have been times of brutal repression as the imperial government sought to consolidate its control in this remote, and often troublingly independent, region. Repression was not just directed against indigenous peoples. Chinese (usually Han) migrants often integrated with non-Han peoples, and were on occasion punished for it (Giersch, 2006: 7).[5] During the Yongzheng reign (1724–1735) the Qing invaded twice, once in 1727 and again in 1732, ostensibly to calm unrest between Han (*bin haw*) and Dai. Qing rulers were unwilling, however, to spare the resources and troops necessary to exert direct control over Banna (62). Although Qing emperors sought to manipulate intergroup conflicts in border regions, they recognized that in certain situations indirect rule, through indigenous institutions, was better than direct military occupation (222). Since the Han (206 BCE–220 CE) peripheral regions had been ruled by tributary leaders who came to pay homage to the Chinese Center. This was known as the *tusi* system (Waley-Cohen, 1999: 15).

Daile (Tai Lue) literature suggests that Dai peoples moved to the banks of the Mekong River in present day Banna sometime in the eighth century (the Daile text *Lesipsongpang* cited in Liu, 1999: 1; Yun, 1998: 1–54). There was also a large inward migration of Tai speakers into the region during the Mongol-led Yuan Dynasty (1279–1368), as Dai living further north in Yunnan fled the invaders. In prerevolutionary times Dai heads of state (*Tsau Phaendin*) ruled while paying tribute to both Chinese and Burmese courts and on occasion the Thai court as well.[6] The phrase used by Tai speakers to explain this situation was *Ho pen pho, Man pen mae* (Han/Yunnanese is the father, Burmese is the Mother) (Ratanaporn, 2000: 324). In China the Tsau Phaendin were recognized as indigenous leaders within the tusi system.

Chinese influence on local affairs in Banna increased after the Nationalist Revolution of 1911. Considerable numbers of Chinese troops moved to the region initially at the request of the Tsau Phaendin to protect him against rebellious local factions, but they stayed on to maintain order once the Revolution began (Hsieh, 1990: 2). When the Communists took power they negotiated with Dai leaders. As Giersch (2006: 222) points out, "Official seals were issued to various Tai rulers, much as they had been in Qing times." Xishuangbanna Dai Autonomous Prefecture was established in 1953. Yet by the 1950s major land reforms had been implemented that broke the Tai aristocracy and ended the Chinese Center's dependence on local Dai rulers. During the Cultural Revolution (1966–1976) local ritual practice and Theravada Buddhism were strongly (on occasions brutally) discouraged. Since the 1980s Dai cultural and religious practice has been more or less tolerated (Komlosy, 2002; Davis, 2005). Unlike during the Qing, the borders between China and Southeast Asia are now firmly delineated. But people and ideas continue to flow across them, and Southeast Asian influence (curtailed during the Maoist era) has been growing since the 1980s.[7]

Banna covers a little over 19,000 square kilometers and lies in the southeast of Yunnan province. The area is home to a multiplicity of peoples, many of whom are, like Dai speakers, cross-border peoples. The 1996 census gives figures for eighteen non-Han peoples, though not all—like the Bai and Naxi economic migrants, for example—are indigenous to the region. At a little under 35 percent, Dai peoples constitute the largest section of the population. This figure represents a significant fall in the percentage of the Dai population, however, since they numbered over 50 percent in the 1950s.[8]

Today Han peoples move to this fertile subtropical region as tenant farmers, traders, and laborers, and many thousands visit each year as tourists (Komlosy, 2004; Schein, 1997, 2000; Oakes, 1993, 1997, 1998; Rack, 2005; Gladney, 1994). This incoming Han population is highly diverse and stratified. As Hansen (2004: 63) writes, "Many of the poorest Han peasants have taken up jobs in the service sector, which very few Tai people will accept. Many minority people therefore regard these Han peasants as being at the bottom of the local social hierarchy. Differences in social class and level of access to power are so profound among different Han immigrants that they cannot be regarded as a common, unified group of 'colonizers.'"

Feminization and Ethnic Tourism

Images of Dai women have been unashamedly used to promote Xishuangbanna as an enticing travel destination. Most hospitality workers, be they guides, hotel workers, or waitresses, dress in recognizably Dai outfits, and many of them speak Dai.[9] Tourist literature often touches

Feminization, Recognition, Cosmological 129

Figure 7.1 Sculpture in Jinghong's main square, 2005
Source: Photograph by the author with permission.[10]

upon the enchanting character of Dai women or the exotic beauty of their svelte figures enhanced by tight sarongs. One 2004 guide, published by the Yunnan People's Press, is entitled *Xishunagbanna wenrou de youhuo* (Gentle and Soft Seduction of Xishuangbanna) (Li, 2004). In the late 1990s a young woman, wearing a Dai-style sarong, hands held demurely in prayer position, provided the main advertising icon for Yunnan Air. As tourists make their way to the hotels of Jinghong they are confronted by numerous images of Dai women adorning the city streets (see figure 7.1).

At present there is little interethnic or political tension in Banna. Increasing ethnic tourism in the region and its concomitant feminization, however, has bought with it significant changes.[11] The current grave concern over the spread of AIDS, drug use, and prostitution has led to a questioning of the wisdom of promoting the area using tantalizing feminine imagery. Associations of such imagery shift easily between nostalgic images of a lost purity (where Dai women simultaneously represent both the alluring exotic and a lost purity of an uncorrupted China) and more sinister or seedy associations. AIDS and HIV issues are now the subject of high-profile education and health campaigns carried out in both Chinese and Dai. In 2006 new AIDS awareness posters were being erected in Jinghong, including a display made by local school children.

There has been a shift in the government representation of prostitution in the region. When AIDS first emerged as a significant threat the supposed lax morals of the Dai were blamed. This is unsurprising as "minority nationalities" are often associated with societal freedom in the Chinese popular imagination (Gladney, 1994; Schein, 2000). Yet recent studies have demonstrated that AIDS cases are higher among Han peoples in Banna, and so gradually attitudes among the Chinese people in general and health workers in particular have shifted. Today AIDS is often thought of as a Han problem—especially among educated urban Dai (Hyde, 2001; Evans, 2000). Closely related to prostitution are the considerable problems of drug abuse. A report issued by Save the Children (1997) stated that almost all the female sex workers they interviewed in Banna were drug users. Sex workers are usually poor non-Dai economic migrants who dress in Dai style to profit from its exotic allure. Educated Dai women had been quick to point this out to me. They noted, with great anger, the "loss of face" that such activity caused Dai peoples. Thus although there is considerable Dai pride in the beauty of their people and homeland, there is also concern over how outsiders in such a multiethnic context interpret feminized images.

To the Chinese Center, the best way to maintain stability in border regions is through reforms that enable at least some of the benefits of economic growth to be more evenly distributed.[12] The state now actively promotes entrepreneurship and, especially in non-Han regions, ethnic tourism that it views as the key to sustainable development (the "Go-West" strategy). Tourist trips, where Chinese visit non-Han areas, are said by officials to both provide a green alternative to industrialization and to promote societal integration. Through these policies the *economic* (antipoverty drive) and the *educational* (ethnic tourism) are being used together in an attempt to promote harmony within the larger Chinese polity. Such developmental policies, which imply visions of progress and their concomitant assumptions of backwardness, are greeted with varying degrees of ambiguity by their target communities. Public discourse, full of rhetoric invoking harmonious coexistence, is deployed to ensure and perpetuate acceptance of state policy. Images of Dai feminine beauty chime well with this project. To Chinese eyes these images appear demure, obliging, and gentle. They contribute to the feeling that Banna is one border region where the state does not have to concern itself over splitists and rebels. Dai readings of such feminine imagery, however, often vary from that of the Chinese majority. These two different interpretations contribute to a negotiated, ever-shifting accommodation on the ground. The dissociation of Dai peoples (as metonymic embodiments of Xishuangbanna) from the stigma and dangers of AIDS contributes, moreover, to ensuring the continued allure of the region as a tourist destination (Hockx and Strauss, 2005).

In everyday life Tai Lue (Daile) girls are taught to walk tall: to be proud of their beauty. They love dressing up, putting on copious amounts of make-up, and parading about—behavior that can lead to muttering by non-Dai women about Dai arrogance. They often wear large amounts of fine, filigreed gold jewelry, and some elders still have large ornate silver or gold hairpins. DVDs in Dai (and Thai) aimed solely at a Dai audience, showing dancing and singing girls, can be found all over Banna alongside Mandarin versions made for the tourist market. Dai girls do work in the tourist industry, including as escorts, and Dai girls move to destinations throughout China to join dance troupes and work in minority theme parks or restaurants.

Since the time of Erasmus (1466–1536) the power of feminine beauty has been recognized: "[Women] have the gift of beauty which they rightly value above everything else, for it ensures their power to tyrannize over tyrants themselves" (Erasmus, 1508 [1971]: 89). There is also a potential for expression in the images of Dai femininity that Dai people themselves utilize. As Dru Gladney (1994: 117) explains, "Minorities...by allowing the objectivizing gaze of the state-sponsored media, establish their identity and right to a voice in their own affairs, appropriating and turning, whenever possible, these objectivizing moves to their own benefit. In this way, the maintenance and assertion of minority 'culture,' no matter how exoticized or contrived, may be seen as a form of resistance." Through the promotion of a Dai feminized aesthetic Dai peoples are engaged in complex identity negotiations. Below are some of the reasons why Dai peoples are willing to engage in the promotion of feminized images of themselves and their land despite the dangers of misreadings or negative readings, including associations with prostitution or subservience to the Chinese Center.

Feminine Potency:
The Multifaceted Symbols of Blood and Hair

In Dai Theravada Buddhist thought the human body constitutes a vertical microcosm, with the head associated with heaven, the heart with earth, and the loins with hell. Suffering is caused and perpetuated by intentional action and attachment to worldly illusion. Action binds us to the cycle of *samsara*, through the workings of *karma* (action and reaction). Strength and power come from harmonious alignment to the cosmos and its generative (cosmogenic) forces. But destructive earthly potency can also be harnessed through the purposeful disruption of cosmic harmony. Engaging with destructive powers has consequences, often unforeseen, and as such is profoundly dangerous. Menstruating women leak a substance (blood) that is associated with earthly action, through a part of their bodies (the loins) associated with hell or action and reaction, *karma*. Menstruating female bodies, though also microcosmic (head-heaven; heart-earth; loins-hell), do not maintain this microcosm clearly. Their blood, associated with the earthly realm and action, can flow and so disrupt the ideal alignment. Their blood may contaminate parts of the body such as the head, usually associated with the end of suffering and with the heavenly realms.

Tanabe (1991: 188) views menstrual blood as "a morally degraded entity," yet he explains that "such pollution of menstrual blood, while constraining women's activities, also however, represents a power destructive to men's mental and emotional stability and their magical efficacy." Women are not meant to enter temples during their menses, and there are some pagodas that they should not enter at any time. Entering temples during their periods is dangerous because were the substance they leak (blood) to come into contact with things associated with ending suffering and attachment (heaven), such as images of the Buddha, the cosmic alignment could be upset, and the ongoing processes of cosmogenesis put in jeopardy.[13] A similar logic explains why women's sarongs, which may have come into contact with menstrual blood, should not be hung above waist-height even when drying. If the fabric came into contact with a man's head it could harm him.

In daily life (outside the monkhood—*sangha*) the power of the earthly and hellish realms to defeat one's enemies in battle, to attract love, and so on can be useful. Such powers can be harnessed through magical techniques, including tattoo. These practices are neither good nor bad, but merely efficacious (Tannenbaum, 1987: 694). There are many Theravada stories of women using their potency, their access to earthly creative forces inherent in their menstrual blood, to both protect and destroy men. Take, for example, the antics of the Mon leader Queen Camdevi who "defeated the aboriginal chieftain by offering him a gift of a hat. The hat had been daubed with the queen's menstrual blood, and once the chieftain [had] placed it on his head, his notorious fighting powers were destroyed for ever" (Davis, 1984: 66; Tanabe, 1991: 189).[14] Camdevi's opponent had attempted to steal her realm and trap her into a forced marriage. Her reaction that turned the world upside down, literally realigning the cosmos, is still spoken of today, and her spirit still frequently possesses spirit mediums in north Thailand. Camdevi's success is testimony to the fact that "things might have been, and still might be otherwise" (Morris, 1994: 70).

Similarly, destructive power works in the origin story of my fieldwork village near Meng Zhe (Muong Tsae). A young local man remarked,

> Long ago before the pagoda of the village was built there were many huge bees living in this area. These bees were the size of people and were so unfriendly that they would kill adult villagers and abduct small children for food. These huge bees took soil and used it to build the hillock on which the temple is built today. The Heavenly God (Meng Fa) looked down and saw that the people of the village were deeply distressed. To help alleviate their suffering he took a huge sword and cut the earth, letting water run freely in the new trench. This new water supply meant that the people could move up to the present village site. But even after the move the bees went on pestering the people, causing unimaginable hardship and misery.
>
> At that time the King of the area was called Zhao (*Tsao*, King) Jingham. He set out to kill all the bees but nothing was of any use. Arrows and bullets could not penetrate the bodies of the bees. Eventually he strengthened his arm using soil and tattoos and tossed a precious red jewel at the bees with such strength and force that they fell dead.
>
> King Jingham had two wives, an elder and a younger. The elder wife resided in Menghai (Muong Hai) but the king went with his young wife to Jinghong. He said he was going to war. But he did not return and as time went on his older, first wife became more and more angry.
>
> In revenge she took the precious stone her husband had used to rid the village of the bees, which was now set in gold, and set out to destroy it in anger. She took the jewel and draped it in a woman's sarong, then placed it in a glutinous rice streamer. Eventually after being steamed for a long time the stone exploded and was destroyed. Just then the king and his young second wife, still in Jinghong, died.[15]

King Jingham mistreated his first wife by neglecting her and taking a second wife. In revenge she took the king's precious stone, to which he was magically connected, draped it in a woman's *sarong* associated with earthly power and placed it in a glutinous rice streamer cosmologically important in Dai thought. As the gem was destroyed, so were the king and his second wife.

Like blood, hair is a potent symbol in Dai cosmological understandings. The meanings of blood and hair are multiple and overlapping because each symbol represents an "infinite regress" of meaning.[16] In most publicized images of Dai women, they are shown to have long, free flowing hair. There are many manifestations of the potency of long hair in daily life. For example, Dai women should not comb their hair in the house as this is disrespectful to resident household spirits (*phi huen*). Women should tie their hair up in a tight bun while standing on the porch. Women ought also to be careful not to let their hair flow freely near monks as this would be disrespectful, dangerous, and erotically charged. Women usually have their hair tied neatly back and in some areas of Banna they wear a headscarf.[17] Despite and probably because of this free flowing hair is considered most attractive.

Hair has long been a topic of anthropological interest. James George Frazer (1929: 231) links the potency of hair to its proximity to the soul of the head and this can be dislodged if not treated with proper respect. Indeed, the Dai do say that hair cutting can be dangerous because the souls of the head can take flight that can cause sickness. Edmund Leach explains that other early thinkers saw hair as symbolizing "fertility, soul-stuff or individual power (*mana*)" (1958: 160). There are numerous reasons why Dai peoples understand hair to be powerful and dangerous. The most obvious reason is that hair flows between the head and the waist or below, and so upsets cosmic harmony/alignment. The head is also the site of at least three of the thirty-two souls that the Dai say everyone has.

Another reason for the potency of hair in Banna is that Dai women wash their hair in the starch-rich water used to wash rice. This is said to make their hair black and strong. Phya Anuman Rajadhon (1961) has explained that in Thailand, rice, in the form of offerings, bridges the gap between the mundane and spiritual realms. Moreover, the Rice Goddess (*Yaguanhao/Khwankhao*) is of great importance to Dai peoples. Rice is therefore a ritually significant substance that forms part of merit generating ceremonies. An abbot at the Central Temple (Watbajie, Zhongfosi) of Jinghong told me about a brave, young, legendary woman named Namgalani (possibly the Earth Goddess Nantolani discussed below). She had gone deep into a mine to dig for precious stones. The tunnel collapsed but luckily she had recently washed her hair using rice water. She wrapped her hair around her head and survived for seven days before she was rescued.

The Earth Goddess Nantolani is also renowned for the potency of her hair. Ai Liu (1993: 69–70) notes that the hair of this Goddess is the conduit for the water of the everlasting heavenly river. Within her hair the water spirals for a thousand years and then flows slowly out for mankind's benefit. The water flowing from her hair is said to have the power to cleanse people's sins. Nantolani came to the aid of Sakyamundi, the historical Buddha, when he was attacked by the evil Mara's forces during his meditation under the Boddhi tree. When Mara attacked Sakyamundi, all the weapons turned into beautiful harmless flowers. Mara became enraged but did not give up his assault. Eventually Sakyamundi put his hand into the ground and pulled out Nantolani. Nantolani squeezed the water out of her wet hair; it formed a torrent that washed away Mara and his hordes.[18]

The potency of hair is also apparent in a story associated with the origin of "Water Splashing Festival," part of Dai New Year celebrations (*Songkran*). The young Dai girl Nanlimananna, who had been kidnapped by an evil king, used a strand of her hair to sever the tyrant's head from his shoulders. As the head rolled to the floor, it burst into flames and threatened to consume the whole area. The girl and her fellow captives splashed water on the head for three days, until the flames abated. Thus images of young Dai girls with long flowing hair are not examples of passivity or subordination but rather can be seen as displays of the strength, beauty, and the resilience of Dai ways of being.

Theravada Moral Understandings about the Maltreatment of Women

So far in this chapter we have met warrior women, goddesses, and female slayers of demons, but what are the moral consequences when a woman is unable to prevent herself from being harmed? This question is best addressed by referring to the representation of women in the *Vessantara Jataka*, a text of great importance in the Theravada Buddhist ritual cycle in Banna and elsewhere in Southeast Asia (Keyes, 1984). The *Vessantara Jataka* describes a previous incarnation of Sakyamundi Buddha as Prince Vessantara during which he learned complete lack of attachment. He accomplished this by fulfilling a vow to give away whatever was asked of him. Vessantara learned compassion (*karuna*) and self-sacrifice and gained the ability to radiate loving kindness (*metta*) to all beings. The story formed part of the mural painting on the side of the village temple where I carried out my fieldwork, and most Dai people are familiar with it. When the written text of this sutra (*tam*) about compassion is read out in a particular ritual context, it is said to bring rain—compassion from heaven. The text's ability to bring rain is called upon each year during *Dan Tam*, a harvest festival when the text is read in full.[19]

The sutra has two principal female characters: Madi, the virtuous wife of Vessantara, and Amidada. The story of Madi provides great insight into the importance of motherhood in Theravada thought as well as the centrality of the idea of "nurture" in understanding the complexities of gender relations for Theravada peoples. As Charles Keyes (1984: 230) explains, it is women who nurture the *sangha* (monkhood), it is they who make its existence possible; and they achieve this through everyday sacrifice and work. Yet in relation to understanding the feminization of Xishuangbanna it is the experiences of Amidada that we should focus on here. When Amidada was young, her father sold her to repay his debts. She quickly found herself married against her will to a despicable character named Zhuzagapam (Brahmin Jujaka). Circumstances had forced her to marry a man she neither knew nor loved. Despite her misfortune she was the perfect wife and doted on her husband, attending to his every wish and whim. As Keyes writes (1984: 234), "Such a relationship is likely to lead the woman to seek some sort of material advantage from the man in return for yielding to his unwanted sexual attentions." Thus Amidada demanded two children to help her in her work and Zhuzagapam went in search of them. When walking in the forest he came across Vessantara and his young children. He demanded Vessantara hand over his children. As Vessantara had made a vow of total generosity, he did so. But the gods were watching, and they arranged for the lecherous and greedy Zhuzagapam to return the children to Vessantara's father, the king. When Zhuzagapam was in the palace trying to sell the king his own grandchildren he was treated very well. Zhuzagapam, unable to control his own greed, ate so much that his stomach burst and he died (see figure 7.2).

Zhuzagapam's thoughtless exploitation of his selfless wife ultimately led to his death. More harm comes, through the workings of *karma*, to the exploiter than to the exploited, even if the exploited demands material compensation for the sufferings. Keyes (1984: 237) uses this tale to explain the actions of Thai sex workers who refer to themselves

Figure 7.2 Zhuzagapam upon dying. Mural on village temple's outer wall, 2005
Source: Photograph by the author with permission.

as "modern Amittatapanas" (Amidadas) and who "have often found themselves constrained by circumstances beyond their control—often a consequence of coming from rural families in deep financial trouble—to enter into sexually exploitative relations with men. Under such circumstances, a woman can seek [like Amittatapana] to effect some temporary gain through the money paid to her by her undesirable 'clients.'"

The *Vessantara Jataka* adds a new dimension to understanding what at first sight appears to be the passive acceptance of the "feminization" of Xishuangbanna. Dai women have come to stand metonymically for Xishuangbanna and little is done to counteract this image. The Dai seem to internalize this inferior position of female against male, and weak against strong. But a critical rereading of this Jataka suggests that within such an unequal relationship, the moral upper hand falls on the side of the woman, or in this case Banna as an overexploited and feminized area. Ultimately this may be degrading, but through the working of *karma* the perpetrator will pay in the end. Thus, bearing in mind the huge power of the Chinese State, and the futility of resisting its encroachment, it does not seem surprising that pragmatism has led many Dai peoples to engage with processes that generate feminized images of Banna.

Conclusion

Since late imperial times Chinese border regions have been controlled through the manipulation of imagery (Deal and Hostetler, 2006; Hostetler, 2001). Effective control of the border regions was linked to the reputation of the imperial center. In the Qing era colonial expansion was not driven by fiscal considerations. Indeed control of these regions was, more often than not, an economic burden (Giersch, 2006: 47). Rather campaigns of border control were part of proving the imperial center's right (and might) to rule. Today images of the "exotic other" are used in the promotion of China as a multiethnic state unified in its diversity. China's border regions are the recipients of antipoverty campaigns and endless developmental projects. The border regions' continued representation as "exotica" chimes with current sustainable development policy and has similarities with imperial methods of rule. Sarah Davis (2005: 42–44) states that popular images of Tai Lue people "evoke the tributary performances with which ethnic kingdoms welcomed Chinese imperial emissaries in the past...Sipsongpanna Tai Lues still dance for the empire while trying to hold it at bay."

The meanings of labels and images cannot be fixed, captured, or foreclosed—rather they are in a constant flux of contestation, negotiation, and renegotiation. The attractive images of young and beautiful Dai have drawn tourists from all over China and beyond to come to Xishuangbanna and spend money. There is a Dai saying: "beauty is sweet like honey" and "beautiful flowers have bees buzzing round them," meaning beautiful people and places are attractive. But for Dai peoples, the meanings of these images are multifaceted: they speak of potency, strength and loyalty, and the possibility of morally justified compensation for all that is given.[20] The Dai are engaged with the Chinese Center in an ongoing negotiation of and for recognition, a negotiation that dates back to at least the early Qing. They are continually reminding the center of their presence, forcing recognition of them as a distinct and vibrant living culture within the larger Chinese polity. But they do so in their own way. To engage in such an important and dangerous negotiation, with a state that has proven itself destructive, powerful, and very wary of "splitist" activity, using imagery that was threatening would be counterproductive. There is no doubt that the dominant discourse about non-Han peoples feminizes them, but it is not the case that acceptance of such imagery is an acceptance of inferiority. Dai peoples read feminized images, mostly imposed on them but also generated by them, through their own cosmological and moral understandings. This chapter has not outlined a counter, rebellious positioning—Dai against Han. Rather it is an explication of "cross-readings," of a multicultural context in which the same images have multiple and contradictory associations.

There is pragmatism and sophistication in Dai negotiations with the center that have been overlooked in simplified accounts of "Sinification" or "Hanification." The debate needs to move beyond questions of authentic cultural expression. The promotion of Xishuangbanna as a young accommodating woman takes on new meanings when we realize that it is often young women who slay demons in Dai mythic knowledge. When Dai moral understandings are taken into account we see that exploitation leads to justifiable demands for compensation and that the exploiters often come to sticky ends. This provides a new perspective on the economic transactions now taking place in Banna. Furthermore Banna is a multi-ethnic region, home to many non-Dai peoples. Through the active promotion of Banna as "home of the beautiful Dai," they are confirming their historical place as the dominant culture in the region, often at the expense of indigenous hill-dwelling groups. Moreover we must recognize that not all Han in the region are trying to "sinify" Banna; rather Dai peoples and ways of being remain powerfully alluring for Han migrants and cultural exchanges take place in both directions. For example, Han migrants bring their statues of Chinese gods to Jinghong Central Temple for consecration and blessing. The economy of the area is growing; new links to other Southeast Asian countries are being built. A vast regional Theravada study center is under construction. There are problems to be acknowledged: drug use, prostitution, and HIV/AIDS among them. But to think of Dai peoples as feminized and hence subordinate would be to underestimate them, to ignore their own cosmological insights, and to deny the long and complex history of this border region.

Notes

I would like to thank Baas Terwiel, Joanna Overing, and Robert Storrie for their comments on this chapter.

1. Sinification is seen among other things in changes in the language used in markets from Tai to Mandarin-based "Bannahua," in the change of men and women's dress to factory-made Chinese or "Western-inspired" designs, in the use of chopsticks and the eating of white rice

rather than "sticky" varieties, and in the popularity of Chinese language music and television programs (Komlosy, 2008).
2. On the fluidity of Dehong Dai (Tai) ways of being and the complexities of current Han/Dai identities, see Yos (2001: 164–165).
3. See Conway (2006) on Shan shamanism.
4. Much recent scholarship has shown the fuzzy or porous nature of ethnic categories. The work of Mary Rack (2005) on Kho Xiong (Miao) speakers is particularly insightful. In Banna people shift and change ethnic identities and there is considerable blurring of religious boundaries. Nonetheless when you are in a Dai village you are clearly in a Dai village; it is obvious from the language, dress, architecture, food, and so on. As many theorists have noted (not least Toni Morrison and Judith Butler), these categories are both constructed and real, flexible and yet lived as primordial and unchanging. This is the paradox at the heart of lived identity politics. Fanon's comments on the work of Sartre are particularly illuminating (1986: 131–140).
5. It is a common misunderstanding that only Han Chinese invade or migrate to non-Han areas. Indeed this internal Orientalist stereotype of the moving/dynamic Han and the static passive non-Han is a construct that needs to be countered. The realities on the ground are much more fluid and complex. Probably since the Ming and certainly since the Qing, Han and non-Han Chinese (Hui, Manchu, Naxi, Tibetans, etc.) peoples have been moving to Banna. They have come as economic migrants, officials, or as pilgrims and merchants on their way to other lands. For some of these people their inclusion within the Chinese state is problematic but others are profoundly nationalist (Litzinger, 2000: xx; Schein, 2000; Komlosy, 2004, 2008) The terms "Han" and "Chinese" should not be conflated, both are complex multivalent symbols.
6. In the early years after the Communist Revolution of 1949, the Dai were thought to represent the slave owning/feudal societal stage.
7. For a detailed history of "minority nationalities" in China, see Blum (2002), Mackerras (1995), Harrell (ed., 1995), among others.
8. For figures from Xishuangbanna statistical yearbook published by the local area's statistics office and for figures collected after 1949 and published in *Daizu shehui lishi diaocha, minzu wenti wu zhong cong shu* (Societal and historical research on the Dai nationality, Nationality Questions Series) (1983), see Komlosy (2002).
9. Dai language was the lingua franca especially in the hills and smaller market towns and in some areas still is.
10. This blending of exoticism and nostalgia is common in cultural production in contemporary China (Lo, 2005: 183; Komlosy, 2008).
11. Like most "peripheral" areas in China Banna's reputation for lawlessness and chaos (*luan*) is far worse than the actual rates of interpersonal violence experienced on the streets.
12. World Bank China, Quarterly Update 02/05: 8. This report also states that 2005 has been defined as the "year of reform," one in which fiscal and taxation reforms will aim to generate "harmonious society."
13. Female power in the Southeast Asian context is still little understood. The complimentarily of genders that has been widely reported for island Southeast Asia is still denied by many scholars of the peninsular. There is evidence that in some Shan (Tai peoples living within Burma) temples women's sarongs are used to wrap sacred sutras. This is something to do with the power of these garments but the links are yet to be fully explored (Personal communication with Susan Conway and Monica Janowski in 2008).
14. Rosalind Morris (1994: 55) states that in her experience this story only refers to a hat made of a sarong and therefore that the presence of menstrual blood is implicit rather than clearly stated.
15. This story is painted on the inner walls of a small "domain cult" shine dedicated to Zhao Jingham. The Dai villagers regarded the village shrine as the cosmological and political center of the district.

16. I am grateful to Terwiel for his eloquent explanation of the ambiguity of symbolism in Tai thought (Personal communication with author).
17. The wearing of scarves by young Dai women is more apparent in Menghai County than in Mengla or Jinghong. When asked why women wore scarves the women replied that it was the correct thing to do. When pushed they explained that it was due to the cold. Another possible explanation and one that Yao Jide, an anthropologist specializing in Hui studies at Yunnan University, agreed with (although not one articulated by any of my interlocutors), is that the Menghai Dai have been influenced by a neighboring community of Islamic (Pa Shee) Dai who have been living in the region for at least two hundred years (Personal communication with author).
18. This is the explanation given at village level of the moment when the Buddha called the earth to witness his enlightenment, this moment is depicted as the Buddha seated in *bhumisparsamudra*, his right hand touching the ground and his left wresting in his lap.
19. This takes place during Buddhist lent (that is between *Haowassa* [*guan menjie*, closing the door] and *Ochwassa* [*kai menjie*, opening the door] celebrations during the rainy season). The chanting of this Jataka takes place over fourteen hours (06:00 am to 08:00 pm).
20. It should be said that non-Dai women in China also wield considerable power (and arguably always have) even within the confines available to them in an often androcentric environment. Jaschok and Miers (1994: 9) have shown that the "once ubiquitous stereotype of the long-suffering, meek, submissive Chinese woman as simply a victim of family interests, a vision of compliance and self-sacrifice, stands thus revealed for what it is—a stereotype in need of reappraisal and an empirical content" (Bray, 1997; Stafford, 2000).

Bibliography

Ai Liu. 1993. *Nanchuan fojiao yu Daizu wenhua* (Theravada Buddhism and Dai culture). Kunming: Yunnan minzu chubanshe.

Anuman, Rajadhon. 1986. *Popular Buddhism in Siam and Other Essays on Thai Studies*. Bangkok.

Blum, Susan. 2002. "Margins and Centers: A Decade of Publishing on China's Ethnic Minorities." *Journal of Asian Studies* 61, no.4, 1287–1310.

Bray, Francesca. 1997. *Technology and Gender: Fabrics of Power in Late Imperial China*. Berkeley, CA: University of California Press.

Butler, Judith. 1997. *Excitable Speech: A Politics of the Performative*. New York: Routledge.

Conway, Susan. 2006. *The Shan: Culture, Arts and Crafts*. London: River books.

Davis, Richard. 1984. *Muang Metaphysics: A Study of Northern Thai Myth and Ritual*. Bangkok: Pandora.

Davis, Sara. 2005. *Song and Silence: Ethnic Revival on China's Southwest Borders*. New York: Columbia University Press.

Evans, Grant. 2000. "Transformation of Jinghong, Xishuangbanna, PRC." In Grant Evans, Christopher Hutton, and Kuah Khun Eng, eds. *Where China Meets Southeast Asia: Social and Cultural Change in the Border Regions*, 162–182. Copenhagen, Denmark: Nordic Institute of Asian Studies.

Fanon, Franz. 1986. *Black Skin White Masks*. London: Pluto Press.

Frazer, James George. 1929. *The Golden Bough: A Study in Magic and Religion*. Abridged edition. London: Macmillan.

Giersch, C. Patterson. 2006. *Asian Borderlands: The Transformation of Qing China's Yunnan Frontier*. Cambridge, MA: Harvard University Press.

Gladney, Dru. 1994. "Representing Nationality in China: Refiguring Majority/Minority Identities." *Journal of Asian Studies* 53, no.1, 92–123.

Hansen, Mette Halskov. 1999. *Lessons in Being Chinese: Minority Education and Ethnic Identity in Southwest China*. Seattle, WA: University of Washington Press.

———. 2004. "The Challenge of Xishuangbanna: Development, Resources, and Power in a Multiethnic China." In Morris Rossabi, ed. *Governing China's Multiethnic Frontiers*, 53–83. Seattle, WA: University of Washington Press.

Harrell, Stevan, ed. 1995. *Cultural Encounters on China's Ethnic Frontiers*. Seattle, WA: University of Washington Press.

Hockx, Michel, and Julia Strauss. 2005. "Editors' Introduction." In Michel Hockx and Julia Strauss, eds. *Culture in the Contemporary PRC: China Quarterly Special Issues New Series*, no.6. Cambridge: Cambridge University Press.

Hsieh, Shih-Cheung. 1990. "On the Dynamic Ethnicity of Sipsongpanna Tai during the Republican Period." *Thai-Yunnan Newsletter*, nos. 9, 2–8.

Humphreys, Christmas. 1997. *A Popular Dictionary of Buddhism*. Richmond, Surrey, UK: Curzon.

Hyde, Sandra Teresa. 2001. "Sex Tourism Practices on the Periphery: Eroticising Ethnicity and Pathologizing Sex on the Lancang." In Nancy N. Chen, Constance D. Clark, Suzanne Z. Gottschang, and Lyn Jeffery, eds. *China Urban: Ethnographies of Contemporary Chinese Culture*, 146–162. Durham, NC: Duke University Press.

Jaschok, Maria, and Suzanne Miers, eds. 1994. *Women and Chinese Patriarchy: Submission, Servitude and Escape*. London: Zed Books.

Keyes, Charles. 1984. "Mother or Mistress but Never a Monk: Buddhist Notions of Female Gender in Rural Thailand." *American Ethnologist* 11, no.2, 223–241.

Komlosy, Anouska. 2002. "Images of the Dai: The Aesthetics of Gender and Identity in Xishuangbanna." Ph.D. diss., University of St. Andrews.

———. 2004. "Processions and Water Splashing: Expressing Local Affinity and National Identity during Dai New Year in Xishuangbanna." *Journal of the Royal Anthropological Institute* 10, no.2, 351–373.

———. 2008. "Yunnanese Sounds: Creativity and Alterity in the Dance and Music Scenes of Urban Yunnan." *China: An International Journal* 6, no.1, 44–68.

Leach, Edmund. 1958. "Magical Hair." *Journal of the Royal Anthropological Institute of Great Britain and Ireland* 88, no.2, 147–164.

Litzinger, Ralph. 2000. *Other Chinas: The Yao and the Politics of National Belonging*. Durham, NC: Duke University Press.

Li, Zhimin. 2004. *Xishunagbanna wenrou de youhao* (Gentle and soft seduction of Xishunagbanna). Kunming: Yunnan renmin chubanshe.

Liu, Yan. 1999. *An On-the-Spot Investigation into the Southerly Emigration of the Dai Race*. Kunming: Yunnan minzu chubanshe.

Lo, Kwai-Cheung. 2005. *Chinese Face Off: The Transnational Popular Culture of Hong Kong*. Champaign, IL: University of Illinois Press.

Mackerras, Colin. 1994. *China's Minorities: Integration and Modernization in the Twentieth Century*. Hong Kong: Oxford University Press.

Morris, Rosalind. 1994. "The Empresses New Clothes: Dressing and Redressing Modernity in Northern Thai Sprit Mediumship." In Lynne Milgram and Penny Van Esterick, eds. *The Transformative Power of Cloth in Southeast Asia*, 53–70. Montreal, Canada: Canadian Council of Southeast Asian Studies and the Museum for Textiles.

Morrison, Toni. 1992. *Playing in the Dark: Whiteness and the Literary Imagination*. Cambridge, MA: Harvard University Press.

Oakes, Tim. 1993. "The Cultural Space of Modernity: Ethnic Tourism and Place Identity in China." *Environment and Planning D: Society and Space* 11, no.1, 47–66.

———. 1997. "Ethnic Tourism in Rural Guizhou: Sense of Place and the Commerce of Authenticity." In Michel Picard and Robert E. Wood, eds. *Tourism, Ethnicity and the State in Asian and Pacific Societies*, 35–70. Honolulu, HI: University of Hawai'i Press.

———. 1998. *Tourism and Modernity in China*. New York: Routledge.

Overing, Joanna. 1986. "Men Control Women? The 'Catch 22' in the Analysis of Gender." *International Journal of Moral and Social Studies* 1, no.2, 135–156.

Rack, Mary. 2005. *Ethnic Distinctions, Local Meanings: Negotiating Cultural Identities in China*. London: Pluto Press.

Ratanaporn, Sethakul. 2000. "Tai Lue of Sipsongpanna and Mŭang Nan in the Nineteenth-Century." In Andrew Turton, ed. *A Civility and Savagery: Social Identity in Tai States*, 319–329. Richmond, Surrey, UK: Curzon.

Sanharakshita, Urgyen. 1993. *A Survey of Buddhism: Its Doctrines and Methods through the Ages*. Glasgow: Windhorse.

Schein, Louisa. 1997. "Gender and Internal Orientalism in China." *Modern China* 23, no.1, 69–98.

———. 2000. *Minority Rules: The Miao and the Feminine in China's Cultural Politics*. Durham, NC: Duke University Press.

Shi, Zhihua. 1992. *Nanlimananna: Poshuijie de gushi* (Nalimananna: A water splashing story). Beijing: Wenhuaxian chubanshe.

Stafford, Charles. 2000. "Chinese Patriliny and the Cycles of *yang* and *laiwang*." In Janet Carsten, ed. *Cultures of Relatedness: New Approaches to the Study of Kinship*, 37–54. Cambridge: Cambridge University Press.

Tanabe, Shigeharu. 1991. "Spirits, Power and the Discourse of Female Gender: The Phii Meng Cult of Northern Thailand." In Anas Chitakasem and Andrew Turton, eds. *Thai Constructions of Knowledge*, 183–212. London: School of Oriental and African Studies, University of London.

Tannenbaum, Nicola. 1987. "Tattoos: Invulnerability and Power in Shan Cosmology." *American Ethnologist* 14, no.4, 693–711.

Waley-Cohen, Joanna. 1999. *The Sextants of Beijing: Global Currents in Chinese History*. New York: W. W. Norton.

Yun, Gao. 1998. "The Dai Vernacular House in South China: Tradition and Cultural Development in the Architecture of an Ethnic Minority." Ph.D diss., University of Edinburgh.

Yos, Santasombat. 2001. *Lak Chang: A Reconstruction of Tai Identity in Daikong*. Canberra, Australia: Pandanus Books in association with the Thai-Yunnan Project, Australian National University.

Zheng, Peng. 1993. *Xishuangbanna Gailan* (Brief introduction of Xishuangbanna) Kunming: Yunnan minzu chubanshe.

CHAPTER EIGHT

Re-Presenting Women's Identities: Recognition and Representation of Rural Chinese Women

SHARON R. WESOKY

送你一棵果子，只能享用一次；送你一粒种子，可以受用一生。
If you are given a fruit, you can enjoy it only once;
If you are given a seed, you can benefit from it your whole life.

The above slogan captures the mission of a nongovernmental organization (NGO) known as *Nongjianü* in its attempts to promote the social development of China's rural women in the post-Mao era. *Nongjianü*, or the Cultural Development Center for Rural Women (Rural Women), promotes particularistic modes of recognition, representation, and identity-formation among its target group (Nongjianü, 2003: ii). This chapter explains how such promotion happens. It first examines how rural women can be understood as a "minority" in mainland China, especially in relation to hegemonic discursive formations in Chinese society today. Then it introduces *Nongjianü* as an NGO advocating for rural women in China since the 1990s. This study looks particularly at how *Nongjianü* generates recognition, representation, and identity for rural women in a way that is distinctive in its approach. It argues that *Nongjianü* and its subjects mutually constitute an identity for rural women finding assets in their marginality. Together they create a "pragmatic politics of the present moment" that locates in these women liberating and empowering possibilities quite distinct from any sort of utopian solution to the dilemmas they face.

Rural Women and Capitalistic Hegemony

The extent to which rural women are a minority or subaltern population in contemporary China is linked to their position *vis-à-vis* hegemonic structures and discourses, since numerically they are hardly a minority. Structurally, rural women's place in contemporary China is produced through a number of processes that derive from one-party rule, continued patriarchal influences, and capitalist globalization. For instance, China has experienced a feminization of agriculture since rural-urban migration became possible after the death of Mao Zedong and the introduction of economic reform (Jacka, 1997; Judd, 2002). Rural girls also are more likely to be withdrawn from school than boys (Li, 2004), and so face further social and economic limitations.

Discursively, quasi-official-level organs like the All-China Women's Federation regard rural women as suffering from what is sometimes termed "low quality" (*suzhi cha*) that diminishes their capacity to compete in the market economy. Ellen R. Judd regards "quality" as the "crux of the contemporary women's movement in rural China" (2002: 19). More generally, Andrew Kipnis observes that *suzhi* is "central to PRC dynamics of governance," and that "the increasingly competitive nature of Chinese society is one of the driving forces behind the national concern with *suzhi*" (Kipnis, 2006: 295, 310). While several scholars argue that the Chinese regime is in fact ambivalent about the dash to the capitalist market characterizing the post-Mao reforms (Gladney, 2004: 283, 299–300), there is also an overall *telos* to the continuing obsession in China with development and modernity, and the idea persists that the reform process will allow China to "escape its status as a developing country" (Ong, 1997: 175). A market-oriented and consumerist culture with a growing gap between haves and have-nots, despite raising questions within Chinese officialdom about the corrosive effects of the market, would seem to indicate that China is falling in line with global tendencies. Such a formation, while not making rural women a minority, does locate them in a subaltern place in relation to hegemonic forces.

Nongjianü and Cyclical Notions of Time

The Cultural Development Center for Rural Women, *Nongjianü*, was founded in the 1990s at a time when "new" feminists were preparing for Beijing to host the United Nations Fourth World Conference on Women in 1995. The advent of foreign donor funding in China for such activities also facilitated this feminist organizing. *Nongjianü* emerged in 1993 as the magazine *Rural Women Knowing All (Nongjianü baishitong)* by Xie Lihua, one of the editors of *China Women's News (Zhongguo funü bao)*. It was initially formed with a grant from the Ford Foundation's Program on Reproductive Health and Population. The magazine adopts a wide-ranging approach to its target audience of rural women. It includes practical, technical, and agricultural advice, but also contains features of more political and social relevance. These include features on legal consciousness and awareness, political participation and leadership, as well as teaching materials to help eradicate rural women's illiteracy. It frequently publishes the letters, poems, and other writings of its readers, and its editors make it a point to read every letter that is received from readers.

Later in the 1990s, *Nongjianü baishitong* expanded its activities from being a magazine to also becoming a more service-oriented organization, including projects such as the Practical Skills Training School for Rural Women (Nongjianü School) founded in 1998. The Nongjianü School, a central part of the organization's mission, between 1998 and mid-2004 trained over 3000 students in tailoring, computer skills, cosmetology, food service, and educational techniques (Luo, 2004a, 2004b).[1] The magazine, *Nongjianü baishitong*, played a pivotal role in creating the Cultural Development Center for Rural Women in 2006, which was recognized by *China News Weekly* as one of the three NGOs in the country with the greatest "sense of social responsibility." In 2003, the magazine's name was changed to *Rural Women (Nongjianü)* as a way of making "gender consciousness even more prominent" in its title.[2] The Cultural Development Center was spun-off as an independent NGO in 2001 to be better situated to receive global development funding (Jacka, 2006).

It should be noted that *Nongjianü* is very much an NGO in the Chinese framework. To this end, it has *China Women's News*, the official newspaper of the All-China Women's Federation (ACWF), as its *guakao danwei*, or "supervisory work-unit" in the Chinese state. Thus, the magazine is closely affiliated with the state that it sometimes seeks to critique. In addition, the magazine depends on the Women's Federation at the local level to purchase and distribute each issue. The magazine's peak circulation in 1997 of 230,000 was eventually reduced to 70,000 today (China Development Brief, 2006). Hence, the magazine obviously reaches only a small portion of China's vast rural population.

Yet the connections of the magazine to the state do not necessarily mean that it is inherently and continuously subject to state control. In some ways, the magazine epitomizes Xueliang Ding's idea of "institutional parasitism," with organizations described as independent in fact closely connected to the state, but also in some cases engaging in activities that ultimately undermine state authority (Ding, 1994). Elsewhere, I have described the relationship between the Chinese party-state and women's NGOs as one of symbiosis, wherein both sides can obtain benefits (Wesoky, 2002). Thus, the founder and editor-in-chief of *Nongjianü*, Xie Lihua, is a Communist Party member who also finds cause to engage in critique of the effects of some state policies on rural women. In many ways, the magazine is reaffirming the view of Vivienne Shue (2004: 28) that "embedded in the very logic of legitimation advanced by a system of domination we can find the grammar that may be used most effectively by citizens and subjects in making statements in opposition and in resistance to that system." Seen from this perspective, the magazine's publishing and publicizing of state policies is itself a form of resistance; by creating awareness of state-granted rights the state is providing ways for rural women to resist when such rights are violated.[3]

This chapter examines the ways that *Nongjianü* and the status of rural women are mutually constitutive categories, and how together they construct a version of culture that seeks to regard rural women as legitimate bearers of one form of what it means to be Chinese. In fact, it is through their liminal status that rural women become such bearers. In particular, *Nongjianü* upholds a hybrid or syncretic form of culture that sees a type of Confucian virtue as worthy of praise and encouragement. More crucially, it supports rural women, who are typically and traditionally unvalued and marginalized members of society, as potential repositories—even exemplars—of such virtue. It is important to note that *Nongjianü* apparently does not adopt such a position in order to pander to statist interests who also promote Confucian virtues as an antidote to the negative effects of the market (Ong, 1997). Instead, it offers a genuine moral statement regarding the nature of a desirable post-Communist social, political, and cultural order. To this end, *Nongjianü* adopts what I term a "pragmatic politics of the present moment." It promotes a more cyclical concept of time than typical Western-derived and linear visions of modernity.

Such pragmatic politics and their cyclical time horizon are evident in the discourses and practices of *Nongjianü* as an NGO seeking to advance the status of China's rural women. The organization first and foremost sponsors concrete programs to improve the day-to-day lives of rural women. Such programs are predicated on a very real assessment of the prospects for rural women's lives, and what sorts of measures can improve their conditions in the present moment. As discussed below, the organization also has an ethical vision for the good life that draws from Confucian-inspired ideas and regards these community-oriented values as useful now that under market reforms there is a proliferation of "self-propelling subjects" (Ong, 1997: 173). Such a vision even includes a cyclical idea of how rural women should employ what is gained through their affiliation with *Nongjianü* to give back to other rural women, to their own hometown communities, and to *Nongjianü* itself.

Utilizing content analysis of the magazine *Nongjianü* to advance this argument, this study takes a critical look at articles from the 2004 edition of the magazine that discuss programs of the Cultural Development Center for Rural Women. By discussing these programs, the magazine seeks to introduce the organization's activities to a wider audience. Articles are especially authored by personnel in the organization, including Luo Zhaohong, principal of the Nongjianü School, located on a suburban Beijing campus, and Xu Rong, a program officer with the organization who works particularly on the creation of Rural Women's Health Support Small Groups promoting suicide prevention at the village level. Articles were selected for research to allow multiple voices to be heard: the voice of the organization itself as well as the voice of the organization's subjects. Such analysis facilitates an examination of the programs of one NGO in China today, to see how it advances recognition, representation, and identity among rural women.

Recognition: Orientalism/Hybridity and Modernity

Nongjianü promotes a complex discourse that can be regarded as hybrid or syncretic in nature. Hybridity, in the words of Homi K. Bhabha, is an "interstitial passage between fixed identifications...that entertains without an assumed or fixed hierarchy" (Gladney, 2004: 1). The discourse is also syncretic in the terms advocated by Kuan-Hsing Chen in that it "implies the active participation of the involved subjects" and, again in Bhabha's words, "resists the attempt at holistic forms of social explanation" (Chen, 1998: 23–24). *Nongjianü*'s development of hybrid recognition of rural women employs varied lenses to understand their conditions, including elements of Confucianism, statism, feminism, and transnational influences.

With respect to Chinese women, the acknowledgment that Confucianism is valuable to their lives and identities is perhaps the most problematic. Confucianism is historically a gender-hierarchical system of thought, with women being in the inferior position of the male-female relation. Furthermore, employing Confucian ideas can lead to "self-orientalization" (Ong, 1997: 195), or the perpetuation of some aspect of Asian or Chinese cultural essence as unchanging in nature. Yet *Nongjianü* has clearly found aspects of Confucian values to be worthy of its endorsement. Joseph Chan sums up these values as follows:

> Most simply put, Confucianism holds that people should cultivate their minds and virtues through lifelong learning and participation in rituals; they should treat their family members according to the norms of filial piety and fatherly love, respect the superiors and rulers, and show a graded care and concern for all; learned intellectuals above all others should devote themselves to politics and education to promote the Way and help build the good society. (2003: 130)

For instance, *Nongjianü* explicitly encourages filial behavior on the part of the women it assists. In one story, the mother of one young woman who studied at the Nongjianü School wrote a letter to thank the school for transforming her daughter: "My daughter has changed, she has become sensible and is able to speak, she shows filial piety to her aged grandparents—I am grateful to the Nongjianü School for teaching our daughter these things and also teaching her how to be an upright person (*xue zuoren*)" (Luo, 2004d). In a Hebei village, where *Nongjianü* founded a Rural Women's Health Support Small Group, "an atmosphere of showing filial piety to old people gradually formed" due to the Small Group performing a self-written skit titled "Filial Son," based on real events in the village's history (Xu, 2004c).

More generally, *Nongjjianü* frequently advocates the central importance of compassion (*aixin*) to its activities as well as to the conduct of its beneficiaries. Luo Zhaohong opens an article about the Nongjianü School with a description of its overall purpose in relation to *aixin*:

> The Practical Skills Training School for Rural Women is a school brought together by compassion. Every student coming to the school through financial aid has been immersed in a loving sea, wrapped up by love; even more the well-known saying of the elderly writer Bing Xin can be branded on their minds: "If you have love you have everything." Gradually, at the same time as they are enjoying love's comforts, they also are inwardly making a decision, they want to transmit the love they have gained for themselves to people who need help even more, they also want through their own labor to offer a tribute and to repay society, to repay all the loving care and support to these compassionate persons. (Luo, 2004c)

Such emphasis on love and compassion is also consistent with Confucian ideas of overcoming the self, and loving your fellow men (Chan, 2003: 133).

Yet such Confucian ideas are not mere self-orientalizing gestures but in fact are meant to convey a prospective ethical system that is in contrast with the more individualistic-oriented aspects of the market economy. *Nongjianü* seems to promote them because they are human values that allow rural women to improve their own status while also helping others and not losing sight of aspects of tradition that can serve a valuable purpose. Such ideas can especially be regarded as transcending orientalist deployments when some of the other values promoted by *Nongjianü* in its cultural syncretism are added into the mix.

One of these is the influence of feminism. As further noted below, *Nongjianü* seeks to empower rural women in important ways. Along with the Nongjianü School and the Health Support Small Groups, the organization acts to promote "the awareness of gender and citizenship among rural women," and it also "raises rural women's ability and opportunity to participate in politics" (Nongjianü, 2003: 2). For instance, it runs courses for rural women village leaders that introduce concepts on gender consciousness. Such activities do seek to make "the world more hospitable to women than it is" (Di Stefano, 2003: 272). These feminist ideas are quite different from traditional Confucian ideas about the role of women, though not wholly incommensurable with Confucianism as an ethical worldview (Chan, 2003: 142–145).

Another component of the *Nongjianü* cultural formation is an acknowledgment of the role that the state can and even should play in the group's activities and goals, despite the group's self-described non-governmental status. In this sense, *Nongjianü* is not oppositional to the party-state, but rather operates in symbiosis with it (Wesoky, 2002). *Nongjianü* specifically notes that it is operating in line with certain statist policies, and that it benefits from the support of various levels of the party and government. One article in the magazine details the various types of moral and material support received by the Nongjianü School from central and local governments as well as various levels of the All-China Women's Federation. It also notes that the school was praised by Beijing city officials for its "profound inspiration and influence on all educational organs and educational workers" (Luo, 2004b). Such a connection to statist imperatives reveals capitalist globalization need not necessarily diminish state power but can sometimes expand it (Ong and Nonini, 1997: 324). An alternative perspective, however, considers ways globalization lessens the power of the state to promote the rights of citizens (Brysk and Shafir, eds., 2004), and how the state can at times play a useful role in promoting welfare and even rights.

One way *Nongjianü* conceives a state role is through its frequent discussion of the legal system. Since its founding, the magazine has featured columns on the legal system, first titled *Fazhi Tiandi* (The Universe of the Legal System), and later *Falü Bangzhu* (Legal Aid). In many of its writings, the magazine notes that one source of rural women's problems is their inadequate understanding of their constitutional and other legal rights. At the same time, the magazine demonstrates that there is growing awareness of the potential for legal remedies to rural women's problems. In the editor's note for the Legal Aid column in January 2004, the editor writes that the magazine will, in the new year, feature not only "legal experts to exclude difficulties and dispel uncertainties for you" but also a new invitation to "onlookers" to offer their "viewpoints and opinions" (Nongjianü Editor, 2004a). Each issue of the magazine publishes reader letters and expert responses, with legal questions from readers on matters such as property rights, inheritance rights, labor and consumer rights, as well as marriage and divorce law. Urging rural women to utilize the legal system to deal with their problems is another way the magazine finds a use for statist and modern modes of recognition.

Such an understanding of the need for statist intervention is consistent with the views of Chinese intellectual critic Wang Hui, who notes,

> The struggle for social justice and fair market competition is not, therefore, opposed to state intervention, but rather seeks social

democracy in order to use the democratic control of society over the state to oblige the state to implement social insurance and to prevent it from becoming the protector of domestic and transnational monopolies. (Wang, 2003: 123–124)[4]

Also relevant to Wang's discussion of transnational monopolies is the influence on *Nongjianü* of various globalizing forces. While scholars and critics often discuss globalization in terms of its exploitative ramifications on the labor force, the other side of globalization is the introduction of new resources and discourses to social organizations. As noted above, *Nongjianü* was initially founded with a grant from the Ford Foundation, and it has also received numerous grants from other foreign sources. One article in *Nongjianü* discusses how contributions from the German and American embassies upgraded working conditions for teachers at the Nongjianü School (Nongjianü, 2004). Other articles note the contributions of foreigners to creating a financial aid fund to pay for young women to attend the school (Luo, 2004a). Foreign ideas have also been influential—generally in the school's adoption of gender perspectives, but also in work done in specific programs. For instance, a training class for women teachers from Inner Mongolia invited not only Chinese but also Western educational experts to allow the teachers "to understand new concepts and thinking from the outside." Such ideas injected new "passion and energy" into the teachers' work (Chen, 2004).

Syncretic application of Confucian, feminist, statist, and global discourses enables the construction of a form of recognition of rural Chinese women that is simultaneously critical of and conciliatory toward the omnipresence of the market in contemporary China. The Confucian and statist components in particular recognize that the market economy may be inevitable but also that its negative effects on morality and equality are not necessarily so; the feminist and global aspects concede that global ideologies may have useful lessons for rural women.

Such hybrid subjectivity composes what might be described as the recognition of an alternative modernity derived from the standpoint of rural Chinese women, one that diminishes the role of individual initiative under the conditions of modernity (Chen, 1998: 25). This view of individual autonomy in "the pervasive, now globalized, market economy" is "at odds with the emphasis in most classical religious traditions on the individual's embeddedness in society" (Madsen and Strong, 2003: 17). *Nongjianü* in some cases explicitly examines how rural women can arrive at their own notion of modernity, one that is commensurate with their life horizons and prospects. One way that this is done is by examining how village life can become more modern—seeking to value rural existence rather than merely intimating that the only path of improvement of rural life is through migration to urban areas. One article notes how a Health Support Small Group in one village engaged in a campaign to improve the villagers' sanitation habits, leading to a "big change in appearance" of the village. At the Chinese New Year, the Small Group went through the village distributing New Year scrolls reading

> Good policies and good techniques pave the rural family's comparatively well-off road.[5]
>
> New era and new ideas hasten the Divine Land's spring. (Xu, 2004b)

Another village was able to enthusiastically demonstrate its methane gas energy project to visiting Ford Foundation officials, leading the Ford official to declare, "I did not think that rural women would be so capable—we spent so little money and they made such tremendous changes occur in their hometown!" (Xu, 2004c). This methane gas project has allowed women to introduce sustainable practices into village life—a cyclical technology. These are more concrete manifestations of rural women's subjectivity.

Representation: Subalternity and Empowerment

One way that *Nongjjianü* contributes to the formation of a Chinese politics of recognition is by taking subaltern subjects and transforming them into empowered ones. On the pages in the magazine women exist simultaneously as both. But the magazine details how, through the course of encountering *Nongjianü*'s programs, women are converted from victims to agents. The magazine is full of rural women's stories of tragedies as well as hopeful endings in their lives, a common trope in the women's magazine genre.

The stories of rural women, and especially young rural women, who encounter *Nongjianü* are rife with tales of the tragic happenings in their lives prior to *Nongjianü*'s entry. The magazine often describes the dismal conditions of the lives of the rural women recruited to attend the Practical Skills Training School. In many cases, the women are from single parent families or are orphans. For instance, one student at the Nongjianü School had a crippled father and therefore "the entire family's heavy responsibilities of life rested on the work of her mother's thin and weak shoulders." As a result, Little Li, "a sensible child, discontinued her studies after the second year of junior high school in order to work to subsidize the family expenses, but in the bottom of her heart she always longed to be able to return to the classroom" (Luo, 2004c). In another case, program officer Xu Rong, visiting Guizhou on a loan project for rural households, met a Puyi Nationality girl named Luo Meiling whose father was an abusive mute and whose mother abandoned the family after years of abuse. Originally the mother felt that giving birth to a son after two daughters would "end her suffering days," but when her "sea of bitterness did not end" she "mysteriously went missing." Xu Rong observes that "rural feudal thinking is serious, and Meiling's mother was clear in her heart: divorce is even more difficult than running away, so she chose the latter." Meiling was thus left basically alone to rear her siblings, given that her grandfather was a businessman who was usually not in the village and her father was abusive (Xu, 2004a). The magazine's recognition of the role of traditionalism in the suffering of rural women is important, although not discursively diverging from statist discourses on the sources of China's rural dilemmas.

Nongjianü, however, has transcended statist rhetoric in its identification of the problems caused by the market for rural women and the need to find specific ways to assist them. While the state has largely advocated means for rural women to compete more effectively in the economy, *Nongjianü* has been more attuned to the gendered ways that rural women enter and participate in the market. In this sense, *Nongjianü* engages in a form of representation of rural women distinct from that promoted by the quasi-official-level Women's Federation, which primarily promotes a vision of women's "quality" that becomes those attributes and abilities that enable women to compete in the marketplace, individually or collectively (Judd, 2002: 29). This is a strategy that primarily seeks to employ a top-down approach to rural women's needs, defined by officials rather than through processes of self-definition and so in this case reinforcing the claim made by Aihwa Ong:

> These subaltern groups who bear the main burden of Asian capitalist success are almost never mentioned in dominant discourses of the Asian way. Though indispensable to capitalist success in the region, they are rendered invisible and speechless, an effect of the symbolic violence (Bourdieu) of triumphalist Chinese modernity. (Ong, 1997: 192)

Nongjianü renders rural women visible and gives them a voice, which also serves to empower them in a number of ways. It does this by helping them create a variety of capitals: "For Bourdieu, such capitals are different, mutually convertible kinds of culturally defined resources that can be converted into personal power, thereby supporting one's life chances of social trajectory" (Nonini and Ong, 1997: 22). For instance, the financial aid fund established by a Chinese-American artist "changed poor rural girls' fates, particularly the fates of many orphans or girls from single-parent families" (Luo, 2004a). Assistance especially to these sorts of girls indicates awareness of how fragile is the social support system under the market reforms, an implicit critique of the effects of the market on Chinese society. In confronting the effects of the reforms, *Nongjianü* has empowered rural women in certain specific ways that affect their own lives as well as their home villages and society at large.

The Practical Skills Training School not only provides young rural women with employment skills training, but it also imparts certain values that affect how they utilize the fruits of their trainings. Thus, the educational capital provided by the training is manifested in other sorts of capital, such as cultural and symbolic. A persistent refrain in the magazine's discussion of the school is not only that the girls imbue Confucian values such as filial piety as discussed above, but also that they become quite committed to giving back to the school and society at large. One article details how various girls at the school, within a year of finishing their training course and finding employment, are already giving donations back to the school in their quest to repay society. One group of students, originally from a revolutionary liberated area in Jiangxi province, also had the idea (subsequently named the "1 + 1 Model" by the organization's founder, Xie Lihua) of using their earnings for each to provide a scholarship for another girl from their hometown to attend the school. The class leader, Gao Xiaona, read their proposal at their graduation ceremony:

> To be able to come to Beijing to study, we are very fortunate. But in our hometowns there still are very many like us who, owing to being poor, had to leave school early; they don't have the opportunity to get out to receive education. We have compassionately been given financial aid, therefore we even more have the responsibility to take these loving seeds and spread them, to extend the loving spirit... In our new work posts, we will work hard, mutually learn, and improve together. After one year, every person will

voluntarily take 500 *yuan* to aid financially one person from their hometown who like them needs the help of other sisters to come study at the school.

Luo Zhaohong, the school's principal, is convinced that such generosity—equivalent to one month's salary—is evidence that the school is a "transmitter of love" that is also "gaining the 'repayment of love,'" a process she hopes can be continued forever (Luo, 2004c).

The training offered by the Nongjianü School in areas like computer data entry and cosmetology is admittedly highly gendered in nature, focusing on skills more compatible with normative ideas of the types of labor performed by women. To what extent does this truly empower them, and to what extent does it keep them subject to persisting patriarchal structures? One potential effect is that such an approach does confront men's power over women by seeking to empower rural women in their own domains. Given current conditions in China, rural women are more likely to succeed in feminized spheres—and some even aspire to own their own businesses in such spheres, another way of potentially giving back to their hometowns (Luo, 2004a).

The Rural Women's Health Support Small Groups also have empowering effects that go beyond their main intention of preventing rural women's suicides. In two such groups, certain women adopted wider leadership roles in the village. For instance, in Houcheng village in an unnamed province, Zhang Jinxia, a member of the Small Group, "determined to work at first in changing village customs and the village's appearance":

> Since the land was divided to households, the village has not had a woman head, but Jinxia felt that in the farming slack season women always gathering together to play mahjong was not a good thing, and then thought of everyone organizing to do some meaningful things. As time passed, her home eventually became the villagers' most loved place to go, every evening the playing and singing was extraordinarily lively, she virtually became the women's director, and, as a result, she was elected by the villagers to be the Women's Health Support Small Group's head; this decidedly was not by chance.

Under Zhang Jinxia's leadership, women in the village were empowered to overcome their husbands' objections to establish cultural teams; consequently, a "healthy cultural life replaced gambling" in the village (Xu, 2004b). In another village, this one in Hebei province, the Health Support Small Group engaged in similar cultural activities, and also founded a lending library, broadcast entertainment and technical education programs, helped the wife of a paraplegic get her children's school fees and agricultural taxes exempted, and provided "psychological counseling activities and mediating of family conflicts" (Xu, 2004c). In these various ways, rural women were empowered to adopt positive roles in their hometowns as well as society at large, and the positive effects of empowerment of women became evident to villagers.

Such an approach to village life is somewhat different from the emphasis on "low quality" (*suzhi cha*) emphasized by the Women's Federation as a cause of women's subordination. While in some cases *Nongjianü* does refer to the poverty, illiteracy, and "low quality" of rural women, it also transcends such a focus by containing numerous stories on rural women who have overcome these circumstances to improve their lives. In this sense, the magazine offers an implicit critique of the "quality" discourse on development emphasized by more state-oriented agencies, and adopts an approach that is more explicitly oriented toward empowerment (Jacka, 2006).

Identity: Dialogical Constitution and Ideas of the "Self"

Nongjianü the magazine/organization and rural women are mutually constitutive categories, with *Nongjianü* contributing to the creation of new identities for its subjects, and these subjects also asserting agency in both their own identity-creation as well as in *Nongjianü*'s content and activities. For instance, up to 60 percent of the magazine's content is contributed by its rural women readers (China Development Brief, 2001: 107). Such a process epitomizes the dialogical aspect of identity-creation emphasized by Charles Taylor, with "languages needed for self-definition" occurring through the interaction of organization and its subjects (Taylor, 1994: 79). The magazine frequently refers to its readers as "sisters" or "friends"; the column in which editor-in-chief Xie Lihua answers reader letters is titled *Dajie Xinxiang* (Eldest Sister's Mailbox). Often, solicitations to readers refer to them as "peasant friends" (*nongmin pengyou*) (Nongjianü Editor, 2004b). Using such terminology bridges the substantial gap between the urban creators and rural readership, and the rural women become more like peers than subordinates.

The Practical Skills Training School influences rural women's identities in the content of its training as well as its frequent exhortations to them to work hard and reap the benefits they have experienced by studying at the school. Students are often urged to "treasure the opportunity" they have received (Luo, 2004b). Yet the rural women who are the recipients of *Nongjianü*'s programs also shape its identity. Luo Zhaohong writes of the ways that the students constantly remind her of the meaningful nature of her work. Students themselves came up with the "1 + 1 Model," detailed above, to support other girls from their hometowns to study at the Nongjianü School, thus demonstrating how the ideas of rural women have shaped the programs of *Nongjianü*. Indeed, the Cultural Development Center notes that it was through the initial running of the magazine in the first half of the 1990s that "our staff learned much about the needs and aspirations of rural women" (Nongjianü, 2003: 16).

Through this dialectical process, rural women's selves are created in ways that are transformative of their own self-understandings. They continue to be disciplined in certain ways, as detailed above in terms of continuing adherence to Confucian norms, but in other ways they are resistant as well. Merely traveling to Beijing from remote hometowns can simultaneously be an act of resistance and discipline—they are gaining a kind of freedom while still committing themselves to help their families remaining in the village.[6] Luo Meiling, a Puyi girl in Guizhou, had to overcome her intense feelings of responsibility toward her younger sister in order to travel to Beijing to study at the Nongjianü School (Xu, 2004a). Such hesitance indicates conflicts that exist between desires for personal growth and familial responsibilities. *Nongjianü* seeks to allow personal growth while also encouraging maintenance of family commitments—it often notes how the wages the girls can earn following their training can "help their family escape from poverty" (Luo, 2004d).

But its beneficiaries also note how much happier they are after their training, partially from their ability to give back but also through the realization of greater self-identity. This is manifested through their having the autonomy to make their own decisions in life. Luo Zhaohong notes how students, who should use their earnings for their own life needs, instead think "I have finally earned money, I can take my own money to do what I want to do" and decide that what they want to do is contribute some of their earnings back to the Nongjianü School. The students also achieve a sense of value through their ability to engage in studying after usually having dropped out of school in their junior high years. The school gives them the time and opportunity to write, paint, and engage in craft activities (Luo, 2004c). Students of the Nongjianü School gain "confidence and infinite power" as well as an enhanced awareness of their own "latent abilities" (Chen, 2004). Similarly, village-level participants in Rural Women's Health Support Small Groups can show American visitors through their village and demonstrate their accomplishments and abilities, and thus "feel pride in themselves" in a way that "for generations they never experienced" (Xu, 2004c).

Nongjianü is an archetypal example of the type of modern communications and mass media that "are forming new Chinese subjectivities that are increasingly independent of place, self-consciously postmodern, and subversive of national regimes of truth" (Nonini and Ong, 1997: 25–26). Through its discussion of the Nongjianü School and the Rural Women's Health Support Small Groups, *Nongjianü* the magazine presents a vision of the potentialities in rural women's lives in today's China, and thus reaches a wider audience than those who directly experience the School or the Small Groups. In their syncretism, rural women are also increasingly postmodern in their senses of identity, though probably not usually self-consciously so. And, although *Nongjianü*'s ideas are in some significant ways consistent with regime-level discourses regarding the utility of Confucian or Asian values, it also expresses such ideas and others in a way that is not merely sycophantic toward those in authority, but in a way that acknowledges the real values in such ideas as well as how they can ameliorate the excesses of the market policies also promoted by the state. *Nongjianü* inherently subverts certain statist policies, for instance, by essentially ignoring the existence of the putative *hukou* system that divides rural and urban status in China through its encouragement of young rural women to study at the Nongjianü School so they can find work in large urban areas. It also offers an alternative to the placating consumerism offered by the state as a substitute for democratization of political forms. *Nongjianü* encourages rural women to not only exemplify values that rise above those of individualistic consumerism, but also to act as exemplars of such values in their own communities. Such values also diverge from the stereotypes some urbanites have of rural migrants to cities as materialistic and self-seeking (Lei, 2003).

Nongjianü advances an alternative modernity in its quest for recognition, representation, and identity for rural women. It also promotes particular values in order to raise the real standard of living for rural women. In this sense, it seeks to create a stable identity. Sometimes its beneficiaries note that it provides "the sense of a family" (Luo, 2004a) in a world where

> [t]heir sense of fragmentation and even displacement comes out of an ever-increasing sense of being alternatively embedded in and disembedded from various social relationships and the inescapable tension between identification with specific places (or families) and the postmodern flux of many places and many identifications. (Nonini and Ong, 1997: 26)

Conclusion

Certain Western feminist standpoints would find potential problems in the compromises that the *Nongjianü* magazine and organization have made with a patriarchal culture and state, through their syncretic recognition of Confucianist and statist elements alongside feminism and globalized cultures. Such a form of recognition, however, recognizes both the realities of rural women's lives and the very real value that can be obtained from elements of Confucian culture as well as state involvement.

Nongjianü represents women through the promotion of programs that are often reproductive rather than transformative of conventional gender roles and stereotypes, although by doing so it provides women with at least some "requisite resources and opportunities for effective practices of agency" (Di Stefano, 2003: 272). It may draw on certain "customary ways of life" (Pateman, 2003: 305), a strategy often inimical to feminist thought, but, again, it does so in a way that seeks to empower rural women and improve their contemporary existence.

Finally, the dialogical process of identity-formation between *Nongjianü* and rural women tends to influence rural women's senses of self in ways that preserve their connection to patriarchal family structures and obligations. But this can be regarded as a more communitarian and less individualistic manifestation of feminist ideas, one that may be consistent with an ethic of care advocated by some Western feminist thinkers.

Evidently, *Nongjianü* is not only helping rural women find their footing in the reform-era market economy, but it is also encouraging a healthy skepticism regarding the market. Such a skepticism differs from Chinese regime-level concern over the market's corrosion of certain traditionalist moral structures in that it seeks instead to generate a vision of the good life that promotes care, love, and generosity, rather than individualistic profit-seeking. In addition, *Nongjianü* exhibits doubts regarding Western, linear visions of socioeconomic progress by lauding a culture of rural women that differs from the global capitalist consumer culture now taking root in urban China. *Nongjianü*'s "pragmatic politics of the present moment" might stem from the desire to simply improve the lives of rural women, but it also has evolved into a distinctive ethical and sociocultural framework.

Notes

I thank Wang Qiaochu for providing Chinese language assistance.

1. The "gendered" characteristics of the training classes are apparent; the Nongjianü School is not training rural girls to be construction workers or truck drivers.
2. Personal communication with Xie Lihua in Beijing in March 2006.
3. Minxin Pei notes how Chinese are more likely than Westerners to believe that "some of the most basic rights are granted by the state rather than given at birth" (2003: 41).
4. I am not making any claim that China's current government approximates this sort of "social democracy" advocated by Wang Hui; rather, I am using this as one example of arguments that a state role to counter the most egregious effects of the market can be useful, especially when it occurs in conjunction with civil society.
5. *Xiaokang* society is an official rhetoric regarding the goals of the Chinese reform process—it is regarded as a higher standard of living currently enjoyed by most people, especially rural Chinese, but not as lavish as that in the consumerist West.
6. For more on the complex ways that rural-to-urban migration shapes the subjectivities of rural women, see the essays in Gaetano and Jacka (eds., 2004).

Bibliography

Brysk, Alison, and Gershon Shafir, eds. 2004. *People Out of Place*. New York: Routledge.

Chan, Joseph. 2003. "Confucian Attitudes toward Ethical Pluralism." In Richard Madsen and Tracy B. Strong, eds. *The Many and the One: Religious and Secular Perspectives on Ethical Pluralism in the Modern World*, 129–153. Princeton, NJ: Princeton University Press.

Chen, Hu. 2004. "Tuoqi xinling de taiyang" (Supporting the sunshine of the soul). *Nongjianü* (Rural women) (June): 41.

Chen, Kuan-Hsing. 1998. "The Decolonization Question." In Kuan-Hsing Chen, ed. *Trajectories: Inter-Asia Cultural Studies*. New York: Routledge.

China Development Brief. 2001. *250 Chinese NGOs: Civil Society in the Making*. Beijing: China Development Brief.

———. 2006. "Profile: Veteran Fighter for 'Ugly Duckling' That Serves Rural Women." *China Development Brief*. Retrieved on April 3, 2006 from http://www.chinadevelopmentbrief.com/node/526

Ding, X. L. 1994. *The Decline of Communism in China: Legitimacy Crisis, 1977–1989*. Cambridge: Cambridge University Press.

Di Stefano, Christine. 2003. "Feminist Attitudes toward Ethical Pluralism." In Madsen and Strong, eds. *The Many and the One*, 271–300.

Gaetano, Arianne M., and Tamara Jacka, eds. 2004. *On the Move: Women in Rural-to-Urban Migration in Contemporary China*. New York: Columbia University Press.

Gladney, Dru C. 2004. *Dislocating China*. Chicago, IL: University of Chicago Press.

Jacka, Tamara. 1997. *Women's Work in Rural China: Change and Continuity in an Era of Reform*. Cambridge: Cambridge University Press.

———. 2006. "Approaches to Women and Development in Rural China." *Journal of Contemporary China* 15, 585–602.

Judd, Ellen R. 2002. *The Chinese Women's Movement between State and Market*. Stanford, CA: Stanford University Press.

Kipnis, Andrew. 2006. "Suzhi: A Keyword Approach." *China Quarterly* 186, 295–313.

Lei, Guang. 2003. "Rural Taste, Urban Fashions: The Cultural Politics of Rural/Urban Difference in Contemporary China." *Positions* 11, 613–646.

Li, Danke. 2004. "Gender Inequality in Education in Rural China." In Tao Jie, Zheng Bijun, and Shirley L. Mow, eds. *Holding Up Half the Sky: Chinese Women Past, Present, and Future*. New York: Feminist Press.

Luo, Zhaohong. 2004a. "Aixin tuoqi de rensheng" (Love's support of human life). *Nongjianü* (December): 41.

———. 2004b. "Hao da yi ke shu: Geji dangwei, zhengfu, quntuan zuzhi guan'ai Nongjianü xuexiao diandi jishi" (A very big tree: A chronicle of each level of the party, government, and mass organizations showing loving care for the Nongjianü school). *Nongjianü* (July): 41–42.

———. 2004c. "Women ye zai shou huozhe 'ai'" (We are also harvesting "love"). *Nongjianü* (January): 42–43.

———. 2004d. "Yunnan 'Jinhua' chu zhan jing cheng" (The beginning of Yunnan "Golden Flowers" opening in the capital city). *Nongjianü* (May): 42–43.

Madsen, Richard, and Tracy B. Strong. 2003. "Introduction: Three Forms of Ethical Pluralism." In Madsen and Strong, eds. *The Many and the One*, 1–21.

Nongjianü. 2003. *Cultural Development Center for Rural Women*. Beijing.

———. 2004. "Fazhan cong gaishan fengxianzhe de tiaojian kaishi" (Development from starting to improve the conditions of those who offer tributes). *Nongjianü* (October): 40.

Nongjianü Editor. 2004a. "Falu bangzhu" (Legal aid). *Nongjianü* (January): 26.

———. 2004b. "Nongjia zhifu baitong: He nongmin pengyou shuo jiju xinlihua" (Almanac of the rural becoming rich: Speaking some innermost thoughts with our peasant friends). *Nongjianü* (January): 46.

Nonini, Donald M., and Aihwa Ong. 1997. "Chinese Transnationalism as an Alternative Modernity." In Aihwa Ong and Donald Nonini, eds. *Ungrounded Empires: The Cultural Politics of Modern Chinese Transnationalism*, 3–33. New York: Routledge.

Ong, Aihwa. 1997. "Chinese Modernities: Narratives of Nation and of Capitalism." In Ong and Nonini, eds. *Ungrounded Empires*, 171–202.

Ong, Aihwa, and Donald M. Nonini. 1997. "Toward a Cultural Politics of Diaspora and Transnationalism." In Ong and Nonini, eds. *Ungrounded Empires*, 323–332.

Pateman, Carole. 2003. "Feminism and the Varieties of Ethical Pluralism." In Madsen and Strong, eds. *The Many and the One*, 301–308.

Pei, Minxin. 2003. "Rights and Resistance: The Changing Contexts of the Dissident Movement." In Elizabeth J. Perry and Mark Selden, eds. *Chinese Society: Change, Conflict, and Resistance*. New York: Routledge.

Shue, Vivienne. 2004. "Legitimacy Crisis in China." In Peter Hays Gries and Stanley Rosen, eds. *State and Society in 21st-Century China*, 24–49. New York: Routledge.

Taylor, Charles. 1994. "The Politics of Recognition." In David Theo Goldberg, ed. *Multiculturalism: A Critical Reader.* Oxford: Blackwell.
Wang, Hui. 2003. *China's New Order: Society, Politics, and Economy in Transition.* Cambridge, MA: Harvard University Press.
Wesoky, Sharon R. 2002. *Chinese Feminism Faces Globalization.* New York: Routledge.
Xu, Rong. 2004a. "Buyi guniang: Ni hui you xiwang de" (Puyi girls: You can have hope). *Nongjianü* (February): 38–39.
———. 2004b. "Huanhuan xixi guo danian" (Happily spending the New Year). *Nongjianü* (February): 4–5.
———. 2004c. "Huanteng de Shangquyang cun" (Jubilant Shangquyang village). *Nongjianü* (August): 43.

CHAPTER NINE

"This Is My Mother's Land!":
An Indigenous Woman Speaks Out

SIU-KEUNG CHEUNG

Introduction

The politics of recognition by definition urges us to see and respect a clear difference among social groups in terms of their identity and that of the culture at large. Charles Taylor is, therefore, correct to claim that the politics of recognition is dialogical and, by implication, totally relational in character (1992). The presence of asymmetric power relationships frequently spoils this dialogical progress, however, and leads to stereotyping of minorities. No culture is single, pure, or monolithic; the same goes for the individual experience that develops from it (Said, 1994; Rex, 1992). All cultures involve encounter and ongoing negotiations of identity. Heterogeneity of historical experience exists accumulatively and indeterminately. But the politics of recognition, along with those with the power to offer recognition, frequently gloss over the diversity of people in their actual setting and flatten the ever-present complexities of the social group, culture, and identity purportedly recognized (Dyson, 1994; Stiehm, 1994). This phenomenological circumstance of culture is incompatible with the politics of recognition that must fix an identity as static and unitary if it is to be a discernible thing for recognition.

Having said this, one cannot simply reduce the politics of recognition into a matter of power and counterpower. As essential as the matter of power and counterpower is, it is necessary to maintain that the main theme is the drive and search for mutual acceptance. Struggles for recognition should be taken as fights for coexistence within a respectful space. Rather than a one-sided gesture of acceptance based on political correctness, where the more powerful recognize the less powerful, a politics of recognition should develop through mutual adjustments among groups (Goldberg, 1994).

This chapter examines such a fundamental contradiction in the politics of recognition by drawing on my ethnographic findings of village politics in the British colonial New Territories of Hong Kong from 1898 to 1997. It uses the life-story of an indigenous woman, Deng A-Mei, to flesh out the tension between diversity in the practice of people and artificial homogeneity in the politics of recognition. In doing so, it highlights the gendered implications of special recognition that British colonizers adopted for the indigenous Chinese communities. It shows women as real, speaking, and living subjects, engaged in the ongoing struggle for their rights to land through individual and collective actions.

The Invention of Indirect Rule in the New Territories

British colonizers wrestled control of different parts of Hong Kong at different times through different diplomatic agreements made possible by military means. The New Territories was the last piece of territory that Britain acquired from the crumbling Chinese empire. But the British acquisition of the New Territories was conditional. Previously, Hong Kong Island and Kowloon Peninsula were perpetual concessions made through the Treaty of Nanjing and the Treaty of Beijing in 1841 and 1860, respectively. In the case of the New Territories, it consisted only of a temporary lease of ninety-nine years through the Convention for the Extension of Hong Kong Territory in 1898 (Welsh, 1993). The New Territories was also much larger than the rest of Hong Kong and contained many predominant Chinese clans possessing abundant members, land, resources, and power in different villages (Baker, 1966).

When British colonizers proceeded to take over the New Territories, they investigated the area in order to gather local information for administrative control. They also tried to prepare the first flag-hoisting ceremony to demonstrate the colonial sovereignty in the New Territories. But they encountered resistance from Chinese villagers. In April 1899, villagers organized an armed force to attack the British officials in Tai

Po where the British intended to launch the first flag-hoisting ceremony. Although the British swiftly crushed the rebellious Chinese force, they reached a compromise and invoked the age-old policy of indirect rule to conceal their failure to subdue the Chinese people in the New Territories. They justified this indirect rule by claiming respect for Chinese tradition (Wesley-Smith, 1980).

The British claim that it recognized indigenous customs and laws did more harm than good. It seldom consolidated the rule of the colonial authorities. Instead, it generated endless disputes over territorial rights because of the conflicting interpretations of "indigenous tradition" in the governance of the local community. Furthermore, this form of colonial recognition never preserved the preexisting ideas and practices of governance. Instead it engaged in what Eric Hobsbawm and Terence Ranger call "the invention of tradition" by selecting customs and creating new ones to serve current political needs (Ranger, 1983). British colonization depended on the co-optation of the local elites and the creation of alliances of power-sharing with them (Moberg, 1992; Friedman, 2005).

Subsequent to the completion of the first flag-hoisting ceremony in the New Territories, the British in 1899 made the first noninterventionist announcement to the Chinese villagers in line with the notion of indirect rule and the promise to recognize indigenous traditions (Hong Kong Government, 1899: 532). But, in practice, the British only focused upon the issue of land, and conducted a thorough survey of the existing land tenure and ownership in every Chinese village in the New Territories for administrative and tax collection purposes (Nelson, 1969). In 1905, they passed the New Territories Land Ordinance and legally recognized Chinese villagers' customary rights to land property: "In any proceeding in Supreme Court in relation to land in the New Territories the Court shall have power to recognize and enforce any Chinese custom or customary right affecting such land" (Hong Kong Government, 1905: 8).

This ordinance also had a special clause that maintained what the British thought to be the existing collective ownership in the Chinese lineage organizations and that allowed Chinese villagers to appoint their managers (*sili*) in handling the land and estate of communal halls (*tong*). In 1910, after the legislative tasks had been completed, what ensued was the New Territories Land Ordinance, a specialized socio-political governance order for the New Territories (Hong Kong Government, 1910).

This colonial recognition of Chinese traditions in the New Territories under the notion of indirect rule had long been taken for granted by scholars. For example, Maurice Freedman argued that the New Territories under British rule was an excellent site for the anthropological and historical study of traditional Chinese practices (1958, 1966, 1976). Freedman's studies have been taken as a powerful paradigm in academia. The following scholarly discourse on the New Territories highlights the issue of how British colonial power became conventional or received knowledge in the social sciences:

> We should probably credit this "enlightened colonialism" as the only reason why traditional Chinese kinship organization, land tenure system, and beliefs have been preserved in their authentic form.... I would contend that they have not only been fossilized, but also been pushed into their "pure" and "ideal" manner. (Huang, 1982: 66)

In reality, it is egregious to take the New Territories as the prototype of traditional Chinese society. No matter whether the researchers were politically naïve or insensitive, their studies were easily used to justify the colonial notion of indirect rule that the British used to dominate the New Territories for almost a century.

This long-standing notion of an authentic traditional Chinese society that existed in the New Territories is a pure conceptual construct almost entirely of the making of these early sinologists. The British had codified Chinese laws and customs into a more strict fashion than what had existed before in China. The British had introduced new legislative terms and categories forcing people to negotiate over their land with new legislative procedures. A good example was the new legislative requirement to appoint *sili* for overseeing the communal ancestral land and estates as there was no such formal position in the Chinese lineage in the past. By applying the new rule, the British also intensified their bureaucratic control of land in a more forceful and systemic manner than the Chinese authorities had done. They produced land records and cadastral maps, required people to register their land, issued new official deeds to landowners, narrowed people's right to land, introduced new land policies and even abolished existing local practices thought to be incompatible with the new British ruling system. This superimposition of new legislative and bureaucratic practices upon land tenure and practices was so extensive that British indirect rule succeeded in undermining the many flexible arrangements, negotiable areas, self-autonomies, and informal local conventions or obligations that the Chinese had normally held in the past (Chun, 2000).

Recent studies also reveal that the precolonial Chinese society in the New Territories was seldom as lineage-centered as the British colonizers and early sinologists had claimed (Watson, 1985; Faure, 1986). Rather, it was the result of the British colonial recognition of Chinese tradition that transformed the lineage organizations in the New Territories into the central authority in governing communal village life. Most critically, Chinese lineage organizations are not gender-neutral. These organizations were extremely patriarchal and maintained many male-dominated practices such as patrilocal residence, patrilineal succession of family land and property, male-only participatory right to communal corporation in control of ancestral estate, and male-only right to participate in communal affairs and decisions on an agnatic basis (Jones, 1995). The colonial recognition of Chinese tradition worked as an official authorization of the patriarchal interests and practices in Chinese lineage organizations. Thus, the notion of indirect rule perversely served as a convenient rhetoric that covered up the British colonizers' complicity with the Chinese patriarchs in this game of *realpolitik*.

In 1926, the British went so far as to empower the Chinese patriarchs and normalize their power in the New Territories by integrating the New Territories Association of Agricultural, Industrial and Commercial Research (*Xinjie nonggongshang yanjiu zonghui*) into the colonial government and renaming it the Rural Consultative Committee, widely known as Heung Yee Kuk in Hong Kong today. In 1959, the British institutionalized the Heung Yee Kuk as the highest statutory advisory body of the New Territories by enacting the Heung Yee Kuk Ordinance. Therefore, the Heung Yee Kuk became a formal institution in the British colonial representation system. It contained 27 Rural Committees with 651 villages at the bottom. The council members of the Rural Committees were made up of the village representatives, who came from the male-only election among the patriarchs in each village. All the chairmen and vice chairmen of the Rural Committees, in turn, became the council members of the male-controlled Heung Yee Kuk (Lam, 1986). By so recognizing the Chinese villagers' traditional practices, the British "modernized" their communal political structure and reinforced the institutionalized androcentric rule in order to facilitate the colonial governance of the New Territories.

In 1972, when the British introduced the Small House Policy in order to settle the overwhelming number of land disputes among Chinese villagers, they formally called the villagers in the New Territories "indigenous inhabitants." But they used the term to refer only to the patrilineal male descendants of those men who were living in the villages in the New Territories on July 1, 1898. The Small House Policy therefore became a sexist colonial land policy because it specified that only the "indigenous inhabitants" (males) were eligible for an official allowance to build one premium-free village house during their lifetime (Ng, 1996). Accordingly, it entailed a critical bias that not only reinforced the boundary between the "indigenous inhabitants" and the urban population in Hong Kong, but also privileged the patriarchs by normalizing the patrilineal practice within the Chinese village communities with essential land interest in the long run.

The British control of the New Territories was to end on June 30, 1997 under the ninety-nine years' lease. During the Sino-British negotiations over the future of Hong Kong in the 1980s, the British agreed to transfer the sovereignty of Hong Kong entirely to China. In turn, China introduced the policy of "one country, two systems" to maintain the status quo of Hong Kong for fifty years. China also drafted the Basic Law of the Hong Kong Special Administrative Region of the People's Republic of China to specify the constitutional framework of Hong Kong after 1997 (Nicholas, 1999).

Despite the formal ending of British colonialism, the legacy of an invented tradition continued. In the New Territories, both the Chinese and Hong Kong authorities have proceeded to preserve the British policy of indirect rule for the village communities in the New Territories. The Basic Law Article 40, Chapter 3: Fundamental Rights and Duties of the Residents, states, "The lawful traditional rights and interests of the indigenous inhabitants of the 'New Territories' shall be protected by the Hong Kong Special Administrative Region." Article 122, Chapter 5: Economy, Section 2. Land Leases, specifies,

> In the case of old schedule lots, village lots, small houses and similar rural holdings, where the property was on 30 June 1984 held by, or, in the case of small houses granted after that date, where the property is granted to, a lessee descended through the male line from a person who was in 1898 a resident of an established village in Hong Kong, the previous rent shall remain unchanged so long as the property is held by that lessee or by one of his lawful successors in the male line.

Is this a case of indirect rule a la Chinese in the postcolonial era? Is there to be a Chinese reinvention of the age-old British invented "Chinese tradition" in the New Territories? Evidently, the colonially authorized notion of Chinese tradition obtains a new official recognition at the constitutional level. The postcolonial Chinese government also continues to rule the village communities in the New Territories on a patriarchal basis.

The selective and partial recognition in the British colonial government, and continuing with the postcolonial Chinese government as well, represents a crude fiction of the Chinese communities in the New Territories. This crude fiction is so perverse that it has already jeopardized many essential social and cultural values of the people in the practice of their domestic and communal life. It does not, however, mean that the people who were subjected to this crude fiction did not develop their own politics of recognition by taking action themselves. What follows is a story of an indigenous woman who struggled for the recognition of her right to land from the late colonial to the early postcolonial period.

The Story of Deng A-Mei

Deng A-Mei is now seventy years old and lives in the village of Dashu (Big Tree Village) in the New Territories. She was the elder of her parents' two children. Her father was a fish hawker and her mother a farm laborer. Her younger brother died when he was an infant leaving her as the only child in the household. From early childhood, she lived frugally with her family and worked laboriously with her mother to cultivate the family's land. She deeply cherished her memories of working with her mother in the farm as described below:

> In the daily rounds, my mother and I needed to wake up just after dawn and start to work in the farm.... But, we really were good at work. We could sow many paddies and make good yields. Annually, we could produce 3 piculs in the first yield and 3 more piculs in the second yield. You see! This was how terrific my mother and I managed to work and how hard it was in our past. So far, I have not yet talked about of how we worked together to keep the two pigs and three cows in our home.

But her marriage was less fortunate. She married her husband at the age of twenty, but unlike other village daughters she did not move out of the village after marriage. Sadly, she eventually divorced her husband after he became a drug addict. She had to raise the children—five daughters and one son—on her own by working on a construction site.

Deng A-Mei said that her father passed away in 1984. To take care of her mother's health, A-Mei continued to visit her every day. She also asked her second daughter Zhou Shaofen to move into her mother's home to assist with home care. But her mother passed away in 1987. Her death was not only an emotional loss to A-Mei but also led to an acrimonious property dispute over the family land.

According to Zhou Shaofen, when her grandmother died in hospital, A-Jin, as a close relative, came to the hospital. But A-Jin abruptly explained to Zhou that since her grandparents had no son, A-Jin's three sons would inherit the estate according to Chinese tradition.[1] The estate included three ancestral houses and two farms owned by Deng A-Mei's parents. If Zhou Shaofen wished to continue staying in her grandmother's home, she would have to pay rent to A-Jin's three sons. On hearing this, Zhou was deeply infuriated and found it totally ridiculous. She simply ignored A-Jin's claim and continued to live in her grandmother's home.

Deng A-Mei indicated that this was not the first time A-Jin had made such a claim over her parents' estates. On many previous occasions, A-Jin had asked Deng A-Mei's father to pass his family estates on to her three sons, but he refused to do so. Since her father's demise, A-Jin had already pressured her mother and had publicly claimed that Deng A-Mei's father had adopted her three sons and thereby her sons were the rightful heirs of the family estates. But, Deng A-Mei rejected this claim, and argued that her father had never adopted A-Jin's three sons and that A-Jin's husband had been adopted by another Deng family. Therefore, A-Jin's family worshipped another ancestor of the Deng family, and her sons were not entitled to inherit the family estates. As Deng A-Mei asserts,

> Yes, it is true! My deceased father was her (A-Jin) deceased husband's real brother.... But A-Jin's husband was passed to another Deng family through adoption among close kin (*guoji*).... The ancestral altar in their home was that of another family, too.... But, that woman (A-Jin) makes whatever ridiculous story for herself. To take other people's things, she can now say that she had given my father her three sons by *guoji*. But, this is absolutely impossible! How would a person in this world give all the sons to another person? Would they have no need to have a son to be the heir of their family at all?

It was about a month after the death of Deng A-Mei's mother when A-Jin hired a lawyer to act on behalf of her three sons. She officially and legally pressed the claim to inherit the family estates. She also spread gossip in the village claiming that Deng A-Mei had no right to the family estates because she was adopted and had no real blood relationship. As Deng A-Mei complained,

> That woman (A-Jin) is absolutely terrible! As if one story is not enough, she makes another one. She now keeps talking in the village that I originally was an adopted child. What is more, she added that I was actually taken as a servant girl to work in my parents' home. Otherwise, the people would not usually call me a servant (*meici*)!

Moreover, Deng A-Mei pointed out that A-Jin had mobilized a village leader to support her case and to require the tenant of her mother's farmland to pay rent to A-Jin. Deng A-Mei recalled the incident:

> I helped my mother to collect the rent from her tenant all along. But, A-Jin secretly went to see our tenant (for collecting rent) shortly after my mother died.... To begin with, our tenant felt very puzzled. She refused to give me the rent. As far as I know, she did not pay any rent to her. But, later, A-Jin found a village leader to help her and went with him to see our tenant again. So, how could our tenant understand what was going on? With the presence of the village leader, our tenant was afraid. At the end, she paid rent to A-Jin, not me.

A few words should be said about the role of A-Jin in the property dispute. A-Jin is fifteen years older than Deng A-Mei. In local kinship terms, A-Jin is a "married-in-woman" whereas Deng A-Mei is a "married-out-daughter." When A-Jin was eighteen years old, she married the brother of Deng A-Mei's father. Then she had three daughters and three sons with him. Her husband passed away many years ago. Her three daughters got married and moved out to live with their husbands and children a long time ago. Her three sons migrated to the Netherlands. But they kept contact with their kinsmen and fellow-villagers and occasionally returned home. They also continued to participate in the communal meeting and obtained their shares of the produce from the ancestral estate. In any case, A-Jin frequently seized any opportunity to undermine Deng A-Mei's credibility in daily conversations with others. She reminded people of A-Mei's transitory status as a married-out-daughter in the lineage and continued to argue for her three sons' right to inherit her parents' estates. She once repeated her main stance in the dispute and openly stated:

> The thing is of being out; it is really being out. If not, what does "out" mean? The married-out-daughter is another family's people once they are married out. They could not come back and take things out! In our past, we would even find it inappropriate to go back to our home village, as we have become another family's people.... But, that nasty bitch (Deng A-Mei) is shameless!

Local information also had it that A-Jin publicly remonstrated with Deng A-Mei on behalf of her three sons for the right to inherit the estates of Deng A-Mei's parents. At the public funeral for Deng A-Mei's father in the village, an elderly woman recalled how A-Jin competed with Deng A-Mei to be the chief mourner in the event:

> It was really ridiculous! How could they (A-Jin and A-Mei) quarrel with each other even over the funeral ritual! Is it not sad enough? But, that A-Jin truly came to compete with Deng A-Mei to take charge of the event and said that she only worked to represent her three sons who were in the Netherlands.... While she worked to take the cup (a key ritual instrument) from A-Mei, her swearing against A-Mei was horrible. At that moment, I really didn't want the others to know that I lived in the same village with her. That cup was almost torn apart, if A-Mei had not given up finally and said that she did not want her father's funeral to become an open farce.

There are indications that many fellow-villagers generally supported A-Jin's position in the dispute. Another married-out-daughter commented on Deng A-Mei's social status, "As she (Deng A-Mei) was born a girl, she should already expect that a girl would not have any inheritance! Just like me, I never ask about my deceased father's things and fight for them with my brothers." On a public occasion, a village leader made a similar statement of not passing over any property to the married-out-daughters. He even justified A-Jin's case by invoking the Qing Law Code, the legal code of the Manchu dynasty from 1644 to 1911. He argued, "Deng A-Mei is just a 'servant girl.' She married an outsider. We should stand for the tradition of 'bequeathing property to the male heir.' The Qing Law Code only gives the male heir the right of inheritance. Otherwise, all of the Dengs will lose face."

In the end, A-Jin won her case in 1990. Her sons could officially acquire her family's estates. She then went to the Court to obtain an official injunction that prevented Deng A-Mei and her second daughter Zhou Shaofen from staying in the ancestral house. In effect, Zhou Shaofen was driven out of the house by the bailiff from the government. Two of A-Jin's sons returned to the village from the Netherlands and applied to the government to build a small house onto the two farmlands in the family's estates.

Deng A-Mei said that this turn of events frustrated her. The most unacceptable fact was the loss of the two plots of farmland where she had worked with her mother since childhood. "This is my mother's land!" Deng A-Mei could not control her tears but cried it out in my interview. She also described how the land reminded her of the legacy of her mother's hard acquisitions from her lifelong savings with all her laborious sweat and toil. A-Mei said,

> These two plots of farmland absolutely belonged to my mother and were earned by her sweat and toil. Up to now, I still clearly remember how hard she had worked on the farm. How difficult it was for her when she went to find money to buy the land from the landlord.... Her legs would suffer from serious rheumatism and sharp pains while she was alive. It is also because she had worked too hard on those two farms.

Deng A-Mei could not control her anger but furiously berated the traditional authority of the Qing Law Code:

> What is that god damned Qing Law Code to allow people to rob other people's things! Why as a daughter who looked after my parents would that mean I have no right to my family things at all?... When my father died, my mother was not entitled to get any land or house from him. But, when my mother died, why could they come to take all her land? Even the Qing Law Code upholds the rule: "bequeathing to men not women," they at most are able to get my father's things. Why could they also take my mother's land?

Deng A-Mei had tried everything to fight for her parents' property. She subsequently hired a lawyer to act on her behalf. She also worked on her own to pursue all possible avenues for her case. She had tried many times to photograph the ancestral altar in A-Jin's home so as to produce evidence that A-Jin's family was under another branch of the Deng clan. But, she could not take this photograph because A-Jin always closed the door of her house. A-Mei had gone out of her way to reach some of the fellow-villagers who could prove her status as her father's real daughter. But no one was willing to help her, even though in private they were sympathetic to her claim.

Deng A-Mei's case coincided with the handover of Hong Kong's sovereignty to China in 1997. The issue of land ownership in the New Territories suddenly reemerged as Hong Kong's return to China approached in the early 1990s. Strong social and political pressures called for change in the British authorized "Chinese tradition" in the New Territories. This unique moment opened a new door for Deng A-Mei's personal struggle.

In the spring of 1994, the Hong Kong government had to rectify a legal anomaly in the practice of the New Territories Ordinance under the separate territorial policy of indirect rule. This legal anomaly derived from a misconception that the New Territories Ordinance referred *only* to the indigenous population and *only* applied to the rural areas of the New Territories. However, the New Territories Ordinance legally covered *all* the people and *all* the land in the New Territories. This could require the High Court to enforce the traditional (patrilineal) inheritance laws as regards to landownership, unless exemption had been made by the legal owner (Hong Kong Government, 1984).

Neither the Hong Kong government nor any of the 2 million urban migrant dwellers (40 percent of Hong Kong's total population) in the urbanized area of the New Territories registered any exemptions. Most public and private buildings fell under the jurisdiction of the New Territories Ordinance, even though this was not part of the owners' expectations (Hong Kong Legislative Council, 1993: 1040–1042). Accordingly, the Legislative Council pressed the Hong Kong government to amend the New Territories Ordinance. The Hong Kong government finally expanded the existing exemption clause in the Ordinance into the New Territories Land (Exemption) Bill. The government endowed the new bill with retrospective legal power to exempt all nonrural land in the New Territories from the Chinese customary law recognized by the British in the New Territories Ordinance since 1910 (Hong Kong Legislative Council, 1994: 4539–4589).

But it was difficult for the Hong Kong government to correct their juridical anomaly. An elected independent legislator, Christine Kung-Wai Loh, seized the moment to challenge the policy of indirect rule and the rigidified Chinese feudal patrilineal inheritance practice. She cited Article 26 of the International Covenant on Civil and Political Rights that was to guarantee nondiscrimination on sexual grounds and was incorporated into the Law of Hong Kong by Article 22 of the Hong Kong Bill of Human Right (Jones, 1995). Combining the principle of this international covenant with the contemporary principle of gender equality, Loh claimed that the existing colonial policy of indirect rule in the New Territories was discriminatory based on sex. It was totally outdated from the contemporary context of the New Territories that was as well-developed as the rest of urban Hong Kong (*Ming Pao*, March 31, 1994).

Then Legislator Loh drafted an amendment to the New Territories Land (Exemption) Bill presented by the government to the Legislative Council. She proposed to extend the New Territories Land (Exemption) Bill to include the rural land in the New Territories, not only the non-rural land there as the Hong Kong government had initially suggested. Loh intended to place the entire area of the New Territories under the General Law of Hong Kong wherein if a deceased did not prepare any will, his property would be divided into two equal shares; one for the spouse and the other one would be equally shared among his children. Accordingly, the indigenous women would have the same right of inheritance as men. The existing Chinese custom of male-only inheritance institutionalized by the New Territories Ordinance under the British policy of indirect rule would be abandoned (Zhang, Jiang, and Liu, eds., 1995: 126–128).

Confronted with such a challenge from Legislator Loh, the Hong Kong government stated that they had "no strong objection" to her amendment (Chan, 1996: 13). However, numerous indigenous men and women in the New Territories vehemently reacted against Legislator Loh and the Hong Kong government's supportive posture on her amendment. The Heung Yee Kuk denounced the Hong Kong government for abandoning the policy of indirect rule and for interfering with their traditions. To counter Legislator Loh's juridical movement, the Heung Yee Kuk rallied hundreds and thousands of indigenous men and women under the slogan of "protecting our families and clans." They organized collective resistance by creating the Communal Headquarters of Struggle in Protecting Families and Defending Clans (*Ming Pao*, March 26, 1994). Swiftly and intensively, the Heung Yee Kuk launched numerous assemblies, large-scale marches and protests. More and more people, village communities, rural bodies and authorities were mobilized to join their fight. Throughout their protests against Legislator Loh and the actions of the colonial government, their people sang various national songs to show their "Chineseness" (Chan, 1996: 21). They staged some mock traditional trials of effigies of Legislator Loh and other key figures, sentenced them to death, and set them on fire (*Eastern Express*, April 18, 1994). They recalled the past histories of the armed resistance against the British colonizers in 1899 (Heung Yee Kuk, 1996: 78–79). They publicly worshipped the sacrificed ancestors of the armed resistance to gain media coverage (Zhang, Jiang, and Liu, eds., 1995: 50). One of the protestors even announced that he would bite and rape Legislator Loh if she entered the New Territories (*South China Morning Post*, March 23, 1994).

Important officials and agencies of the Mainland Chinese Government became involved in this incident. On the one hand, they urged the British to uphold the indigenous traditions as stated in the Basic Law of Hong Kong. On the other hand, they opposed the proposed amendment by Legislator Loh as part of the British conspiracy to destabilize Hong Kong before 1997 (*South China Morning Post*, March 27, 1994). However, Legislator Loh won substantial support from different political parties, women's groups, religious institutions, nongovernmental organizations, academics, celebrities, and other public figures (Zhang, Jiang, and Liu, eds., 1995). She even referred to the articles in the Chinese Constitution about the principle of gender equality to counter against the Chinese officials' arguments (*Xiandai ribao*, March 30, 1994). The oppositions from the Heung Yee Kuk and their people may have been vehement but they proved to be futile. The membership of the Legislative Council contained only one seat for the Heung Yee Kuk. The Heung Yee Kuk also only managed to obtain one additional supporter in the Legislative Council. Christine Loh's private amendment was passed in the Legislative Council and won thirty-six out of thirty-eight votes (Hong Kong Legislative Council, 1994: 4539–4589).

Deng A-Mei participated intensely in Legislator Loh's camp. She joined an ad hoc committee created for this issue along with many feminists and other indigenous women. A-Mei spoke to the media about the dispute with A-Jin. She visited Legislator Loh and attended the assemblies and demonstrations to support Loh's juridical action. However, her dispute with A-Jin did not end after Legislator Loh's private amendment was passed. A-Mei still needed to wait for the procedures of the Court in dealing with her case. Her fellow-villagers viewed her as a hateful troublemaker who had created the whole Legislator Loh controversy in order to destroy their customs. For example, many village men and women continued to spread a sexist rumor that A-Mei had become a low-priced prostitute since she had divorced her husband.

They even claimed that she would engage in disgusting "wild fights" in the forest for some of her clients. In a similar vein, they talked about Deng A-Mei's "real relationship" with the existing male tenant. In the daily gossip, this male tenant was said to be Deng A-Mei's secret lover. As her second daughter Zhou Shaofen had now moved in with A-Mei, the gossip intensified. It was rumored that Deng A-Mei's "that-part" could not service her secret lover because she had overused it in making money in her past. Her second daughter had now replaced her since she had divorced her husband because of a lack of sexual life. On top of these personal attacks, many people in Big Tree Village completely isolated Deng A-Mei from the community. Some villagers even claimed that they would remind their children to avoid going to her home and playing with A-Mei's grandchildren. The villagers' attempts to undermine Deng A-Mei's right to inherit her mother's land were further implicated with the character assassination of Deng A-Mei.

Judgment of Deng A-Mei on the part of her villagers was not entirely one-sided. Their aversion to Deng A-Mei, which arose from her involvement with Legislator Loh's campaign, never caused them to hold back their appreciation of her as an extraordinarily filial daughter. There were also some sympathies for her case. One elderly woman in the village talked about Deng A-Mei favorably:

> She surely is the model of a great daughter, one I seldom see.... Since she was a little child, she worked extremely hard to help her mother. When her mother became old and suffered from paralysis, her life in looking after her mother was extremely tough indeed.... But, that A-Jin was really overpowering! Even though her sons have the right to Deng A-Mei's parents' property, she should not treat Deng A-Mei so overpoweringly and always swear at her. After all, she (Deng A-Mei) was her parents' direct child. She should have some rights to her parents' matters.

Conclusion

At first sight, the rise of Deng A-Mei's land dispute appears to be "present" and "local," and profoundly "personal" and "domestic." The issue concerns the ownership of three village houses of a family with two plots of farmland. The participants were from members of an ordinary kin group. The venue was no more than a village community. But the development of this dispute and its relations to Legislator Christine

Loh's campaign shows that the issues involved in this land dispute were deeply "historical" and "global," and they were extremely "political" and "social." The sequence of events became entangled with the intense conflicts between the colonial state, the postcolonial state, and the patriarchs on one side, and the unique interconnections of Deng A-Mei's personal struggle with Legislator Loh's juridical movement on the other side.

In the first place, this case makes it clear that society in the New Territories is not silent and inert. It is, instead, a highly complex congeries of experiences configured by multiple historical memories and practices. The village reflects a dynamic society full of diverse agents who act relative to internal and external forces. This results in practices of collusion, competition, and very occasionally, consensus. These multiple historical memories and practices range from the personal as indicated by the story of Deng A-Mei, through the regional as indicated by the demonstrations of the Heung Yee Kuk, to the national as indicated in the reinvention of the feudal authority of the Qing Law Code, and the international as indicated by the arguments of Legislator Christine Loh and the interventions of the colonial and postcolonial states. Traditions and different legal systems at different levels enabled different agents to legitimatize their specific positions and to challenge one another. The Qing Law Code, the separate territorial New Territories Ordinance, the General Law of Hong Kong, the Basic Law of Hong Kong, the Chinese Constitution and the International Covenant on Civil and Political Rights had been drawn upon by these different agents. The contemporary principle of gender equality and the historic values of Chinese traditionalism had been used in collision with each other. The liberation of women and the reincarnation of the old Chinese patriarchy led to a situation where protagonists pursued conflicting strategies. The locality of the New Territories is in a state of play where heterogeneous subjects, historical dynamics, and socio-political forces interact. None of these factors were as simple as what the British colonizers legislatively and administratively claimed and maintained in their manipulative politic of recognition.

Importantly, Deng A-Mei's case highlighted the critical patriarchal nature of the version of Chinese tradition authorized, reinvented, and reinforced by the British colonial government. By operating as an honorable patriarch, A-Jin benefited from this colonial policy of recognition simply because her three sons could claim to be the lawful male heirs. Not only did the village leaders and other powerful patriarchs directly help A-Jin, but also the whole community in the village generally supported her. The British colonial state enabled A-Jin to reinstate her claim over the heritage of Deng A-Mei's parents through both legal and bureaucratic means. "Gender blindness" made possible the British colonial control by adopting the British policy to Chinese patriarchy. This reinforced the British hegemonic claim to sovereignty by being culturally sensitive to indigenous practices. As a result, this enabled A-Jin to obtain many institutional and practical advantages and to normalize her patriarchal oppression over Deng A-Mei.

However, Deng A-Mei's case also suggests that both the colonial state and the Chinese patriarchy were never that all-powerful and well-coordinated. The politics of recognition had opened a critical terrain of unending contestation. As the episode of the Legislator Loh's controversy shows, the British colonial state had significant self-contradictions in its administration and was ignorant of some applications of indirect rule. Their alliance with the Chinese patriarchs quickly collapsed and dramatically turned out to be totally irreconcilable as well. In practice, the patriarchs even invoked their "Chineseness" to play out their *realpolitik*. They collectively reinvented various Chinese practices in order to demonstrate the so-called authentic "traditional Chinese identity." They suddenly shifted to the role of aggressive anticolonialists and expediently drew a new alliance with the postcolonial Chinese state, which was making use of political prerogatives and diplomatic positions against the British.

Alain Touraine is right when he points out that society is not without its reflexivity in questioning its historicity and transforming its dominant cultural model (1988). The real essence of this case does not rest upon the long-standing coalition of the British colonial state with Chinese patriarchs. Neither is it essential that the colonial New Territories actually contained a concurrent patriarchal and colonial (and now a postcolonial) discourse, which suppressed women through its claim of respecting indigenous custom and order. Rather, the importance of these events is that it demonstrates that neither the colonial state nor the Chinese patriarchy in the New Territories could totally determine the lives of the local community and turn it into a governable object. Even with their long coruling of the New Territories, they were not able to suppress dissent when people demanded justice. Ultimately, there was no "male-only" to speak of when women could still be denied their rights.

Throughout their blow-by-blow confrontation in the village, both Deng A-Mei and A-Jin actively used the patriarchs to reach specific ends. To legitimize their different claims over the inheritance, both drew upon their patriarchs to "act" whether they were absent, dead, or alive through their manipulation of cultural symbols and powers. To obtain the official intervention from the colonial state into their private dispute, both took legal action to fight for their specific interest. Whatever the circumstances, neither the patriarchy nor the colonial powers could be really effective but instead they revealed their internal disorders, contradictions, and vulnerabilities.

In these matters, I find Deng A-Mei's dissent from the coercive (patriarchal and colonial) arrangement of her parents' inheritance to be extremely significant and historically meaningful. Her struggle produced an immediate interruption of the manifestation of the patrilineal and patriarchal colonial order via the claimed cultural notion of "Chinese tradition." Her rebellion represented a radical departure in a fight for an essential female interest: the existential right to land. In particular, her case posed a sharp gender question: why would a woman who put her lifelong labor in the land not be entitled to the rights of that land? Her case also makes clear a crucial point that land remains a matter of critical territorial control and economic interest. But it should be also seen as a fundamental cultural right of people and, as Chun once coined it out, "land is to live."[2] It is the essential domain where people undertake their common livelihood, develop their intimate relationships, and create shared experiences among themselves. The loss of their land is a critical deprivation that challenges their existence.

Deng A-Mei's position was not alone. Her dissent had wide-ranging effects. In the context of the Legislator Loh's intervention into the land issue of the New Territories, A-Mei's struggle obtained extensive support from the society. A "war of position" (using Gramsci's term) was aired out in society at large, as she "spoke out" and worked with other radical activists like Legislator Loh, feminists, and women's groups. In this event, forces or bodies ranging from the ordinary indigenous villagers, and the Heung Yee Kuk to members of the Legislative Council, the British colonial government, and the Mainland Chinese officials, could not ignore the dissent.

It is at this point that I can put forward my last remark on the politics of recognition. Thanks to the case of Deng A-Mei, it is now clear that the pursuit of recognition should not be simply a search for normative rules to hold differences together by setting up a common ground, as Charles Taylor has suggested (1992). The pursuit of recognition must also come through many bottom-up struggles in order to open up one's room for maneuver by making sense of and acting upon one's differences. The matter of power and counterpower should not be the only issue. But it should not be entirely removed as a matter of concern either. Continuously reflecting upon the dominant cultural model in specific historical circumstances is of central importance in the dialogical process in the creation of recognition.

British colonial legacy in the New Territories continues down to the present day. It is correct to say that there has been a postcolonial reinvention of the colonial rule in the New Territories. Deng A-Mei's struggle for recognition interestingly elaborates a famous notion of Karl Marx with renewed feminist meaning: "*Man* makes history, but they do not make it just as they please" (Cohen et al. eds., 1979: 103) (emphasis added by the author).

After her ten-year-long struggle came to an end, Deng A-Mei told me that in 1997 she obtained a largely successful result to her land dispute. She compromised with A-Jin through mediation outside the court. A-Mei agreed to allow A-Jin's sons to possess her father's ancestral houses in exchange for the return of her mother's two plots of farmland. In 1998, Deng A-Mei recalled this compromise as follows:

> To begin with, they (A-Jin and her sons) surely did not want to give anything back to me. But, they gradually started wondering about whether they could win the suit in court or not since the law also has been changed. So, they found a village-fellow whom I am also familiar with to talk to me. I told the mediator, "as they said that my father's three ancestral houses were the men's things, it was fine. I could give them to her three sons and would never fight for them. But, I must have my mother's land back as it belonged to my mother. The land was by no means their thing!" By the end of the day, they once again reached me through the mediator and asked me to see the lawyer to finalize the return of my mother's land to me. So, I also went to see my lawyer to cancel my suit against them.

One winter morning, Deng A-Mei led me to see her farms. Upon arriving there, she was overwhelmed by her emotions and once again repeated the many details of her struggle for her land. Out of habit, she unconsciously squatted down, cleared some weeds, and gently felt the surface, checking the soil. With mixed emotions, she picked up some soil and drew in the smells deeply savoring the aromas, an intimate act that she had shared with her mother whom she had sadly missed.

Notes

1. I will discuss the complex lineal relationship between Deng A-Mei's household and A-Jin's household in succeeding account. Now one should be clear that A-Jin's three sons are the closest kinsmen of Deng A-Mei's deceased father in the lineage. The rule of family succession that A-Jin invoked was precisely the patrilineal inheritance practice that required a sonless household to pass their estate to their closest kinsmen's household that has a son in the lineage.
2. In 1985, Allen Chun first coined out this notion of "land is to live" and used it as the topic of his doctoral thesis in contrast with Walter Neale's renowned work *Land Is to Rule* (1969). However, his discussion of this notion in his doctoral thesis was few. He seldom continued to develop it in his later studies too. Even he once again mentioned this notion by using it as a subtopic in one of his recent studies, he still simply showed this notion without enough explicit illustrations (2000). Therefore, I find it necessary to try to extend this important notion from his initial discussion with my ethnographic materials for a better understanding of the substantial meaning of land in the practice of people.

Bibliography

Baker, Hugh D. R. 1966. "The Five Great Clans of the New Territories." *Journal of the Hong Kong Branch of the Royal Asiatic Society* 6, 25–47.

Chan, Selina. 1996. "Negotiating Coloniality and Tradition: The Identity of Indigenous Inhabitants in Hong Kong." *Working Paper Series* 131. Singapore: Department of Sociology, National University of Singapore.

Chun, Allen. 1985. "Land Is to Live: A Study of the Concept of *Tsu* in a Hakka Chinese Village, New Territories, Hong Kong." Ph.D. diss., University of Chicago.

———. 1990. "Policing Society: The 'Rational Practice' of British Colonial Land Administration in the New Territories of Hong Kong c. 1900." *Journal of Historical Sociology* 3, no.4, 401–421.

———. 1996. "The Lineage-Village Complex in Southern China: A Long Footnote in the Anthropology of Kinship." *Current Anthropology* 37, no.3, 429–450.

———. 2000. *Unstructuring Chinese Society: The Fictions of Colonial Practice and the Changing Realities of "Land" in the New Territories of Hong Kong*. Australia: Harwood Academic.

Dyson, Michael Eric. 1994. "Essentialism and the Complexities of Racial Identity." In David Theo Goldberg, ed. *Multiculturalism: A Critical Reader*, 218–229. Oxford: Blackwell.

Eastern Express. 1994. "Villages Pledge to Fight for Tradition." April 18.

Faure, David. 1986. *The Structure of Chinese Rural Society: Lineage and Village in the Eastern New Territories, Hong Kong*. Hong Kong: Oxford University Press.

Freedman, Maurice. 1958. *Lineage Organization in Southeastern China*. London: Athlone Press.

———. 1966. *Chinese Lineage and Society: Fukien and Kwangtung*. London: Athlone Press.

———. 1976. "A Report in Social Research in the New Territories of Hong Kong." *Journal of the Hong Kong Branch of the Royal Asiatic Society* 16, 191–260.

Friedman, John. T. 2005. "Making Politics, Making History: Chiefship and the Post-apartheid State in Namibia." *Journal of Southern African Studies* 31, no.1, 23–50.

Goldberg, David Theo. 1994. "Introduction: Multicultural Conditions." In Goldberg, ed. *Multiculturalism*, 1–44.

Heung Yee Kuk. 1996. "Nanwang de shiyue, nanwang de guanghui, nanwang de chuantong: Xiangyiju qishi zhounian jinian tekan" (Unforgettable Time, Unforgettable Glory,

Unforgettable Misery). *Special Issue for the 70th Anniversary of Heung Yee Kuk*, 78–79. Hong Kong: Heung Yee Kuk.
Hong Kong Government. 1899. "Despatches and Other Papers Relating to the Extension of the Colony of Hongkong." In *Papers Laid before the Legislative Council of Hong Kong*. Hong Kong: Hong Kong Government Printers.
———. 1905. "New Territories Land Ordinance." In *Hong Kong Government Gazette* 3. Hong Kong: Hong Kong Government Printers.
———. 1910. *Law of Hong Kong, Chapter 97, New Territories Land Ordinance*. Hong Kong: Hong Kong Government Printers.
———. 1984. *Law of Hong Kong, Chapter 97, New Territories Land Ordinance*. Hong Kong: Hong Kong Government Printers.
Hong Kong Legislative Council. 1993. *Report of the Meetings 1993/94, PT. 2*, 1040–1042. Hong Kong: Hong Kong Government Printers.
———. 1994. *Report of the Meetings 1993/94, PT. 6*, 4539–4589. Hong Kong: Hong Kong Government Printers.
Huang, Shu Min. 1982. "Hong Kong's Colonial Administration and the Land Tenure System." In Shu Min Huang, ed. *Rural Hong Kong: The Anthropological Perspectives*, 56–72. Ames, IA: Iowa State University Department of Sociology and Anthropology.
Jones, Carol. 1995. "The New Territories Inheritance Law: Colonization and the Elites." In Veronica Pearson and Benjamin K. P. Leung, eds. *Women in Hong Kong*, 167–192. Hong Kong: Oxford University Press.
Lam, Cheong-Yee Eric. 1986. "An Assessment of the Role of the Heung Yee Kuk in the Formulation of Rural Politics in the New Territories." Ph.D. diss., University of Hong Kong.
Ming Pao. 1994a. "Xiangyiju chengli baojia weizu kangzheng zongbu, cu gangfu guangfan diaocha yuanjumin yixiang" (Heung Yee Kuk established the communal headquarters in defense families and clans, and urged the Hong Kong Government to collect people's opinion by full investigation). March 26.
———. 1994b. "Yuanze zhide budaibiao chuantong zhishi" (The fight for principle will not result in the loss of tradition). March 31.
Moberg, Mark. 1992. "Continuity under Colonial Rule: The Alcadle System and the Garifuna in Belize, 1858–1969." *Ethnohistory* 39, no.1, 1–19.
Neale, Walter. 1969. "Land Is to Rule." In Robert Eric Frykenberg, ed. *Land Control and Social Structure in Indian History*, 3–15. Madison, WI: University of Wisconsin Press.
Nelson, Howard G. H. 1969. "British Administration in the New Territories of Hong Kong and Its Effects on Chinese Social Organization." Paper presented at the London-Cornell Project for East and Southeast Studies Conference, Adele en Haut (August 24–30).
Ng, Wai Man. 1996. "Village Revitalization/Disintegration: An Assessment of Suburbanization, Land Administration and Small House Development in the New Territories." Ph.D. diss., University of Hong Kong.
Nicholas, Thomas. 1999. *Democracy Denied: Identity, Civil Society and Illiberal Democracy in Hong Kong*. Aldershot, Hampshire, UK: Ashgate.
Ranger, Terrance. 1996. "The Invention of Tradition in Colonial Africa." In Eric Hobsbawm and Terrance Ranger, eds. *The Invention of Tradition*, 211–262. Cambridge: Cambridge University Press.
Rex, John. 1992. *Race and Ethnicity*. Milton Keynes, UK: Open University Press.
Said, Edward. 1994. *Culture and Imperialism*. New York: Vintage books.
South China Morning Post. 1994a. "Inheritance Protest Ends in Violence." March 23.
———. 1994b. "Rural Visit Passes off Peacefully." March 27.

Stiehm, Judith. 1994. "Diversity's Diversity." In Goldberg, ed. *Multiculturalism*, 140–156.
Taylor, Charles. 1992. *Multiculturalism and the Politics of Recognition*. Princeton, NJ: Princeton University Press.
Touraine, Alain. 1988. *Return of the Actor: Social Theory in Postindustrial Society*. Minneapolis, MN: University of Minnesota Press.
Watson, Rubie. S. 1985. *Inequality among Brothers: Class and Kinship in South China*. Cambridge: Cambridge University Press.
Welsh, Frank. 1993. *A History of Hong Kong*. London: HarperCollins.
Wesley-Smith, Peter. 1980. *Unequal Treaty 1898–1997: China, Britain and Hong Kong's New Territories*. Hong Kong: Oxford University Press.
Xiandai ribao. 1994. "Xiuding tiaoli wu yingmou, peng dinghang: Shunying nannu pingdeng" (No conspiracy behind the Amendment Bill, Chris Patten: This is just to meet the call for gender equality). March 30.
Zhang, Yuefeng, Jiang Qiongzhu, and Liu Yanfen, eds. 1995. *Cong zhe yitian kaishi: Zhengqu pingdeng jichengquan zilaice* (From the present day on: A resource book on the fight for equal inheritance right). Hong Kong: Funu Tuanti Zhengqu Pingdeng Jichengquan Lianxi.

CHAPTER TEN

Making Rights Claims Visible: Intersectionality, NGO Activism, and Cultural Politics in Hong Kong

LISA FISCHLER

Introduction

Since the late nineteenth century many Hong Kong groups have been fighting for formal governmental and societal recognition of their rights. Women's struggles have been a significant part of that history: activism has led to prowomen's rights legislation and to the gradual public awareness of gender issues. However, the local women's movement both evolved as part of broader civil society mobilization and emerged at the intersection of gender, race, class, ethnicity, and other markers of cultural identity. During Hong Kong's political transition to China (1984–1997), the scope of political debate and action over gender issues broadened tremendously, not just through the actions of local women nongovernmental organizations (NGOs) but also due to the activism of other local political actors. The struggles between "pro-Beijing" and "prodemocratic" groups during the transition showed local politics to be gendered—that is "gender [was] present in the processes, practices, images and ideologies, and distributions of power in the various sectors of [socio-political] life" (Lee, 1998: 164). Yet, gender was not the only form of cultural identity that shaped and was shaped by local activism. Groups other than local women's NGOs deployed notions of gender, class, ethnicity, and locale to press for the formal recognition of rights claims by government and legislators.[1]

Since Hong Kong became a Special Administrative Region (SAR) of the People's Republic of China (PRC) in 1997, government efforts to effectively meet the challenges of globalization by turning Hong Kong into a world city have been paralleled by increased Hong Kong NGOs' local alliance building and regional networking. A significant part of NGO activity has been in response to globalization's negative impact on multiple social sectors in Hong Kong. In this context, diverse political groups' use of different constructions of cultural identity, including gender, to push for formal recognition of their moral claims continues to shape postcolonial Hong Kong politics. Political consolidation, globalization, and responses to each by NGOs have made women issues into visible transnational, regional, and local concerns, though this has not translated into greater government and legislative recognition of women's rights than in the colonial period. How has the interconnectedness of cultural identity, politics, and gender that continues to shape and be shaped by the activism of women's groups and NGOs in post-1997 Hong Kong impacted the public awareness of these organizations' moral claims? To answer this question, this chapter utilizes the notion of "intersectionality"—a framework that considers "historically constructed and hierarchical power systems and the politics of personal interactions, including meanings and representations in the experience of individuals" (Dill et al., 2001: 4).

During the pre-1997 transition, when opposing conceptions of womanhood were politicized by contending national identity projects (political struggles between pro-Beijing and prodemocratic groups) two competing discourses emerged. One espoused rapid electoral reform, the executive's accountability to a legislature, the rule of law, and individual freedoms. The other advocated a Singapore-like, conservative Confucian-based, collective social responsibility to the ruling regime (Fischler, 2000). These discourses were undergirded by rival conceptions of gender: the "process and the patterning of difference and domination based on perceived differences between the sexes" (Lee, 1998: 164). The local prodemocratic camp, pursuing a liberal agenda of democratization, made political causes of grassroots women's, female workers', single parents', and housewives' individual entitlements. The local pro-Beijing contingent, seeking a conservative, colonial-modeled, executive-led system, stressed women's collective obligations to family and community (Fischler, 2000). Gender issues related to politicized conceptions of womanhood became active political concerns. But they were cross-cut by conceptions of class (blue collar versus white collar), ethnicity (indigenous versus local), locale (urban versus rural), family status (single versus married), occupation (unemployed versus employed), and race (Hong Kong Chinese versus Asian migrant). In short, intertwined forms of cultural identity, the hallmark of intersectionality, were the factors shaping particular injustices and campaigns to remedy them (Rooney, 2007).

The post-1997 conservative Hong Kong government faces the challenges of an unconsolidated regime, the presence of both pro-Beijing (now progovernment or pro–status quo) and prodemocratic (now "pro–social justice" or "pro–human rights") actors in formal politics, and the constitutionally unresolved limits to Hong Kong's sovereignty. Such new crises and actors distinguish the post-1997 era from previous decades in Hong Kong's history. The aftermath of the 1997–1998 Asian financial crisis brought home how interconnected globalization affected the East Asian region, prompted government efforts to meet the obstacles of the global era more effectively, and evoked local NGOs' collective responses to globalization's negative impact (Ku and Pun, eds., 2006; Chiu and Lui, 2004; Forrest et al., 2004). Diversified migration, housing and land availability, educational concerns about the language of instruction, citizenship, autonomy from the PRC, and rising poverty and unemployment all acquired a new immediacy as political issues. Hong Kong NGOs took up these issues, accompanied as they were by long-standing concerns like increased social exclusion and social divisions "in terms of class, ethnicity, and gender" (Ku and Pun, eds., 2006: 9). Local political struggles, consequently, employed intersecting constructions of cultural identity in their campaigns for rights recognition, which were simultaneously struggles for "'redistribution' of economic, political, and cultural state power" readily revealed by intersectionality (Rooney, 2007).

The conflicts and cooperation among NGOs and the Hong Kong government during the transition period strengthened local identity, propelled NGO members into formal politics, fostered NGOs' views of themselves as watchdogs of local politics, and connected the same NGOs more solidly to international activist networks (Chiu and Lui, eds., 2000). Against this background of Hong Kong's global integration, many NGOs in the post-1997 era have dealt with the challenges of globalization. For example, migrant women workers in Hong Kong today come from a wider range of countries in South and Southeast Asia than they did several decades ago. This not only gives rise to a more diversified membership for NGOs, but also challenges the organizations to address the different needs of both Hong Kong women and migrant women workers in local society.[2] Two ways in which Hong

Kong NGOs have met such issues are through fluid local coalition-building and regional networking with transnational and East Asian NGOs. To examine how these strategies impact the visibility of rights claims, this chapter looks at the employment of varied cultural identity constructions by local and regional NGOs as ways to press for formal recognition of their rights as shown in the Fifth East Asian Women's NGO Forum in 2003 and the Sixth World Trade Organization (WTO) Ministerial Conference in 2005. These events, convened in post-1997 Hong Kong, provide a lens through which to evaluate the complicated relations between the international-regional-and-local links of Hong Kong NGOs' activism, cultural politics, and the growing awareness of rights by a public that has also become more globalized since Hong Kong's handover.

Precursors: Cultural Politics and the Local Democracy Movement, 1997–2003

The years leading up to the Fifth East Asian Women's NGO Forum revealed the primary factors shaping public visibility of local NGOs' and women activists' struggles for formal recognition of rights in Hong Kong. Following the handover of Hong Kong to China on July 1, 1997, the executive-led SAR regime and legislators faced the immense task of debating and effecting laws by which to govern. One basis for deriving rules of governance was the Basic Law, Hong Kong's mini-constitution. A controversial "blueprint" rather than a legally ratified document, the Basic Law contained numerous gray areas left to Hong Kong's governing officials to implement constitutionally. One of these gray areas was Article 23 of the Basic Law, designed to "prohibit acts of subversion against the central government, sedition, theft of state secrets, and to control political activities by foreign organizations and ties with local organizations" (Lee, 2003: 202). Concerned with local organizations' global connections, Article 23 sought to monitor membership in local NGOs, financial resources, and family networks that became global as local residents emigrated overseas. The SAR government began legislating Article 23 in 2002, but the newness of Hong Kong's relationship with its sovereign in Beijing posed problems for the SAR's autonomy in governance. As Thomas Tse notes, "there [were] doubts about the precedence of 'one country' over the 'two systems,' and there [was even] talk of Hong Kong reverting quickly to 'one country, one system'... given that Hong Kong [was] on the verge of recolonization" (Tse, 2006: 67).[3] In short, Hong Kong's status in relation to the central government in Beijing is still unclear.

In 2003, the SAR's announcement of a legislative bill regarding Article 23 drew a huge wave of local resistance representing a revival of the local democracy movement that had gained so much experience of collective action during the pre-1997 transition period (Lam, 2003). On July 1, 2003 the Hong Kong government learned, as had its British colonizers, that whether hard or soft, authoritarian regimes need a modicum of local support to maintain power.[4] Local organizers of the demonstration united under the slogan "Against Article 23; Return Power to the People." But most people participating in the march were neither activists nor affiliates of local organizations (Chan and Chung, 2007). Evidence suggests that on July 2, 2003, people of Hong Kong were extremely angry and dissatisfied with the SAR's economic and political performance over the past six years, and that they came out to protest in huge numbers—500,000 by the end of the day (DeGolyer, 2003; Lam, 2004). Economic downturn after the Asian financial crisis, the SARS epidemic, and the failed official promises of reform and accountability were the reasons for popular protest against the legislation of Article 23 (Hong Kong Transition Project, 2005). Although mobilization efforts by Human Civil Rights Front, the demonstration's local organizer, resonated with local residents, media communication by newspapers and radio programs, political communication concerning Article 23 by lawyers and social communication about the march by friends and family using the Internet and other technology also prompted local residents to turn out on July 1 (Chan and Chung, 2007). As a result, the government withdrew its antisubversion bill indefinitely from legislative consideration (Lam, 2004).

Progovernment groups as well as activists against Article 23, through competing public events, deployed intersecting but not necessarily compatible forms of cultural identity to support local political agendas. Progovernment groups held a carnival wherein a troupe of young women rehearsed a contemporary dance number under the direction of a rather stern older man.[5] The vivacious young women featured in the carnival have been a stock component of events organized by progovernment political groups to push for community unity, political status quo, and regime support. This construction of a paternalistic, protective approach toward young women was gendered and generational, deferential to male leadership and to youth's public appeal. In contrast, at events sponsored by pro–social justice, prodemocracy grassroots groups, young women were more likely to be seen speaking out against gender discrimination, advocating women's independence, and pushing for women's individual empowerment. On July 1, 2003, women in the "pro–social justice" camp appropriated symbols of Chinese cultural nationalism from a song called "Dream of China" (*Jung Gwok Muhng*) to rally residents in support of local, pro–human rights, and social justice causes. A dynamic, prodemocratic, local woman organizer, Gum Gum, took center stage at the antigovernment bill march to sing "Dream of China." She attempted to mobilize local people by appealing to a common Chinese cultural heritage in Hong Kong.[6] Gum Gum, as a visible political figure and women's activist, advocated gender empowerment through her performance. But she also employed an ethnic notion of "Chinese united" to raise public awareness of Human Civil Rights Front's moral claims. These strategies of progovernment and pro–human rights groups demonstrated how social and cultural categories intertwined locally, and how "the different perspectives connected to power" shaped the "mechanisms of inclusion and exclusion" (Knudsen, 2006).

The revival of the local democracy movement in July 2003 was tightly linked to stronger, pro–social justice women's activism. Prodemocratic candidates, including Gum Gum, won directly elected seats in the District Board elections of November 2003. While the District Boards represented the lowest and least powerful level of Hong Kong's political system, their focus on neighborhood affairs and local livelihood issues often made them a weathervane of shifting political currents. The November 2003 election represented a landslide victory for the Democratic Party, whose support at the polls had been slipping since the 1997 handover. But greater dissatisfaction with the government's performance reduced the electoral support for progovernment groups and led to surprising victories for local women activists such as Gum Gum, who were affiliated with the July 1 demonstration (Member of local women's group, 2003).[7] Gum Gum was a very multifaceted grassroots activist. Having been a longtime member of two different women's NGOs that were highly active during Hong Kong's political transition, she helped organize the July 1 protest, won a seat in the District Board election in Wan Chai, and globalized women's issues at the Women's Conference in Beijing in 1995. Hong Kong women's activism shows that gender and class intertwined to shape public visibility of political causes in 2003. Collaboration among different class sectors in Hong Kong has been important for local politics because previous coalitions of nonelites and elites brought about sustained momentum for campaigns that had successfully abolished women's bonded servitude in the 1950s, waged a war against rape in the 1970s, pressured the colonial government to sign a Bill of Rights in 1991, gained the rights of inheritance for rural women in 1994, and helped bring about freer and fairer elections in Hong Kong during the early 1990s (Wong, 2000; Choi, 1995).

The Fifth East Asian Women's NGO Forum

Legal Recognition and Gender Discrimination

The Fifth East Asian Women's Forum shows the ways in which the use of different, intersecting cultural identity constructions by local and regional women's NGOs influenced informal recognition of women's rights by a regional rather than a local public. NGO Forums at each of the United Nations World Conferences on Women have become politically complex arenas in which to press for formal recognition of women's rights by home governments and communities (Meyer and Prűgl, ed., 1999). Following the 1995 Women's Conference in Beijing, regional East Asian Women's NGO Forums were held in South Korea, Mongolia, Taiwan, and Hong Kong. But the local political context, which is structured by inclusionary and exclusionary processes based on interconnected differences like gender, class, and ethnicity, has often been the gauge of local women's global involvement. When the East Asian Women's Forum was held in Taiwan, for instance, PRC women did not attend because of the opposing interpretations of Taiwan's political status among the PRC, Taiwan, and the international community (Member of a local women's organization, 2003). In effect, the majority of the local women's movements in East Asia function within ambivalent political spaces wherein the essentialism or pureness of culture and identity are disputable.[8] However, resource-based inequalities, gender differences (including those among women), local politics, and international connections have conditioned the particular and often conflicting ways different women's NGOs address gender issues, deal with women's rights, and organize on behalf of women throughout East Asia. Addressing, dealing with, and organizing on behalf of women represent informal kinds of recognition of gender issues by East Asian women themselves. But different approaches to women's rights translated into a process of negotiation among East Asian women's NGOs over what types of formal recognition were desired from respective societies and governments. Discussions over gender mainstreaming, migrant labor, and sexual violence at the Fifth East Asian Women's Forum, held at the Hong Kong Baptist University on December 19–22, 2003, reveal the complexities of achieving informal recognition of women's rights among East Asian women's NGOs.

Gender Mainstreaming and Migrant Labor

Migrant women laborers and gender mainstreaming are transnational issues in East Asia, but "intersectionality" best captures how women's NGOs in different places within the region proposed to resolve these issues. At the Forum, many East Asian women's NGOs saw the economic restructuring that followed the Asian financial crisis as reinforcing the feminization of poverty and devaluing women's works (EAWF, 2003). Compared with the past, the feminist movement in Japan had broadened positively to include the issue of migrant women laborers, which underscored the class, ethnic, and racial differences among East Asian women that intertwined with gender relations (Buckley, ed., 1997). In one workshop, Oshita, the representative for the Solidarity Network for Migrants in Japan, described the lack of support by women's NGOs in Japan for helping migrant women laborers who had married Japanese men to gain citizenship. Japan's gendered nationality law was a government project,[9] but Japanese women's NGOs wanted migrant women to be respected as "Thai" or "Filipina" rather than being assimilated as "Japanese" (Fischler, 2003). The reasons put forward by Japanese women's NGOs reflected their own local fight for all women to be recognized as full citizens in Japan. Their refusal to support migrant women laborers' struggles for citizenship, however, denied a basic civil right recognized in the United Nations Declaration of Human Rights to women of a different ethnicity and class. Ethnic and class constructions of Asian migrant women within Japanese NGOs highlighted the gender differences among women and obstructed the formal recognition of migrant women laborers' rights in Japan.

Yet, women's NGOs from the PRC discussed the issue of gender mainstreaming in ways that indicated that local constructions of women could be mediated by international contexts. Drawing from international symposiums on development, women's NGOs from the PRC and South Korea defined "gender mainstreaming" as strategies to fully incorporate women's and men's "concerns and experiences" into political, social, and economic policymaking mechanisms to achieve gender equality (Chung, 2003: 8). One of the main reasons cited by women's NGOs in the PRC for continued gender inequality was a "lack of gender sensitivity" on the part of men domestically; yet, "promoting gender mainstreaming" also meant working more closely with men to promote gender equality. Women's issues are not highly visible in PRC policymaking because discussion of them is often confined to women. On the other hand, limited opportunities and resources go to men, and effective tools for gender analysis in politics and the economy are scarce (Fischler, 2003). Caught in a dilemma, women's NGOs in the PRC draw on international practices to bring about change for women, but have to face local limitations to their implementation.[10] Local gender inequalities condition the ways formal recognition of women's rights works out in practice for women's NGOs in the PRC, yet the Forum provided an arena where gender differences could be informally acknowledged by participants who might have been reluctant to discuss these differences in their own polity.

Women and Sexual Violence

Migrant women's labor in East Asia is intimately related to issues of transregional sex work, multinational trafficking in women, the cross-border keeping of second wives and mistresses (*baau yih naai*), and sexual violence against women. The workshop on sexual violence at the December 2003 Forum demonstrated that power inequities based on cross-cutting forms of cultural identity, specifically ethnicity, class, and gender, partly shaped not only the outcomes of women's organizing but also plans for gaining socio-political recognition of women's rights. Hong Kong women's NGOs, for example, discussed how they turned their 1970s war on rape campaign into a legal victory.[11] Drawing on international legal standards and local expertise, Hong Kong women's NGOs and legislators shared how they made marital rape a legal offense in 2002.[12] Yet, they also noted that implementing the law was problematic: the police refused to take reports of marital rapes, and public education to change husbands' views lagged behind. In addition, the issue of migrant women being raped by their employers was not addressed. Women's NGOs in South Korea and Taiwan discussed how they helped to expand the meaning of sexual violence in the law by drawing on international precedents. In South Korea, the law came to include physical, verbal, psychological, and cyberspace violence; in Taiwan, the law addressed crimes against sexual autonomy. Once again, the local situation of migrant women workers was not discussed. Not addressing "other" Asian women, who were of a different ethnicity and class, however, shows the inequalities that emerged discursively at the intersections of cultural identities and rights claims (Rooney, 2007).

East Asian Women and Forum Politics

Interconnected markers of cultural identity and global politics shaped the process by which East Asian women's NGOs formulated a summary document concerning women's rights at the December 2003 Forum. This document, given its regional political audiences in the form of other NGOs and governments, constituted a type of informal recognition of gender issues and women's rights by the East Asian women's NGOs at the Forum. In an overnight session prior to closing ceremonies, six women from the Forum's steering committee, who all represented different ethnicities, classes, generations, and women's interests from East Asia, produced a draft for participants in the Forum to debate. Some of the significant discussions over wording and clauses included sexuality, migrant labor, and peace. There were only two sentences about the contribution of the Young Women's Caucus to the Forum's proceedings. As it stated, "traditional notions of women's body, sexuality, and gender identity are strongly challenged by young women."[13] The more established, elite women activists in South Korean and Japanese NGOs objected to this sentence. They asked that older women be included in this sentence as each generation of feminists had challenged traditional notions of women's identity. Yet, Gum Gum, the well-known Hong Kong activist, moderated the Young Women's Caucus. She insisted that the real issues at stake were sexual orientation and freedom over one's sex life at an early age, and that these issues were new for East Asian women's movements (Fischler, 2003). The debate among women's NGOs over sexuality revealed how the Forum's discussions were intersectional: through the use of generational differences among women to negotiate the wording of a document pressing for formal recognition of women's rights by respective East Asian governments.

Feminist perspectives that took into account the intertwined gender, class, ethnic, and demographic differences among women contributed to a better understanding of the dynamics of rights recognition at the Fifth East Asian Women's Forum.[14] One early paragraph in the draft declaration listed the negative effects of globalization in East Asia as "feminization of poverty, feminization of agriculture, marginalization of women in employment, deterioration of labor standard[s], intensification of trafficking in women."[15] The discussion over this phrase showed the influence of local politics on women's organizing and the informal recognition of women's rights at this international forum. Delegates from South Korea, Japan, and Hong Kong asked for the addition of "forced migration" to the list of globalization's negative effects. The only objection came from women's NGOs in the PRC who wanted to use "displaced persons" (*lixiang renshi*) instead of "forced migration" because, as they argued, migration was not always forced. The objection of the PRC delegates can be interpreted in light of the international concerns and domestic protests over the relocation of people along the Three Gorges. It is estimated that the construction of the Three Gorges Dam forced more than 2 million people to relocate (Chetham, 2004). The inclusion of "forced migration" in the final published version of the document (EAWF, 2003) shows the mediating impact of international contexts on local crosscutting cultural identity constructions. Formal recognition of women migrants might not occur domestically, but the enhanced regional public awareness of their situation took place through the Forum's summary document.

Cooperation across Borders

As surmised from the Fifth East Asian Women's NGO Forum, increasingly diverse women's NGOs, different women activists' participation in formal politics, a reinvigorated local prodemocracy movement, intersectional cultural politics, and growing international and regional ties with local organizations in Hong Kong have shaped much informal and some formal recognition of women's rights. The issues of comfort women, sexual violence, and migration have produced broader informal recognition and regional collaboration among women's NGOs. Within Hong Kong, women's NGOs continue to gain some formal recognition for some of the rights of different women. Yet, attention to women's issues internationally has been accompanied by more dramatic reasons for concern about women and their rights. One cause for such concern is growing humanitarian crises wherein human rights violations become a basis for peacekeeping operations or international military intervention (Chandler, 2002). Increasingly austere structural adjustment packages that ameliorate debt but grossly impede sustainable local development and impoverish more women on balance are also a concern (Naples and Desai, eds., 2002). In addition, concern is raised by the greater complexity in the ties between migration due to global economic inequities, and drugs, disease, trafficking in humans (especially women and children), and sexual slavery (Uçarer, 1999).

Adding to these, recognition of women's rights has been shaped by intersectionality: intertwined factors such as class, ethnicity, and gender that are mechanisms of inclusion and exclusion, as is evident in the variety of lived experiences of East Asian women. The concerns of the Young Women's Caucus at the Fifth East Asian Women's Forum are indicative of new issues such as sexual orientation and sexual freedoms that are not being addressed by mainstream women's movements, both conservative and liberal, in Chinese polities and East Asia due to generational and class differences among women activists. Gum Gum is an important example of how a local grassroots activist has been determined to reconcile these new women's issues with the preexisting political agendas in Hong Kong's grassroots activism. Moreover, local politics and legal customs allow for expedient solutions that result in the formal recognition of some women's rights, but leave gaps in implementation and enforcement. A good example was Japan's Equal Opportunities Law of 1986, which failed to create effective legal and financial mechanisms of rewarding employers who provided women with equal job opportunities (Buckley, 1997). Another example was Hong Kong's amendment to the inheritance law for indigenous (ethnically distinct from Hong Kong Chinese) women of the rural New Territories in 1994, as discussed by Siu-Keung Cheung in chapter nine. The Hong Kong government failed to address the indigenous women's rights to vote or run for election because the long-established "small house policy" had prevented some indigenous women from inheriting and some women such as divorcees, widows, and single female parents from exercising the same housing rights that the urban females enjoyed (Wong, 2000; Tong, 1999).

The Sixth WTO Ministerial Conference

A similar combination of political dynamics, NGOs' strategic use of interconnected cultural constructions, and responses to globalization's influences that shaped outcomes at the Fifth East Asian Women's NGO Forum also helped structure the informal recognition of livelihood entitlements at the Sixth WTO's Ministerial Convention held in Hong Kong in December 2005. The year prior to the Sixth WTO Ministerial Conference was an eventful one in terms of both NGO activism and local Hong Kong politics. In January 2005, more than 200 NGOs met in Hong Kong, during another international conference, to begin organizing antiglobalization movements that would take place during the Sixth WTO Ministerial Conference in Hong Kong.[16] The coordinating organization for these NGO efforts was the Hong Kong People's Alliance (HKPA), headed by the Hong Kong Confederation of Trade Unions (CTU).[17] The antiglobalization efforts under the HKPA began several days prior to the official opening of the Sixth WTO Ministerial Conference (hereafter referred to as "the Conference") in the form of a well-attended public protest march. At this point, the gender dimensions of these events were quite muted because, unlike other UN forums wherein a gender perspective has become an integral part of the proceedings, official WTO conferences deliberately lack a gender focus (Hernandez, 2006).[18] Globalization has disproportionately disadvantaged women, particularly impoverished rural women in developing countries, through the unequal terms dictated by structural adjustment programs of the World Bank. Consequently, there also were class and demographic (urban versus rural) dimensions to antiglobalization struggles (Naples and Desai, eds., 2002). As partly evidenced by the Fifth East Asian Women's Forum, globalization also had broadened cooperation among regional, local, and international NGOs. The prominent spokesperson of the HKPA was an active and visible HKCTU member, Elizabeth Ying-Ngo Teng, who was a pro-social justice, pro-women's rights supporter.

Despite lacking an explicit gender perspective for WTO Ministerial Conferences, in contrast to other UN forums, the Sixth WTO Ministerial Conference brought greater public awareness of women's rights, but in ways that were dependent on both the broader issues upon which antiglobalization activists were focused and the strategic constructions of class, gender, and ethnicity that sustained their campaigns. As far as the East Asian region was concerned, these broader issues related to the problems of agriculture and services within the context of economic inequities and power disparities between developed and developing nations. Such larger concerns emerged from the focus of the Doha Development Round of the Sixth WTO Ministerial Conference. On the other hand, globalization, in this case the highly uneven spread of capitalist free trade, had and continues to have a profoundly negative impact on migrants, sex workers, and rural farmers, a substantive percentage of whom are women. These issues helped shape the informal recognition of rights and entitlements that emerged, both locally and internationally, from antiglobalization protests during the WTO Conference in 2005.

Services, Agriculture, and South Korean Farmers

In December 2005, intersections of class, ethnicity, and demographic constructions of cultural identity shaped and were shaped by antiglobalization NGOs. The legacy of the Fifth WTO Ministerial Conference in 2003 at Cancun, Mexico was strong at the Sixth WTO Ministerial Conference in Hong Kong because of both a South Korean farmer's suicide and the Hong Kong government and local media in a post-9/11 world. Korean farmer, Lee Kyung-hae, whose ethnicity was not Hong Kong Chinese, had committed suicide at the Fifth WTO Ministerial Conference in Cancun over great anger and despair at the negative impact, to the point of impoverishment, of the WTO on agricultural jobs in countries like South Korea (Kelsey, 2005). Due, in part, to the lack of WTO attention devoted to Lee's fatal protest and the inability of the antiglobalization demonstrators in Cancun to present their case at the Fifth Ministerial Conference, the South Korean farmers cooperated with the Hong Kong People's Alliance in organizing antiglobalization protests for the Sixth WTO Ministerial Conference, but also came with their own agenda of interrupting the actual meeting to have their case heard (Fischler, 2005).[19] In the context of a post-9/11 U.S.-generated climate of fear, the Hong Kong government and local media helped fuel the potential explosiveness of the South Korean farmers' presence at the antiglobalization protests. They issued public warnings and took visible and pervasive security precautions against the "terrorists," the relatively poor, rural, ethnically non-Chinese farmers, who were soon to arrive from South Korea to disrupt the Conference (Member of local human rights organization, 2005; Fischler, 2005).

Hong Kong residents braced for what they presumed was to be an onslaught by antiglobalization protestors, especially South Korean farmers, as constructed by the Hong Kong government and media. Shop owners either closed their doors and risked losing much-valued business, barricaded their main entrances with the metal gates and directed customers to enter by side doors, or hung protective netting across large business windows to stop any projectiles thrown by protestors (Fischler, 2005). The Hong Kong police and antiriot police came out in full force during the Conference; government officials designated a single protest route; city workers created and barricaded a demonstration site, well away from the Hong Kong Convention Centre where the Conference convened; police redirected traffic around Hong Kong to accommodate the daily scheduled protest marches; and security covered walkways and overpasses in strong netting.[20] Amidst this tense atmosphere, first-day disruption of the Conference by 50 of the 200 NGOs accredited to attend the actual meeting in the Convention Centre, and second-day aggressive efforts by South Korean farmers to push back against antiriot police shields and reach the actual Convention Centre, reinforced the local public's negative perceptions about the antiglobalization demonstrators.[21] Yet, the South Korean farmers did something to alter popular prejudices. Using a "three steps, one prostration" marching style that involved taking three steps walking upright and forward, then sliding one's body flat with face to the ground and arms outstretched over one's head before beginning the sequence again along the designated protest route, they demonstrated they were not violent but loyal to the earth and occupation, and good, ethical Buddhists (Local historian, 2005).[22]

Like the pilgrimage-style marches, television-prompted association of the protesting Korean farmers with the heroine of a contemporary Korean drama, "Jewel in the Palace," abruptly shifted Hong Kong residents' views of the NGOs. "Jewel in the Palace," a drama that first aired in 2003 on South Korean television, rapidly gained popularity in many Asian countries.[23] The drama is about the life of the first female physician, Jang Geum (*Cheung Gum, Chang Jin*), in medieval Korea, a time and place when women had few rights by contemporary UN standards. In Hong Kong during the 2005 WTO Ministerial Conference, Jang Geum became a female icon that virtually eradicated the Hong Kong public's antipathy toward the South Korean farmers as well as apathy toward local politics. South Korean antiglobalization activists became "filial sons and daughters" and "moral workers" fighting for their legitimate rights for a now aware local and regional public. Moreover, the Hong Kong media's use of a regionally popular female icon, in the form of Jang Geum, constructed a softer, feminized public persona for the once "terrorist," rural, poor, Korean farmers. Jang Geum's position as a female in an exclusively male occupation incidentally drew much public attention to livelihood entitlements in many modern Asian societies. In addition, women, through the actions of the South Korean NGOs and the media's coverage, could now be perceived, similarly to the rural, poor, South Korean farmers, as victims of the WTO's policies and globalization. Women, too, became empowered to struggle for their deserved rights. Public awareness of women's rights emerged at the intersections of class, ethnic, and demographic constructions that shaped and were shaped by East Asian NGO activism.

NGOs and Women's Rights: Migration, Sex Work, and Violence

During the Sixth Ministerial Conference in 2005, many of the antiglobalization local, regional, and international NGOs held indoor forums, teach-ins, networking sessions, collaborative book signings, victims' tribunals, and workshops that highlighted the interconnectedness between cultural factors affecting informal recognition of rights claims. Important women-related concerns were migration, sex work, and violence (Fischler, 2005). Given its parallels with "intersectionality" as it focuses on inclusionary and exclusionary mechanisms, one analytically useful way of categorizing the presentation and discussion of these issues both within antiglobalization protests and at other NGO activities during the Conference is the "inside-outside" dichotomy employed by Jane Kelsey to describe physical, material, and symbolic divisions between protestors and accredited Ministerial Conference participants at Cancun in 2003 (Kelsey, 2005).

While media-driven public attention was garnered through the gendered relationship between the South Korean farmers who were protesting the WTO and the icon of Jang Geum, NGO-organized, in-depth discussions and presentation inside small tents, classrooms, and meeting halls mostly located on Hong Kong Island offered informal recognition of Asian women's rights. Such informal recognition came in the form of written declarations for change directed to WTO leaders, collaborative research studies, and recommendations on migrant women of different ethnicities and working-class women laborers published and distributed at NGO workshops, and tribunals, to name but a few. Rural women negatively impacted by WTO policies were encouraged to claim legitimate entitlement to their rights for social and economic justice (Fischler, 2005). In contrast to the media's shaping of public awareness of women's status through the gendered figure of Jang Geum, NGO activities had a more directed focus: awareness that women indeed were deserving of specific rights. Several examples of local NGO activism in Hong Kong lend credence to this definition of informal recognition of women's rights.

Although protest activity directed toward the plight of sex workers around the Asian region was clearly visible on signs and placards in the antiglobalization marches, informal recognition of sex workers' rights also was an objective of NGO activism. One leader of a local Hong Kong NGO fighting for sex workers' entitlements explained that sex workers from other parts of the world, including mainland China, were coming to Hong Kong to join the antiglobalization demonstrations in order to protest the violation of their rights by police and the laws that criminalized prostitution. For this NGO member, there was an intertwined gender, class, and ethnic relationship between WTO policies, globalization, and the impoverishment that brought about these women's entry into sex work, especially the unemployment of their husbands. When asked what she would want from the WTO, this activist replied that she would ask the WTO to give sex workers a voice to speak to the WTO because they had no representation in the organization. She also added that she wanted the WTO to give sex workers rights as legitimate workers (Member of local women's NGO, 2005). How she recognized the rights of sex workers and how she would have demanded the WTO's recognition of the sex workers' rights indicated an intersectionality in cultural identity factors influencing informal recognition of women's status by Hong Kong NGOs.

During the daily antiglobalization marches, WTO monitors were busy writing down slogans and observing NGOs involved in the protests. While this may have raised awareness within the WTO about the situation of migrant women throughout Asia, it was the deliberate efforts by local and regional NGOs following arrests of South Korean farmers on the second-to-last day of the Conference that show an emerging informal recognition of women's rights. Over 900 demonstrators, many of them South Korean farmers, were arrested by Hong Kong police in what proved to be the most violent clash between antiglobalization protestors and antiriot police.[24] While some of the farmers were female, the Hong Kong media once again constructed those arrested as masculine, violent protestors. In contrast, the majority of local NGOs trying to gain the release of the arrested protestors constructed their concerns in terms of rights for protective, caring, humane treatment while incarcerated and of a fair hearing. This portrayal represented a culturally feminized way NGOs felt officials ought to treat arrested protestors. The failure of the Hong Kong police to provide the arrested protestors with entitled necessities such as food, water, blankets, and adequate shelter angered local NGOs, under the umbrella of the Hong Kong People's Alliance. Police coercion directed against all of the protestors was a concern, but most especially against the female South Korean farmers. Whether this deeper concern was due to the local media's employment of the icon of Jang Geum is unclear, but the local NGOs' intentional demands for the recognition of the female farmers' rights by Hong Kong police are indicative of an informal recognition of these specific women's rights by these particular Hong Kong NGOs.[25]

Conclusion

Given the diverse profiles of the international, regional, and local activists, and political players at the Fifth East Asian Women's Forum and the Sixth WTO Ministerial Convention in Hong Kong, it is understandable why different levels of awareness about women's rights would emerge in each case. The difference between the two cases explored in this chapter hinged on two issues. First, discussions of women's rights at the Fifth East Asian Forum took place in a UN-based forum that already recognizes gender as a legitimate perspective for international meetings.[26] This formal recognition of a gender perspective has yet to occur within WTO Conferences (Hernandez, 2006). Second, the Forum's explicit focus on women's issues was more conducive to a greater degree of informal and formal recognition of different women's rights at the group level of political players and NGO activists. Comparative studies on gender and women's movements support the argument that previous experience with and activism on women's rights and women's culturally based differences matters for future developments in legal recognition of gender discrimination (Bystydzienski and Sekhon, eds., 1999; Rueschemeyer, ed., 1998; Gilmartin, 1995).

In contrast to the 2003 Forum, activism on behalf of women's issues at the 2005 WTO Ministerial Conference in Hong Kong, while a part of the antiglobalization protests, was not the primary focus of NGO activity. At the workshops and gatherings centered on women's issues, informal recognition of women's rights by NGOs was clear. Yet intersectionality in strategic cultural constructions by multiple and competing groups created significant ambiguities. The ethnic, class, and demographic (rural versus urban) focus of the Hong Kong government, police, media, and society on the South Korean farmers, for example, also shaped the degree of public attention centered on women and their rights. This pattern is visible within the comparative gender studies literature, too. Whenever the state is faced with severe crises such as war, security threats, and internal unrests, it tends to co-opt women's rights to a degree that opportunities for autonomously initiated recognition are foreclosed (Fischler, 2000). Softening public perception toward South Korean farmers through the cultural construction of Jang Geum by the media, for instance, raised awareness of women but did not directly result in official recognition of their rights. Likewise, prominent women's organizations in China, as documented by Sharon R. Wesoky in chapter eight, even as they aim to help rural women gain independence and empowerment through training and education, have a semisymbiotic relationship with the Communist state because of the formal registration requirements for all NGOs and the unofficial links with the local authorities (Wesoky, 2001). Ambiguity and differences exist among Hong Kong women's NGOs as regards their culturally constructed approaches to women's issues. Unlike the women's NGOs in Mainland China, however, they do not have the same semisymbiotic ties to government that are often a severe stumbling block to raising public awareness and gaining informal or formal socio-political recognition of diverse women's rights.

In the final analysis, what does this conclusion suggest about particular styles of recognition for the rights of women in Chinese societies, such as Hong Kong? For one, similarities in political practices may lead to comparable degrees of formal recognition of rights at the law-making level. There are sufficient similarities in Hong Kong's politics during its late colonial "transition" (1982–1997) and post-1997 periods to warrant more in-depth comparisons as far as the processes defined by intersectionality that shape formal and informal recognition of women's rights and the extent of continued social inequalities and injustices. Cross-border comparisons and contrasts to the PRC, Taiwan, and Singapore are worthy of further exploration in this context. The strength and past experiences of women's movements with campaigns for informal and formal recognition of women's rights, moreover, appear influencing factors, along with other markers of cultural identity, in present and future developments over women's rights. The degree of independence or autonomy of women's organizations in relation to government institutions is only part of the picture when analyzing the extent to which women's rights are formally recognized in law and in policymaking. In addition, the severity of political and economic crises facing governments, the numeric strength of women's organizations and their cohesiveness within a given polity, external political ties and events, and the distribution of material and political resources to local NGOs matter as well. While these suppositions are limited to a political analysis of two Hong Kong cases, they also represent a first step in suggesting avenues for further research on the relationship between cultural politics, NGO activism, and both the informal and official recognition of rights claims in Chinese societies.

Notes

1. For some documentation of these early collective action efforts, see Tsai (1993). For documentation of struggles over women's rights, see Lee (2003), Wong (2000), and Pearson and Leung (eds., 1995).
2. A similar increase in the diversity among migrant women workers is also evident in research on Japan, the Koreas, East Asia, and the Asian region. See Taguiwalo (ed., 2005) and Fujimura-Fanselow and Kameda (eds., 1995).
3. Related changes in the language of China's own constitution reveal an international influence on issues facing the Beijing leadership. The articles in the PRC constitution that used to condemn "counterrevolutionary" crimes have been replaced by ones concerning crimes "endangering national security." See Saich (2001: 127).
4. For a study that applies this idea to both Hong Kong and the PRC, see Fischler (2000).
5. Scene for Hong Kong screening of the film, "July" (*Chaat Yuht*), December 20, 2003.
6. The scene described, and not its interpretation, is part of the film, "July," as screened in Hong Kong on December 20, 2003.
7. Since Hong Kong became part of the PRC in 1997, the sensitivity of interviews among activists and those involved in politics has increased. Due to this, names of interviewees are not disclosed.
8. Mariana Valverde, "Review of Robert J. C. Young, *Colonial Desire: Hybridity in Theory, Culture, and Race*" (New York: Routledge, 1995). *Canadian Historical Review* 78: 1 (March 1997) provides the definition of "hybridity." See also Friedman (ed., 1994) for the relevance of nonessentialism in East Asian cultures, identities, and politics.
9. Up until recent changes in the law, this meant that children who were the product of legal unions between Japanese women and foreign women could become Japanese citizens, but children of legal unions between Japanese women and foreign men could not.
10. In a way their dilemma is reminiscent of debates among women's movements worldwide about whether to work within the state or outside of it. See Sonia Alvarez, *Engendering Democracy in Brazil* (Princeton, NJ: Princeton University Press, 1990) and Amrita Basu, ed., *The Challenge of Local Feminisms* (Boulder, CO: Westview Press, 1995).
11. Material in this paragraph, except where noted, is based on the author's participant observation at the Fifth East Asian Women's Forum.
12. Marital rape is still not a legal offense in many countries, including some in East Asia.
13. The written draft of the "Declaration of the Fifth East Asian Women's Forum," December 22, 2003.
14. For the importance of differences among women to understanding political contexts, see Georgina Waylen, *Gender in Third World Politics* (Boulder, CO: Lynne Rienner, 1996).
15. The written draft of the "Declaration of the Fifth East Asian Women's Forum," December 22, 2003.
16. The Focus on the Global South's website, www.focusweb.org, has some of the more extensive coverage of the planning and implementation of antiglobalization activities prior to and during the Conference. Accessed December 30, 2003.
17. During Hong Kong's political transition (1982–1997), the CTI more often than not affiliated with the prodemocratic camp. The CTU's main opposition, in terms of local and regional trade unions and labor issues, was the Hong Kong Federation of Trade Unions (FTU) that usually fell within the pro-Beijing camp during transition. However, this seemingly clear-cut division between the CTU and FTU is more complex. On local labor issues, both trade unions have sometimes allied in the interests of Hong Kong, as a community and polity, against Beijing's opinions.
18. Retrieved on December 7, 2007 from http://www.wide-network.org/index.jsp?id=34

19. "Nothing will stop us now, vow Korean militants," *South China Morning Post*, December 14, 2005.
20. Given the holiday commercial season in Hong Kong, Christmas decorations were placed on this netting around the walkways to "cover up the cover up," according to one local activist (Local activist, interviewed by the author, Hong Kong, December 13, 2005).
21. "Curtain rises on summit with call for unity," *South China Morning Post*, December 14, 2005; "Police fear escalation in protests," *South China Morning Post*, December 15, 2005.
22. This style of prostration also is used by Tibetan Buddhists on their religious pilgrimages.
23. There are many Web sites that document the drama's popularity in Asia. Retrieved on January 2, 2006 from http://www.igma.tv/show.php?showid=148; http://asianfanatics.net/forum/Jewel_In_The_Palace_enthralls_Chinese_viewers_Wednesday_September_28_2005_Korea-talk145873.html; http://www.spcnet.tv/reviews/review.php?rID=1048.
24. Unless otherwise noted, the information in this paragraph is drawn from the following sources: Member of local human rights organization, interviewed by author, Hong Kong, December 18, 2005; "Korea send envoy as 800 remain in jail," *South China Morning Post*, December 19, 2005; and local television news broadcasts in Hong Kong on December 19, 2005.
25. This comparison in the particular degree of recognition by Hong Kong NGOs of Korean women's rights is based upon fieldwork at the Second East Asian Women's Ngo Forum in Seoul, South Korea, 1996; interviews of Hong Kong NGO members from 1994 to 2000; and interviews in Hong Kong during the protests at the Sixth WTO Ministerial Conference in 2005.
26. While this does not imply that the UN is liberally sensitive to women's issues, it does acknowledge the substantive degree of progress that has been made toward gender equality at this level, through the auspices of the UN decade for Women (1975–1985), the UN World Conferences for Women (1975–1995), and their regional counterparts, such as the East Asian Women's NGO Forums.

Bibliography

Buckley, Sandra, ed. 1997. *Broken Silence: Voices of Japanese Feminism*. Berkeley, CA: University of California Press.

Bystydzienski, Jill, and Joti Sekhon, eds. 1999. *Democratization and Women's Grassroots Movements*. Bloomington, IN: University of Indiana Press.

Chan, Joseph Man, and Robert Ting-Yu Chung. 2007. *A Revelation of July 1: Internet Mobilization Gives New Life to Democracy*. Retrieved on December 7, 2007 from http://hkupop.hku.hk/english/columns/columns24.html

Chandler, David. 2002. *From Kosovo to Kabul: Human Rights and International Intervention*. London: Pluto Press.

Chetham, Deirdre. 2004. *Before the Deluge: The Vanishing World of the Yangtze's Three Gorges*. New York: Palgrave Macmillan.

Chiu, Stephen W. K., and Tai-Lok Lui, eds. 2000. *The Dynamics of Social Movements in Hong Kong*. Hong Kong: Hong Kong University Press.

———. 2004. "Testing the Global City-Social Polarization Thesis: Hong Kong since the 1990s." *Urban Studies* 41, no.10, 1863–1888.

Choi, Po-King. 1995. "Identities and Diversities: Hong Kong Women's Movement in 1980s and 1990s." *Hong Kong Cultural Studies Bulletin* 4, 95–103.

Chung, Hyun-Back. 2003. "Gender Mainstreaming in Korea after the UN 4th World Conference on Women in Beijing in 1995." In East Asian Women's Forum (EAWF). "Embracing New

Challenges: Women in Action." *Report by the Hong Kong Hosting Committee 5th East Asian Women's Forum, Hong Kong* (December 19–22).

DeGolyer, Michael. 2003. "Political Tsunami." *District Council Election Forecast November 2003.* Hong Kong: Civic Exchange/Hong Kong Transition Project.

Dill, Bonnie Thomton, Sandra Murray Nettles, and Lynn Weber. 2001. "What Do We Mean by Intersections?" *Connections Newsletter of Consortium for Research on Race, Gender, and Ethnicity* (University of Maryland) (Spring): 4.

East Asian Women's Forum (EAWF). 2003. "Embracing New Challenges: Women in Action." *Report by the Hong Kong Hosting Committee 5th East Asian Women's Forum, Hong Kong* (December 19–22).

Fischler, Lisa. 2000. "Women at the Margin: Challenging Boundaries of the Political in Hong Kong, 1982–1997." Ph.D. diss., University of Wisconsin-Madison.

———. 2003. Participant observation by author (December 18–23). Hong Kong.

———. 2005. Participant observation by author (December 12–19). Hong Kong.

Forrest, R., A. La Grange, and N. M. Yip. 2004. "Hong Kong as Global City: Social Distance and Spatial Differentiation." *Urban Studies* 41, no.1, 207–227.

Friedman, Edward, ed. 1994. *The Politics of Democratization: Generalizing East Asian Experiences.* Boulder, CO: Westview Press.

Fujimura-Fanselow, K., and A. Kameda, eds. 1995. *Japanese Women: New Perspectives on the Past, the Present, and the Future.* New York: Feminist Press.

Gilmartin, Christina. 1995. *Engendering the Chinese Revolution.* Berkeley, CA: University of California Press.

Hernandez, Maria Pia. 2006. *The Outcome of Hong Kong: Reflections from a Gender Perspective.* Retrieved on December 7, 2007 from http://www.igtn.org/pdfs//441_WTO%20Update%20-%20January06.pdf

Hong Kong Transition Project. 2005. "Hong Kong Constitutional Reform: What Do the People Want." *Constitution Reform Survey.* Unpublished summary of findings.

Kelsey, Jane. 2005. "Selections on Contributions to Plenary Panel and the Ministerial Meeting in Hong Kong." Paper presented at the Christian Conference of Asia's Globalizing Economic Justice and Social Sustainability, Hong Kong.

Knudsen, Susanne V. 2006. "Intersectionality: A Theoretical Inspiration in the Analysis of Minority Cultures and Identities in Textbooks." Retrieved on June 5, 2008 from http://www.caen.iufm.fr/colloque_javtem/pdf/knudsen.pdf

Ku, Agnes, and Ngai Pun, eds. 2004. *Remaking Citizenship in Hong Kong.* New York: Routledge.

Lam, Willy Wo-Lap. 2003. "Heat on Hong Kong's Tung." Retrieved on December 7, 2007 from http://www.cnn.com

———. 2004. "Once Again: A Rude Shock for Beijing." Retrieved on December 7, 2007 from http://asiamedia.ucla.edu/article.asp?parentid=6436

Lee, Ching Kwan. 1998. *Gender and the South China Miracle: Two Worlds of Factory Women.* Berkeley, CA: University of California Press.

Lee, Eliza Wing-Yee, ed. 2003. *Gender and Change in Hong Kong.* Vancouver, Canada: University of British Columbia Press.

———. 2003. "Prospects for Development of a Critical Feminist Discourse." In Eliza Wing-Yee Lee, ed. *Gender and Change in Hong Kong,* 200–216.

Local activist. 2005. Interviewed by author (December 13). Hong Kong.

Local historian. 2005. Interviewed by author (December 16). Hong Kong.

Member of local women's group. 2003. Interviewed by author (December 20). Hong Kong.

Member of local women's organization. 2003. Interviewed by author (December 23). Hong Kong.

Member of local women's NGO. 2005. Interviewed by author (December 12). Hong Kong.
Member of local human rights organization. 2005. Interviewed by author (December 18). Hong Kong.
Meyer, Mary K., and Elisabeth Prügl, eds. 1999. *Gender Politics in Global Governance*. Lanham, MD: Rowman and Littlefield.
Naples, Nancy, and Manisha Desai, eds. 2002. *Women's Activism and Globalization: Linking Local Struggles and Transnational Politics*. New York: Routledge.
Pearson, Veronica, and Benjamin K. P. Leung, eds. 1995. *Women in Hong Kong*. Hong Kong: Oxford University Press.
Rooney, Eilish. 2007. "Intersectionality in Transition: Lessons from Northern Ireland." *Web Journal of Current Legal Issues*, no.5. Retrieved on July 16, 2008 from http://webjcl.ncl.ac.uk/2007/issue5/rooney5.html
Rueschemeyer, Marilyn, ed. 1998. *Women in the Politics of Postcommunist Eastern Europe*. Armonk, NY: M. E. Sharpe.
Tong, Irene Lik Kay. 1999. "Re-inheriting Women in Decolonizing Hong Kong." In Bystydzienski and Sekhon, eds. *Democratization and Women's Grassroots Movements*, 49–68.
Tsai, Jung-Fang. 1993. *Hong Kong in Chinese History*. New York: Columbia University Press.
Tse, Thomas Kwan-Choi. 2006. "Civic Education and the Making of Deformed Citizenry: From British Colony to Chinese SAR." In Ku and Pun, eds. *Remaking Citizenship in Hong Kong*, 54–73.
Taguiwalo, Judy M., ed. 2005. *Intensifying Working Women's Burdens: The Impact of Globalization on Women Labor in Asia*. Manila, The Philippines: Asia Pacific Research Network.
Uçarer, Emek M. 1999. "Trafficking in Women: Alternate Migration or Modern Slave Trade?" In Meyer and Prügl, eds. *Gender Politics*, 230–244.
Valverde, Mariana. 1997. "Review of Robert J. C. Young, *Colonial Desire: Hybridity in Theory, Culture, and Race*" (New York: Routledge, 1995), *Canadian Historical Review* 78 (March): 1.
Wesoky, Sharon R. 2001. *Chinese Feminism Faces Globalization*. New York: Routledge.
Wong, Pik-Wan. 2000. "Negotiating Gender: The Women's Movement for Legal Reform in Colonial Hong Kong." Ph.D. diss., University of California, Los Angeles.

CHAPTER ELEVEN

Institutionalizing the Representation of Religious Minorities in Post-1997 Hong Kong

LIDA V. NEDILSKY

Introduction

When the British colony of Hong Kong reverted to Chinese sovereignty on July 1, 1997, a majority ethnic-Chinese city became a special administrative region of the People's Republic of China with the promise of "Hong Kong people ruling Hong Kong." One visible change in governance was the replacement of a British-appointed, British-born governor with a Chinese-ethnic, Hong Kong resident chief executive. In this chapter I analyze a related and overlooked aspect of the "Hong Kong people ruling Hong Kong" formula: the selection of religious representatives to fill 40 seats on an 800-person election committee (*syungeui waiyuhnwui*)[1] that determines who will run Hong Kong as chief executive. In doing so, I focus attention on continuity rather than change: religion as a significant minority in Hong Kong.

As discussed in chapter one, the term "minority" implies numeric and social meanings, being at once part of and alternative to mainstream society, being named and naming oneself a distinct identity group. Not only do religious people constitute a minority of Hong Kong's total population, but those unaffiliated with religion represent a growing majority: 58.3 percent in 1988, 60.2 percent in 1995 (Cheng and Wong, 1997: 302). Social indicators, too, show that religions occupy a minority position within Hong Kong. While some religions like

Roman Catholicism have historically exercised influence and enjoyed privilege disproportionate to membership, Taoism, Confucianism, and Islam have existed in relative obscurity. Privilege, however, changes with the political climate of the times. In the postreunification context the Catholic Diocese of Hong Kong must increasingly manage political conflict with the the Hong Kong government and within its own community over government initiatives including civic education (Tan, 1997), language of instruction (Leung, 2001), and anticult legislation (Nedilsky, 2008). And for religious and ethnic minorities in Hong Kong as in other global cities, maintaining culture through moral, ritual, or symbolic commitment can bring marginalization and discrimination (Nedilsky, 2002; Ho, 2001; Ku, 2006). Taken together, these indicators suggest religion in Hong Kong offers an alternative rather than standard way of being.

But there is another consideration when gauging religion's minority status: naming through formal recognition. Along with territorial autonomy and group-specific rights to protect cultural integrity, representation rights like those reserved for Hong Kong's religions on the election committee are the central measures for naming minorities and accommodating diversity in modern states (Kymlicka, 1995: 26). In democracies these measures respond to the need to recognize national and ethnic differences in a stable and morally defensible way by promising a space for self-definition (26, citing Gutmann). A less than democratic polity, Hong Kong raises questions about the implications of state invitation to representation, as well as the implications of a new relationship between state and society where relatively autonomous social groups like religious communities are drawn into closer proximity with the state. The flip side of stability is control, and a state's fixation on control can stifle or distort minority representation (Kung, 2006; Chan, 2005). Consequently, one must underscore the negotiation of these terms of asserting a distinct voice, the role of state and society in asserting and rejecting such measures as representation rights, and the use of power in the political resolution of any claims-making efforts.

I have based the following analysis on archival work and interviews conducted from July to August 2003 and from May to June 2005 with institutional leaders including heads of the central religious bodies in Hong Kong, directors of member organizations participating in these central bodies, as well as individual electors designated to represent the religions.[2] Institutional leaders like the seventeen men and six women interviewed for this project have had to judge the meaning of involvement in Hong Kong's election committee, both in terms of complying with the call to engage and generating a method of engagement. In assuming the role of spokespeople and decision makers, these twenty-three people have taken an active part in putting a face on the religions in Hong Kong's current identity politics. As Robert Bellah and his colleagues emphasize, "This process is never neutral but is always ethical and political, since institutions...live and die by ideas of right and wrong and conceptions of the good" (Bellah et al., 1991: 11–12). Tough political fights, like the one around Protestant churches' plans for celebrating National Day (Chan, 2000), and everyday tensions between religious leaders can threaten to further marginalize a community that sees engagement with political power as inevitably compromising.

But these players are not new to the game of representing religions in so-called church-state relations. For decades prior to the return to Chinese sovereignty, religions in Hong Kong responded to pressures to formalize their communities. They founded associations with leadership hierarchies and systems of governance, petitioned the government to build places of worship and schools, and responded to natural disasters and population surges. In addition, the religious bodies produced newsletters, demonstrated faith through ritual as well as charity, and engaged in protest. In other words, they established the patterned ways of living together and expected action that sociologists refer to as institutions (Bellah et al., 1991: 4).

As Hong Kong religious communities face the future in a special administrative region of China, and assume a public and political role, how do the institutions they have constructed limit and enable these communities? What face do institutional leaders present as they represent religion and minority in Hong Kong? Looking at how and why election committee representatives were named reveals modern moral ideals that are formally reproduced and globally promoted, or institutional virtues. In such a way, minority politics project future implications for both religion and politics, quite possibly beyond one Chinese polity. Anointed "minority" by the Hong Kong Special Administrative Region government, religions are representing a wider conception of the Hong Kong minority population.

Naming the Minority: The Election Committee

It was a morally charged and politically contested process that established the place of religion in Hong Kong's formal system of representation after 1997. To begin with, the method for determining the chief executive was left ambiguous in the document laying down general guidelines for post-1997 Hong Kong. The Sino-British Joint Declaration of 1984, a product of negotiation between Hong Kong's future and current sovereigns, hedged that "The chief executive of the Hong Kong Special Administrative Region shall be selected by election or through consultations held locally and be appointed by the Central People's Government" (Sino-British Joint Declaration, Annex I). Future debates among delegates to political advisory boards on the Basic Law, which became Hong Kong's mini-constitution, revealed the breadth of these guidelines.

In consultations arranged locally during the mid-1980s in the form of a Consultative Committee on the Basic Law, an election committee was but one option on the table for determining the chief executive. More democratic methods included unrestricted nomination and universal suffrage, as well as universal direct election with restriction to nomination. Two religious organizations involved in local consultations recommended the latter. The Hong Kong Christian Council's Commission on Public Policy, in agreement with the Hong Kong Bar Association, recommended universal direct election once candidates secured a threshold of support from standing legislature members. Similarly, The Fraternity for the Sharing of the Christian Way proposed universal direct election once a "candidature body" of former, local representatives did a preliminary selection of candidates and registered electors generated a formal nomination.

Religions were rarely singled out in forums like the Consultative Committee on the Basic Law as a relevant, representative group in Hong Kong society. Nor were they specified by the religious representatives to the Consultative Committee. As previously mentioned, consultation records reveal a multiplicity of ideas that emerged from various citizens and groups of society, weighing the pros and cons of different systems of governance within the broad parameters set down in the Joint Declaration. Exceptional for its specificity was one proposal for a grand electoral college naming six religions (Protestantism, Buddhism, Catholicism, Islam, Taoism, and Confucianism), women, foreign nationals, National People's Committee deputies from Hong Kong, People's Consultative Congress representatives, and grassroots interests like hawkers and students (Special Group of the Political Structure, 1987: 12–22).

Finally, which religions, and what form of each religion's community, were formally specified only after the handover in 1997. The Consultative Committee's proposal for a grand electoral college noted above identified six religions in a society where more than six flourished and drew public recognition. Its subgroup on social lifestyle and religious policies, in contrast, produced a document that included Sikh, Hindu, and Jewish traditions as identifiable elements in Hong Kong religious society (Working Group on the Report on Religious Issues, 1987: 1–2). The electoral college proposal, moreover, did not indicate who could justifiably represent these religions—whether their representative organizations, largest communities of worship, or centers of learning and letters.

The decision to give six religions minority status came from the top. In summer 1993, after months of squabbling over Britain's promotion of direct elections, Chinese and British negotiators agreed to constitute an election committee upon four sectors: industry, commerce, and finance; the professions; unions, social services and religion; and prominent former politicians (Yeung, 1993). Four months after Hong Kong's 1997 return to Chinese sovereignty, the Provisional Legislature, itself constituted by a selection committee approved by the People's Republic of China to replace the democratically elected Legislative Council of 1996, enacted an ordinance designating an existing dialogue group of six religions to nominate and select forty electors (Provisional Legislative Council, 1997, Schedule 2 Part 2). When asked by a journalist in August 1999, a spokesman for resident Hindus expressed his community's desire to also have a say in naming electors, but Hindus have yet to secure such recognition in China (Evans, 1999).

Ultimately, institutional leaders from six religious bodies—the Catholic Diocese of Hong Kong, Hong Kong Christian Council, Chinese Muslim Cultural and Fraternal Association, Hong Kong Buddhist Association, Hong Kong Taoist Association and Confucian Academy—faced a wide-open and novel situation requiring timely response. Whether they wanted them or not, the religions had 40 seats on the 800-person election committee reserved for them by act of the Provisional Legislature. Unlike other constituencies, the religions were not required by law to elect their electors, but could determine for themselves how to assume the responsibility of political representation (Electoral Affairs Commission, 1998). Even the unequal distribution of forty seats among six communities was left to the discretion of the religions themselves.

Man-King Tso, at the time general secretary for the Hong Kong Christian Council, described the job of identifying electors as an "impossible task," more difficult than selecting the chief executive (Sung, 1997). He was concerned about criticism from within the

Protestant community that the election committee was not broadly representative of the Hong Kong public, and thus antidemocratic. Also among his worries were that his group did not have the mechanisms to handle an internal election and did not fully represent the Protestant community. From Tso's uncomfortable vantage point it appeared the religions were called upon to create something out of nothing. Yet, as Tso himself revealed in cataloging his concerns, religions were already mining their communities for resources—values, practices, people, and goals.

Creating Something Out of Nothing: The Six Religions

Formally recognized through the electoral mechanism of the new regime, six specific religions faced the challenge of representing themselves as minorities. Buddhism, Confucianism, Taoism, Islam, Catholicism, and Protestantism could arguably be called Chinese-dominant religions, depending on who in Hong Kong counted (both in terms of who mattered, and who did the tallying). This preexisting grouping, originally coordinated in the 1970s by the Catholic Diocese of Hong Kong, had been coming together regularly in the Colloquium of the Six Religious Leaders of Hong Kong (*Heunggong luhkjunggaau lihngjauh johtaahmwui*), practicing ecumenism and fashioning a public image.

Approximately 270,000 Roman Catholics are registered with the Catholic Diocese of Hong Kong, established in 1841 with the founding of the British colony. Comprised primarily of ethnic Chinese, Hong Kong's Roman Catholics also include Europeans and Asians who have made Hong Kong their home. This figure does not count metics, or those whom the state has never intended to secure resident or citizen status despite accepting their entry, such as Filipinas. The Diocese is currently headed by Bishop Joseph Zi-Kuen Zen, appointed by the Holy See in 1997 and elevated to Cardinal in 2006. Born in Shanghai, he grew up in Hong Kong, returning to the mainland to teach seminary there six months out of the year between 1989 and 1996. The Bishop leads a single yet differentiated community, including clergy and laity, Curia, Diocese Commission, Justice and Peace Commission, and parish committees. Local Catholics take part in a regular synod, and leaders connect across the region (including Taiwan) and with Rome.

Protestants in Hong Kong are more difficult to count, although estimates consistently put the figure between 250,000 and 300,000.

The Hong Kong Christian Council (HKCC), founded in 1956, is an umbrella organization of mainline churches who reckon some 100,000 believers among them. Denominations include Hong Kong Church of Christ China, Salvation Army, Anglican Church, German-speaking Evangelical Lutheran Congregation, Japanese Christian Fellowship, and English-speaking Methodist Church. Charismatic churches tend to group under a separate umbrella, the Hong Kong Chinese Christian Churches Union. HKCC facilitates not just local representation, but also representation of Hong Kong Protestants in international religious affairs via membership in the Christian Conference of Asia and World Council of Churches.

Hong Kong Muslims, like their Roman Catholic counterparts, exclude a sizeable contingent of temporary migrants from their tally of members. Not counting the young women who come from the Philippines or Indonesia to find work as domestic help, Muslims in Hong Kong number some 80,000. Half the believers are Chinese and the rest includes nationalities that have found their way and chosen to stay in Hong Kong: Malaysian, Indonesian, Indian, Pakistani, Bangladeshi, African, and Middle Eastern. The Chinese Muslim Cultural and Fraternal Association (CMCFA), which was founded in 1922 and singled out through the election committee to represent all Muslims, is Sunni, as are its related, and mostly Chinese-ethnic, organizations. There are other known Sunni organizations in Hong Kong, including the Pakistani Muslim Association and the Indian Muslim Association, but they do not work closely together with CMCFA. Also in Hong Kong is Dawoodi Burra, a South Asian, Shia group. Dawoodi Burra, through its place on the Board of Trustees, is jointly authorized with the ethnically diverse Islamic Union to oversee mosques and cemeteries.

Official local estimates suggest that Hong Kong has 700,000 Buddhists (*Hong Kong Report 1995*), although the same source in a different year indicates "the vast majority" of the population may be classified as Buddhist and Taoist (*Hong Kong Report 1997*). With 400 or so temples in Hong Kong, member populations vary widely—typically with 2 or 3 people formally attached to a temple, occasionally with more than 100. Founded in 1945, the Hong Kong Buddhist Association (HKBA) is an umbrella body based on individual, voluntary membership rather than temple or sect affiliation. Its members tend to be of the Mahayana, or Daai Sing, northern tradition, and include Taiwanese and Japanese sects whose members have Hong Kong resident status, but have less affinity with Tibetan and Nepali traditions. HKBA, in addition to representing Buddhists locally, enjoys membership in the World Fellowship of Buddhists. In 1998, the Buddhist community succeeded in securing a public holiday to mark the birthday of the Buddha.

Taoists and those who follow the teachings of Confucius explain the difficulty of counting the number of their believers: Chinese have over millennia absorbed the influence of each of these two sets of teaching, and these religions, along with Buddhism, meet in various forms. In fact, my own interviews with representatives revealed doubt and indecision in self-classification—a sense of fence-sitting between Taoism and Buddhism. This may explain why the Hong Kong Taoist Association (HKTA) was founded upon the demand of the Home Affairs Department that adherents coordinate their independent and scattered altars for better management and oversight. Recognized in 1961 as a legal body, HKTA gained nonprofit status in 1967. Formal registration enabled it to petition the colonial government for land and resources to build schools, medical clinics, and elderly homes. In turn, it became open to government scrutiny in its funding sources, forbidden from securing support from Communist China. Today there are more than 100 Taoist temples in Hong Kong. Corporate members of HKTA include Ching Chung Taoist Association, Fung Ying Sin, Wang Tai Sin (associated also with HKBA, it contains a statue of Confucius), as well as Yuen Yuen Institute (jointly a Buddhist, Taoist, and Confucian learning center). The Confucian Academy, established in 1930, maintains a single school in Kowloon. The organization has been seeking a public holiday of its own, as well as hastening the process to secure land for building a Confucian temple adjacent to Wang Tai Sin.

In 2003, the Six Religions, as they came to be known collectively, marked twenty-five years of interfaith dialogue rooted in an informal, social exercise in civility. An ecumenical push within the Roman Catholic Church on the heels of Vatican II prompted a reorientation in Hong Kong, encouraging the Bishop at the time to take initiative in reaching out to other faiths. He did so through the Hong Kong Diocese Commission, whose first step was to send friendly signals for interreligious visits around the occasion of Chinese New Year. As one of the original actors in the dialogue explained this small gesture's import, it placed a Chinese face on the composition and style of the group: "[It was] [v]ery Chinese to pay visits and finally to invite all the religious representatives, the various leaders on Chinese New Year. Before that, people didn't cross the religious line" (Representative to Six Religions, HKCC, 2005).

These unofficial visits to gain mutual understanding became part of a gradual process of relationship-building. Neither did they include from their inception the six religions today associated with the activity, nor did they retain their basic form. And since syncretism was a concern among certain groups, they did not originally occur with the ease and predictability associated with the gatherings today. From New Year's greetings the process continued to take shape, in 1975 assuming the form of an unofficial dialogue among four religions: Buddhism, Taoism, Protestant Christianity, and Roman Catholicism. In reaching out to the Muslim faith, existing members acknowledged that two distinct Muslim communities were visible in Hong Kong: Chinese and non-Chinese. The dialogue approached the Chinese contingent of the Hong Kong Muslim community because the Buddhists and Taoists already involved in the dialogue were Chinese. Eventually the five religions invited the "folk" religion tied to Confucius to participate, and added to the roll as a nonvoting guest the Orthodox Metropolitanate of Hong Kong and Southeast Asia after it located to Hong Kong in 1997.

In 1978, the now six religions had their first formal gathering, making it the founding year of the Colloquium of the Six Religious Leaders. Not long thereafter, Protestant members floated the idea that religious leaders should be concerned about issues affecting Hong Kong society. Hong Kong Christian Council played the critical role in forming a religious leaders' forum to address social issues around crime, youth, and old age. The religious leaders then began the practice of annually issuing joint, public statements in the major newspapers.

> Every year, the Six issued a New Year statement addressing more and more people of Hong Kong. All twenty major Chinese-language newspapers today receive the statement [and then it is translated into English.] But the statements are so harmless.... [W]hen the leaders sign anything, they are cautious, preachy: "[You] must do something or all moral standards will go down the drain!" At least they have never stopped making statements. (Representative to Six Religions, HKCC, 2005)

From cautious social engagement and civil sharing of theology, the Six gradually moved toward signing on to a common cause.

Consensus-building was ritualized in the colloquium's informal format. When it came to issuing a statement, members—the six religious leaders in the forum and an additional two representatives from each religion, totaling eighteen participants—did not necessarily vote on anything.

> WE never voted. Let's say I was one of the three [from the Protestant group]. Number Two would say something very mild.... something usually acceptable. I would then say something a little radical. Someone else would say, "Let me put it another way." Somehow we'd maneuver the discussion to arrive at a middle way. And then the Number One says, "This is right, this is right." (Representative to Six Religions, HKCC, 2005)

In order to put the name of the Six Religions down on paper and make its voice known, it was required within the group that all members exercise full agreement. The dialogue achieved agreement through harmony-building exchange among participants.

It took years for the group's visibility to emerge, but today the Six Religions are a recognized group, tied to known religious leaders including the Chief Buddhist Abbot, Gok Gwong, as well as Bishop Zen. "The Six Religions organization has a good name, public image.... Among the Chinese business people, they say, 'Oh, the Six Religions...!'" (Representative to Six Religions, HKCC, 2005). As another source reflecting on the colloquium saw it, in addition to the Six Religions representing the majority of religious community in Hong Kong, their system of dialogue likely provided an attractive and ready solution to representing religion in Hong Kong politics (Bishop, Catholic Diocese, 2003). The Six Religions functioned on a common understanding that there had to be unanimity on issues, agendas, and resolutions. They produced an arrangement of three representatives from each religion, with leadership on a rotating basis. They held respect as the core value, as well as the means to get around the group's diversity. In devising the post-1997 system, officials approved by the central government in Beijing named the Six Religions directly, charging individuals already practiced in representing their distinct worldviews to represent them to a wider public.

Constituting Community: Systems of Representation

Institutional leaders among the Six Religions responded to government recognition within existing parameters of faith and conceptions of community. Especially at this early and politicized juncture, representation through the election committee involved making themselves known to Hong Kong society as minorities even more so than representing the interests of community members to the government. Having been named a minority, each religious community relied on its directors and executive officers to accept the task of the election committee, construct a system of sending representatives, and ultimately impart meaning to the name "minority." In what follows, I show how in three markedly different cases—the Hong Kong Christian Council, the Chinese Muslim Cultural and Fraternal Association, and the Hong Kong Buddhist Association—institutional leaders widened their community boundaries as they produced systems of representation.

The Case of the Hong Kong Christian Council

Despite calls by some Protestants and Catholics to boycott the election committee the Hong Kong Christian Council and Catholic Diocese of Hong Kong both awkwardly accepted responsibility of representation. For the Catholic Diocese, its preexisting hierarchy dictated the Bishop was the sole rightful representative for the entire community (Bishop, Catholic Diocese of Hong Kong, 2003). Requiring by law an alternative to this arrangement disregarded the Church's own structure, and exposed the Diocese to potential litigation and internal divisions if individual members were denied the right to sit on the election committee. The only way to participate in self-rule was for individual Catholics to voice their views directly: "The people must shout them, because there's no other way" (Bishop, Catholic Diocese of Hong Kong, 2005). Indicating opposition to the election committee, the Catholic Diocese agreed only to "passive vetting," or confirming the Catholic membership of anyone nominating him/herself an elector.

Lacking such clear guidelines, the Hong Kong Christian Council listened for parameters. One complaint aired among Protestants was that the election committee undermined Hong Kong's wider pursuit of self-rule, promised in the Basic Law. An election committee of 800 functioned as a "small circle," cutting millions of Hong Kong residents out of the selection of local leadership. A second argument opposing representation directed at HKCC was that as an umbrella organization of mainline denominations it did not represent all Protestants in Hong Kong. Responding to these complaints, HKCC held elections in 1998 for Protestantism's representatives to the election committee, opening representation to any Protestant Christian, whether a member of a denomination affiliated with HKCC or not, whether clergy or laity, whether a Christian for a day or one for life. On a single Sunday voting day, church-goers cast ballots for candidates at twelve sites, with the top seven vote-getters named electors. Candidates needed neither official confirmation of congregational affiliation by a minister, nor nomination by a mediating party. By recognizing universal suffrage within the Protestant Church, HKCC sought to silence critics and make a civic exercise in democracy out of a debatably undemocratic process. Protestants, stated one elector associated with the faith, were the only one of the Six Religions to elect their people rather than nominate leaders en bloc. "Protestants are so independent minded!" he explained (Protestant Elector 1, HKCC, 2003).

In determining that all Protestants were eligible to run for and/or elect a representative to the election committee that in turn elected the chief executive or representatives to the legislature, HKCC did not resolve all issues concerning representation. One could argue that by instituting unrestricted universal suffrage within its own sector of society the organization required itself to accommodate more diverse interests and theological positions, not to mention additional political squabbles. In fact, the very same Protestant participant seemingly proud of his faith's independence referred to the election exercise as a "big mess." For the time being, HKCC pacified public struggle over being a voice for only part of the Protestant community of Hong Kong. It even managed to participate in yet distance itself from the small circle election. But once representation was extended beyond its own member churches, HKCC had several other problems.

One problem spawned by universal suffrage was the contention that religious representation in the election committee crossed the line separating church and state. Some congregations refused to participate in the vote. The Baptists were mentioned as one such church, although, ironically, lay Baptists were among both cohorts of electors. Explaining his own position a Baptist elector pointed out, "Baptists are involved in politics—it's not true that they can't or shouldn't participate. No decision was ever made whether they should or shouldn't. There's a clear understanding that Baptists as a whole must keep a distance: the Church/Baptists and politics are separate. But with elections, I don't represent Baptists as such. I'm not elected by them to perform such a role. I became a representative because I am Christian. (Protestant Elector 2, Baptist Convention of Hong Kong, 2005). Others complained that outside his/her own denomination, an elector was unknown. The individual could be popular enough inside a single denomination to secure votes, but how could the elector be considered representative? Finally, with mostly laymen running—some seemingly motivated to get onto the election committee via the religious route as an easier alternative to election within a professional constituency—the representation of a religious community was further called into question.

For the second call for representatives in the year 2000, HKCC employed a "passive vetting" strategy limited to confirming Protestant electors, more along the lines of the Catholic Diocese. The Hong Kong government requested HKCC submit seven names and a recommendation letter from a minister so that each candidate was qualified by his/her own congregation. Within a month of the deadline, mostly in the eleventh hour, HKCC received twenty applicants. Its solution was to submit the applicants to a random selection (drawing seven names from a hat) since universal suffrage had not proven a good way to unify Protestants and get Christians concerned for Hong Kong's future (General Secretary, HKCC, 2003). Moreover, HKCC desired that the electors represent the Protestant sector in its entirety, not just their own denomination. Only one clergy—an officer in HKCC—emerged among the electors. Most electors were, instead, people not involved in any committee work, even greater unknowns than were the electors Protestants had actually voted into power in 1998. The most striking example was a merchant confirmed an elector despite being absent from church for twenty years.

With an open approach to representing a diverse body of believers, there was neither corporate action nor public accountability established through the process. Instead, each elector was an individual Christian with the freedom to follow his or her own conscience. While collective deliberation was encouraged by the one clergy, the idea never got off the ground with his cohort. Faxes, face-to-face discussions, one-on-one consultation seemed plausible approaches to representative voting, yet none of these deliberating strategies was viewed as necessary or exercised collectively. Protestant electors, instead, expressed their desire to hold to their own positions. In electing legislators in 2001, for example, electors received massive information from campaigners. Each elector then held individual meetings with the candidates. With only one candidate slated for the position of chief executive in 2002, Protestant electors finally met as a group for an audience with Chee-Hwa Tung. The clergy, dressed to represent his role, was singled out as spokesman for the group. But when he refused to permit a photograph with the candidate, fellow electors grew aloof. There was no common position or protocol established among the seven electors.

Only after the group met with candidate Tung did HKCC offer a clue to its own position. The organization issued a statement, a "public gesture, emphasizing issues of social justice, caring for elderly...a liberal agenda...not aimed to influence Protestant electors, but to add a voice totally divorced from the electors" (General Secretary, HKCC, 2005). The electors took it as such, acting as individuals with their own criteria for backing a candidate. The Baptist elector, verbalizing the spirit behind Protestant electors' actions to date, explained his approach to voting this way: "I follow my own, personal decision. That's the rule for all Protestant representatives. We do not need to vote collectively or consult with anyone" (Protestant Elector 2, Baptist Convention of Hong Kong, 2005). In his own private view the chief executive should be a person with a good track record, trusted to maintain stability, prosperity, and economic benefit for Hong Kong. Positions on poverty or the elderly were not part of his own calculations.

Clearly accountability to HKCC, to Protestant believers or specific Protestant beliefs was complicated by the messy details of representation. Nor was it considered the guiding virtue. "If [an elector] is not appointed, if everyone is given the chance to be selected, if selection is left to *chance*, then there is no accountability"(Protestant Elector 1, HKCC, 2003). From this clergy's perspective, "It's not an accountability thing. It's who has the *right* to represent. *Equality* matters—not [whether one is] Bishop, or if Christian for a day—for it's a Protestant notion of the individual's relationship with God–being accountable to God" (ibid.).

The Case of the Chinese Muslim Cultural and Fraternal Association

Consideration for participation in the election committee was explained to me by a Muslim elder in the following way: "[It would have been a] simple thing to just keep all seven votes for CMCFA, since the association was singled out by the Hong Kong government. But some members suggested that the Hong Kong government gave the votes to the Hong Kong Muslim society, not really CMCFA. So, as a matter of fairness, CMCFA shared among those who were quite close" (Secretary, CMCFA, 2005). From the beginning, representation was divided among five established and interconnected organizations: the Chinese Muslim Cultural and Fraternal Association, Chinese Muslim Federation, Islamic Union, Islamic Youth, and Hong Kong Muslim

Women's Association. These organizations are in close physical proximity to one another. If they are not housed within the same building, they are located within short walking distance of each other, as well as prayer hall, mosque, and halal restaurants. They relate through common membership and complementary purpose. In the elder's own words, "The five organizations have worked together in the past. The circle is small and familiar" (ibid.).

Together, the five understand themselves as meeting the needs of distinct segments within a largely ethnic-Chinese Muslim community. With a history going back to 1922 and 99 percent Chinese-ethnic membership, CMCFA is the oldest organization among them. It has a prayer hall with Mandarin-speaking Imam from Shandong province, and directs educational, charitable, and religious functions in Hong Kong as well as relations with Chinese religious groups across China. Chinese Muslim Federation (again estimated as 99 percent Chinese) focuses its work around social activities. Predominantly Chinese, Hong Kong Muslim Women's Association was begun in 1949. Islamic Youth has both Chinese and non-Chinese groups, and membership is not limited to young people. Many who started out in this organization early in life have remained involved, and it is not the case that an actual youth serves as an elector. Islamic Union, along with Islamic Youth, is housed in the Masjid Amar and Osman Ramju Sadick Islamic Center, a complex including mosque, library, restaurant, meeting rooms, and school. The most ethnically diverse of the five groups, Islamic Union includes ethnic Chinese, overseas Chinese via Malaysia and Indonesia, and Muslims from beyond Asia. Its library, with materials in English donated from various Arab states, reflects this diversity. In the elder's words, many members have multiple memberships because it is such a small community, a small circle. "We Muslims can be members, and so we know who is doing what, who is the 'elector' of *all* the groups" (Secretary, CMCFA, 2005).

The elder, who himself refused the invitation to be an elector, explained the system of representation according to a standard set of criteria rather than procedure. Representatives are selected from among active members in existing organizations. There are both objective and subjective criteria to assess the suitability of any candidate nominated among members for the role of elector. Primary among all considerations is membership in one of the five Muslim groups recognized by CMCFA. Objective criteria apart from basic membership include maintaining a permanent address in Hong Kong, establishing resident status, and supporting the "one country, two systems" principle developed to peacefully integrate Hong Kong with the People's Republic of China. These criteria are meant to ensure electors are aware of the Hong Kong environment. Other considerations for role of elector, such as connections or reputation and prestige (*mihngyuh*), are meant to ensure beneficial representation of Chinese Muslims both individually and collectively. For instance a vote-carrying Muslim businessman, one who already enjoys visibility through business contacts, gains face in social circles as a known elector, and further builds up the network.

Within CMCFA—the organization with the most votes—electors have been leaders, either of executive member or associate member status. The chairman is automatically made an elector for fear of losing face before the public and other religious leaders, while another executive member is a businessman whose work takes him to China. "Few in the Chinese Muslim community would want to vote as an elector. The community is low key, and wishes to avoid quarrels" (Secretary, CMCFA, 2005). Two middle-aged, female Muslim institutional leaders, accompanied by the elder, echoed these sentiments. Explaining that Islam, their Chinese culture, and gender all discourage them from getting involved in politics, they addressed the obstacles to their own engagement.

> Islam does not desire that we get involved in politics.... Chinese character discourages being political, aggressive.... Maybe it is the character of women. The women's group is a loser since it never makes its work known to the government. Sometimes we receive flyers about gambling, racial equality, et cetera, but we never give feedback to the government. We do not do things like gamble, so it's not a concern. If we already have equality in our community, then there's no need for government action. Regardless of what Chinese assume about Islam, women protect themselves with the head scarf. There is no equality if women are not safe. (Vice President and Secretary, Hong Kong Muslim Women Association, 2005)

Given this chance to speak, the women shared a sense of additional marginalization felt by them as women within the wider Hong Kong society. Regardless of being Chinese, when wearing headscarves they were a misunderstood minority distinct from Chinese.

Despite reluctance to engage in politics, CMCFA, with its related organizations in tow, was given the vote. According to its leaders, each organization was allowed to decide freely on its own how to nominate electors; CMCFA never asked these related groups to account for their votes or confined them to a decision. "It just gave out the vote, never to ask or to follow up. CMCFA is not an association acting as dictator. Even the three voters within CMCFA are not told how to vote. [They are] left to themselves in acting as electors" (Secretary, CMCFA, 2005). An example given of the apparent lack of control and oversight concerned the recent revelation that the Islamic Union, the least interdependent of the five (with its own mosque and separate exchange with mainland China), gave up its vote in 2005. CMCFA was unaware of the decision until government notification that there was an open seat within its subsector. Hassan Robbya, representative from the Islamic Union, did not say why he pulled out. It was suggested the he was probably leaving Hong Kong soon. Yet independent action within an existing small circle must have a different meaning from the one repeatedly articulated by Protestant counterparts. Sharing prayer, celebration, meals among known others encourages a distinct accountability.

Representation, while still new to Chinese Muslims in Hong Kong, is an opportunity, especially in a post-9/11 world, to make known the community's concerns. In so doing, CMCFA exposes the Muslim religion to wider Hong Kong society, including dispelling the "terrorist" image associated with the faithful (Instructor, Islamic College, 2003). "We recognize that Muslims may be an insignificant minority in Hong Kong, but we represent a huge population in Southeast Asia. Gradually we are becoming more active politically. Since the 1979 Iranian Revolution, Islam has been getting a sense of its power, in contrast to being suppressed under British colonialism" (ibid.). Such changes create the chance to have more discussion now that interest in Islam is growing throughout society. Like Taoist leaders interviewed for this study, Muslims note an increase in visits to their institutions by inquisitive Protestants. Through more long-standing pathways to the public like accessing the media, posting its own Web site, petitioning the legislature, and engaging the Colloquium of the Six Religious Leaders CMCFA has articulated an agenda to take up with the chief executive. As Taoists also explained, involvement in the Six Religions allows not only representing beliefs, but a legitimate path to making peace, telling the world that religious adherents are upset for them and can show moral concern (*doihbiu gwaanwaaih*) (Religious Affairs Officer and Spokesperson, Ching Chung Taoist Association, 2005). In contrast, the election committee is functionally and temporally limited. Alluding to the terms of the Joint Declaration and Basic Law, including that Hong Kong remain a special administrative region of China for fifty years, the elder emphasized, "The sole purpose of the election committee is to elect the chief executive (*dahksau*). Their vote has only one use. It has this limitation. To elect the *dahksau* is its only concern. Wasn't around ten years ago; won't be in fifty!" (Secretary, CMCFA, 2005).

The Case of the Hong Kong Buddhist Association

Rather than emphasizing its limited scope, the Hong Kong Buddhist Association projects its authority over resident Buddhists. "We are up till now...still the representative of the Buddhist groups in Hong Kong" (Assistant Chief Executive, HKBA, 2005). Drawing on a general rather than clergy-specific conception of Buddhist community with both historical origins and scriptural validity, HKBA recognizes four key groups it represents, and who, in turn, represent the association: male clergy, female clergy, male laity, and female laity. While community is often understood narrowly to mean clergy, there are historical and scriptural reasons for extending the meaning to encompass laity: chiefly the belief that lay people can be manifestations of bodhisattva, destined for enlightenment. Therefore all four groups are recognized by HKBA, and are made up of recognized individuals, following HKBA's own rules of membership. It is people who independently join in HKBA membership rather than affiliates of member temples or monasteries. And it is among these people that votes are distributed for decision making both within HKBA's own organizational structure and during wider elections.

Each one of these four groups has a place in the executive council of HKBA, its board of directors, as well as the election committee to which HKBA sends electors. Yet there is another way to view membership within the association, to establish if not recognize internal distinctions: distinguishing between general and voting members. Alone entrusted with the task of electing who will be the director of the organization, voting members are part of a privileged, very restrictive group. "Basically, we have to find a way—although the way is not systematic—to validate or verify that they are really devoted Buddhists. It is out of their behavior (*biuyihn*), maybe. Not asceticism, but five precepts: don't kill, don't steal, don't commit adultery, don't lie, and don't drink. Many people can do that, but it depends on the skill or degree of doing it" (Assistant Chief Executive, HKBA, 2005). Without a "sending committee," an official, standing body to constitute the ad hoc election committee, HKBA relies on its elites for functioning as representatives. As one source ruminated, HKBA probably invites its voting members to turn up for a day of voting when it is time to send representatives. Or, perhaps, the central government in Beijing appoints them (Assistant Chief Executive, HKBA, 2005). In fact, according to a higher level source, the board seeks representatives from among the four types, requires their participation, directs their corporate vote, and thus demands accountability (Executive Director, HKBA, 2003). Hong Kong Taoist Association and the Confucian Academy also rely on internal elites, but whereas the Buddhist Association ensures a common vote, the Taoists, mirroring in this respect Protestant electors, view each individual's heart as a unique guide. Known electors for the Buddhist community include Sik Chi Wai, abbot of the Polin Monastery in Hong Kong, as well as Gok Gwong, senior monk and president of HKBA.

As concerns the regular committee and board work, consensus among electors to the election committee is sought and built. Through the course of discussion, group interests that divide women from men, laity from clergy, may be articulated but absorbed or subdued in the association's goal to articulate a common vision and voice so that the vote is cast in a collective manner (Executive Director, HKBA, 2003). In this way the ultimate impact for the association is collectively considered and controlled. In the case of the election committee, part of that voice emerges in evaluating candidates' election materials. Another part comes from the Colloquium of the Six Religious Leaders, which itself serves to build a platform for all religions to come together to have civil dialogue. Moreover, it offers guidance about issues of common concern, as more than one institutional leader indicated through reference to a list of seven expectations for the chief executive, ranging from opposing gambling to looking after the powerless (*Shidai luntan*, May 29, 2005). After 1997, Hong Kong saw changes in its economic base and fortunes, with consequences for social stability. Economic hardship, from the Buddhist perspective, caused vices such as gambling. Approaching the chief executive to encourage resolution has appeared a rational strategy:

> The modern world is advancing in a way we don't want it to go. HKBA understands that sometimes to suppress is not a good way to deal with it. We educate people not to do something like gamble—the damage that this activity can bring to us—rather than ask the government to criminalize gambling. The only

thing we can do is ask the chief executive to deliver the correct message to the people of Hong Kong. (Assistant Chief Executive, HKBA, 2005)

Most likely, it is through direct exchange with the government, including those joint statements that emerge from the Colloquium of the Six Religious Leaders, that HKBA communicates this vision.

Religion's involvement in politics is, some Buddhists argue, both morally and politically appropriate:

> It is out of the history and culture of Chinese people: whether we are Catholics, Buddhists, Christians, we all receive comfort from gods. More or less every Hong Kong person has spirituality, a religion in his heart. That is why the central government finds it important to give a say to religious groups. Why does the central government care? [W]e are executing the "one country, two systems" model in Hong Kong. (Assistant Chief Executive, HKBA, 2005)

Yet both engagement and representation are contested within Hong Kong Buddhist society, with stakes for self-conception, commitment, and action. Politics from both Buddhist and Taoist perspectives is perceived as a worldly affair that can corrupt the heart (Religious Affairs Officer, CCTA, 2005). Political involvement can compromise the Buddhist mission of charity, as vividly maintained by such sects as the Buddhist Compassion Relief Tzu Chi Foundation of Taiwan and Hong Kong. In order to be responsive in an emergency situation like flood or earthquake in the People's Republic of China, to function as a bridge between island and mainland, Tzu Chi refuses involvement in politics (Spokesperson, BCRTCF, 2005). In 2003, as Severe Acute Respiratory Syndrome (SARS) killed hundreds in Hong Kong and mainland China, Tzu Chi responded independently rather than join other Buddhists and the Hong Kong government's relief efforts. Even though affiliated with HKBA, its spokesperson does not recognize the association as representing herself or Tzu Chi in any public capacity, including the election committee. For HKBA, however, its role as representative is broadly conceived. With the selection of the chief executive, HKBA strives to secure a fair administrator to itself as a religion. "Does he really care about the general welfare of the community and not discriminate among the religions? The Catholics [including Donald Tsang, a candidate for chief executive in 2005] are all right.

They are really open-minded. But with the Protestant community in Hong Kong, things may be a little more difficult. Apart from God, apart from Jesus Christ, all others are unwholesome. So this is why in our own mind or in our own hearts we have concern whether the chief executive will be a fair executive, fair to all religions" (Assistant Chief Executive, HKBA, 2005).

Conclusion: The Meaning of Representation

Political representation like the kind involved in Hong Kong's election committee concerns and reflects a process of self-recognition. Whether the task is assumed with trepidation or reservation or enthusiasm it is not simply a matter of getting things done. Each of the Six Religions, in responding to the Basic Law's call for representatives, has been constructing a system around an increasingly formal process of self-understanding going back decades. Although the recognition policy from the Hong Kong Special Administrative Region government identifies and names the minority, breathing a certain new life into it, yet institutional leaders from the religions approach policy implementation from their own positions. As existing community informs representation, so, too, representation further shapes community self-conception, values, and related practices. Meaning for every religion, in other words, comes in part with naming.

While other religions in Hong Kong may be less privileged, more marginal than the six analyzed here, they cannot offer the same lessons the Six Religions have given. Whether their institutional leaders would have jumped at the opportunity, or struggled to maintain their independence, resident Hindus, Jews, Sikhs, Mormons, Hare Krishna, Baha'i, and Falun Gong, just to name some of the more obvious examples, were not anointed recognized minorities. They are among the uncounted. Therefore, they have not been subject to the test of representing themselves through Hong Kong's election committee.

From the cases above we may glean lessons about long-standing practices, contemporary enactments of religious principles and life, as well as the general meaning of religious representation in Hong Kong. For over three decades, religious people have developed and used the Six Religions as a platform for engaging publicly in social concerns. Established through Catholic and further shaped through Protestant initiatives, the Six Religions platform has been an exercise in mutual respect for all faiths. Today, each may refer to the consensual position statements generated through this mechanism as a way to confirm the position of the community in relation to society. For Taoists and Muslims, moreover, the Colloquium of the Six Religious Leaders functions as a legitimate and safe space from which to demonstrate their moral commitment to Hong Kong society. It is the defensible way to be publicly religious.

In comparison, the recently imposed election committee has earned mixed reviews and mixed engagement. Where controversy has accompanied government recognition, most notably in the Protestant but also in the Catholic cases, participation in the election committee has not been a matter of control. Even when institutional leaders have acknowledged a preference for certain criteria and considerations, actual participation has not been limited to any type of political orientation, person, church, organization, theology, or experience. In part denying significance to the election committee as it minimizes or deflects accountability, this approach also serves to recognize liberal equality as a principle established in scripture as well as ideal for Hong Kong's wider society. Where community and representation are open, there is no accountability except through an individual's communication with God: *tuhng Yehsou yauh kautung* (General Secretary, HKCC, 2005). Among the Chinese Muslims the tight and overlapping quality of its community has encouraged openness beyond members of the Chinese Muslim Cultural and Fraternal Association and presumed accountability. The structure of representation is thus a division among trusted brothers. The mixing of age groups, the ritualization of daily rhythms, means the "small circle" outside the CMCFA is familiar, safe. What is unpredictable is the wider society less informed about Islam than is required in an age of Islam's growing presence. As for the Hong Kong Buddhist Association, the diffusion of its members can only be managed in a tight circle, where even the select are required to vote corporately. Openness is sacrificed in the name of accountability, even as a wide array of Buddhist members count among those HKBA represents. Such broad conceptions of community make visible emerging tensions as the faithful grapple with ideas about the sacred versus secular, democratic voice versus corporate action, individual freedom versus collective will and social responsibility.

With attention fixed upon the structure of selecting rather than grooming or connecting representatives to constituents, the meaning of representation (*doihbiu*) has largely been about presenting the religious self to others. Both the newness and the political tone of the "small circle" election committee have warranted such an approach.

But so has the Colloquium of the Six Religious Leaders focusing as it does on sharing theologies, the global concern with Islamic fundamentalism that raises the stakes on public perceptions of religion, as well as the personal struggles of practitioners of traditional Chinese belief systems to classify themselves in neat, countable categories. Self-definition—consideration and communication of each community's unique ways—is increasingly advocated in a world of multiple cultures. That Hong Kong as a special administrative region of China has room yet for minorities to negotiate their unique selves suggests an institutional virtue: Hong Kong minorities are meeting the challenge of defining themselves through the tools they have in hand, not just the tools offered by the state.

Notes

My thanks to Dean Charles I. Peterson and the Development Committee of North Park University for support through an individual development project grant to conduct field research and attend a workshop related to this project. Support from religious leaders in Hong Kong, through voluntary interviews, was invaluable.

1. True to the language of religious testimony documented, all translations are from Cantonese, all transliterations of Cantonese are standard Yale Romanization (Chik and Ng, 1989).
2. In 2003, interviewees assumed the election committee's purpose had been fulfilled, and would be succeeded by direct election of the chief executive in 2007. With the National People's Congress Standing Committee's decision in April 2004 to postpone indefinitely direct elections beyond 2007, and the early resignation of Chief Executive Chee-Hwa Tung in February 2005, the election committee experienced a second wind. My second period of research took place concurrent with stand-in Chief Executive Donald Yam-Kuen Tsang's announcement (May 31, 2005) to seek the post, and commencement of the formal nomination period for chief executive (June 3–16, 2005).

Bibliography

Assistant Chief Executive, Hong Kong Buddhist Association. 2005. Interviewed by author (June 3). Hong Kong.
Bellah, Robert N., Richard Madsen, William M. Sullivan, Ann Swidler, and Steven M. Tipton. 1991. *The Good Society*. New York: Alfred A. Knopf.
Bishop, Catholic Diocese of Hong Kong. 2003. Interviewed by author (August 2). Hong Kong.
———. 2005. Interviewed by author (June 14). Hong Kong.
Chairman of Publicity, Islamic Union of Hong Kong. 2003. Interviewed by author (July 26). Hong Kong.
Chairman, United Muslim Association of Hong Kong. 2003. Interviewed by author (August 3). Hong Kong.
Chan, Kim-Kwong. 2005. "Religion in China in the Twenty-first Century: Some Scenarios." *Religion, State and Society* 33, no.2 (June): 87–119.

Chan, Shun-Hing. 2000. "Nationalism and Religious Protest: The Case of the National Day Celebration Service Controversy in the Hong Kong Protestant Churches." *Religion, State and Society* 28, no.4: 359–383.

Cheng, May M., and Siu-Lun Wong. 1997. "Religious Convictions and Sentiments." In Siu-Kai Lau, Ming-Kwan Lee, Po-San Wan, and Siu-Lun Wong, eds. *Indicators of Social Development in Hong Kong 1995*, 299–329. Hong Kong: Chinese University Press.

Chief Executive Officer, The Confucian Academy. 2005. Interviewed by author (June 9). Hong Kong.

Chik, Hon Man, and Ng Lam Sim Yuk. 1989. *Chinese-English Dictionary*. Hong Kong: Chinese University Press.

Director of Administration, Ching Chung Taoist Association. 2005. Interviewed by author (June 6 and 8). Hong Kong.

Director, Hong Kong Taoist College. 2005. Interviewed by author (June 11). Hong Kong.

Editor, The Confucian Academy. 2005. Interviewed by author (June 9). Hong Kong.

Electoral Affairs Commission. 1998. *Notes on Completion of a Nomination Form for the Religious Subsector*. Retrieved on May 16, 2005 from www.elections.gov.hk/elections/legco1998/ec1.html

Evans, Annemarie. 1999. "Other Faiths to Send Representatives." *South China Morning Post*. August 16.

Executive Director, Hong Kong Buddhist Association. 2003. Interviewed by author (August 1). Hong Kong.

Executive Officer, Hong Kong Taoist College. 2005. Interviewed by author (June 11). Hong Kong.

Former Chair, Hong Kong Taoist Association and Ching Chung Gun. 2005. Interviewed by author (June 14). Hong Kong.

Former General Secretary, Hong Kong Christian Council. 2005. Interviewed by author (May 27). Hong Kong.

General Secretary, Hong Kong Christian Council. 2003. Interviewed by author (July 25). Hong Kong.

———. 2005. Interviewed by author (June 3). Hong Kong.

Ho, Wai-Yip. 2001. "Historical Analysis of Islamic Community Development in Hong Kong: Struggle for Recognition in the Post-colonial Era." *Journal of Muslim Minority Affairs* 21, no.1, 63–77.

Information Services Department. 1995. *Hong Kong 1995*. Hong Kong: Hong Kong Printing Department.

———. 1997. *Hong Kong: A New Era*. Hong Kong: Hong Kong Printing Department.

Instructor, Chinese Muslim Cultural and Fraternal Association and Islamic College, Hong Kong. 2003. Interviewed by author (August 1). Hong Kong.

Ku, Hok Bun. 2006. "Body, Dress and Cultural Exclusion: Experiences of Pakistani Women in 'Global' Hong Kong." *Asian Ethnicity* 7, no.3 (October): 285–302.

Kung, Lap-Yan. 2006. "National Identity and Ethno-Religious Identity: A Critical Inquiry into Chinese Religious Policy, with Reference to the Uighurs in Xinjiang." *Religion, State and Society* 34, no.4 (December): 375–391.

Kymlicka, Will. 1995. *Multicultural Citizenship*. Oxford: Oxford University Press.

Leung, Beatrice. 2001. "Church-State Relations in Hong Kong and Macau: From Colonial Rule to Chinese Rule." *Citizenship Studies* 5, no.2, 203–219.

Nedilsky, Lida V. 2002. "The Web of Voluntary Associations: Christian Community and Civil Society in Hong Kong." Ph.D. diss., University of California, San Diego.

———. 2008. "The Anticult Initiative and Hong Kong Christianity's Turn from Religious Privilege." *China Information* 22, no.3, 423–449.

Protestant Elector 1, Hong Kong Christian Council. 2003. Interviewed by author (July 29). Hong Kong.
Protestant Elector 2, Baptist Convention of Hong Kong. 2005. Interviewed by author (June 6). Hong Kong.
Provisional Legislative Council. 1997. "An Ordinance to Provide for the Constitution, Convening and Dissolution of the Legislative Council of the Hong Kong Special Administrative Region; to Provide for the Election of Members of that Council; and to Provide for Related Matters." October 3. Hong Kong.
Religious Affairs Officer and Spokesperson, Ching Chung Taoist Association. 2005. Interviewed by author (June 8). Hong Kong.
Representative to the Colloquium of the Six Religious Leaders. Hong Kong Christian Council. 2005. Interviewed by author (June 2). Hong Kong.
Secretary, Chinese Muslim Cultural and Fraternal Association. 2003. Interviewed by author (August 1). Hong Kong.
———. 2005. Interviewed by author (May 31). Hong Kong.
Secretary, Hong Kong Muslim Women Association and Hong Kong Islamic Youth Association. 2005. Interviewed by author (June 9). Hong Kong.
Shidai luntan (*The Christian Times*). 2005. "Liuzongjiao caoni dui xin teshoude shizheng qipan" (Six religions draft administrative expectations for new chief executive). May 29.
Sino-British Joint Declaration: Annex I. "Elaboration by the Government of the People's Republic of China of Its Basic Policies Regarding Hong Kong." Retrieved on July 16, 2008 from www.hkbu.edu.hk/~pchksar/JD/jd-full3.html
Special Group of the Political Structure of the SAR. 1987. *Final Report on the Selection of the Chief Executive*. Hong Kong: Consultative Committee on the Basic Law.
Spokesperson, Buddhist Compassion Relief Tzu Chi Foundation. 2005. Interviewed by author (June 6). Hong Kong.
Spokesperson, Hong Kong Taoist Association. 2005. Interviewed by author (June 14). Hong Kong.
Sung, Baby. 1997. "Impossible Task for Churches." *Hong Kong Standard*. October 20.
Tan, John Kang. 2002. "Church, State and Education: Catholic Education in Hong Kong during the Political Transition." *Comparative Education* 33, no.2, 211–232.
Vice President, Hong Kong Muslim Women Association. 2005. Interviewed by author (June 9). Hong Kong.
Working Group on the Report on Religious Issues of the HKSAR: Subgroup on Social Lifestyle and Religious Policies, Special Group on Culture, Technology, Education and Religion. 1987. *Final Report on Religious Issues of the Hong Kong Special Administrative Region*. Hong Kong: Consultative Committee on the Basic Law.
Yeung, Chris. 1993. "Mainland Rejects Compromise Deal as Patten Plan in Disguise." *South China Morning Post*. August 23.

CHAPTER TWELVE

The Limits of Chinese Transnationalism: The Cultural Identity of Malaysian-Chinese Students in Guangzhou

KAM-YEE LAW AND KIM-MING LEE

[D]ifferences between cultural styles of life and communication, despite a similar economic base, will remain large enough to require separate serving, and hence distinct cultural-political units, whether or not they will be wholly sovereign.

Ernest Gellner (1983: 119)

Introduction

In November 2007, two street protests by Malay Indians in Kuala Lumpur revealed that the Malaysian government had failed to tackle the problem of ethnic marginalization in the eyes of ethnic Indians. It was a rare event to witness thousands of ethnic Indians marching down the street and confronting riot police. The ethnic Chinese did not join the protests and the leaders of the Chinese business communities discouraged their members from doing so. Yet the Chinese are also unhappy with the treatment they receive from *bumiputra* Malays. As Lim Kit Siang, the Chinese head of the opposition Democratic Action Party, remarked, "Now, everything is separate, and non-Malays feel like second-class citizens in their own country" (Beech, 2007: 31). Lim had served in the National Parliament since 1969, and he stated that the current ethnic tension was worse than that in the 1970s, even though the national economy had witnessed a steady growth over the past two decades (ibid.).

The problem of ethnic marginalization and the ethnic cleavage between Malays and Chinese has been widely studied by scholars. In Malaysia, each ethnic group maintains its own culture and most social conflicts are coined in ethnic terms. The state's "pro-Malay" policies have institutionalized the ethnic difference between *bumiputra* (Sons of the [Malaysian] Soil) and non-*bumiputra*. Malaysian higher education is an important domain in which the state favors the *bumiputra* Malays against the ethnic Chinese and Indians (Cohen, 2000; Lee, 2002: 5–6). Consequently many well-off Chinese families send their children to study in the West in order to get a higher degree and to secure permanent residence abroad (Pong, 1993: 247; Sin, 2006). As both the rapid expansion of the Chinese economy and the growing economic ties between China and Southeast Asia have changed this picture in recent years, Malaysia is now China's seventh largest trading partner, and bilateral trade has increased by 258 percent since 1999, equivalent to US$18.8 billion (Beech, 2005). Many less well-off Malaysian-Chinese parents are now keen on sending their children to study in mainland China.

This chapter examines the transnational experience of a group of young Malaysian-Chinese students at Jinan University in the city of Guangzhou in South China. Due to a lack of educational opportunities in Malaysia, these young Malaysian-Chinese become "reluctant exiles" as they pursue higher education in China, the homeland of their ancestors. Their transnational experience in China, especially the social encounters with mainland Chinese, is a key to understanding the configuration of their national, ethnic, and cultural identities (Ong, 1999: 17). Beginning with a critical account of the status of ethnic Chinese in Malaysia and their strong ties with mainland China, this chapter discusses the identity problems that a group of young Malaysian-Chinese encountered while studying in Guangzhou. The study draws on qualitative, in-depth interviews to examine their perceptions of "Chineseness," their critiques of Malaysian identity politics, and the emergence of a transnational identity.

Ethnic Chinese in Malaysia: Transnationalism, Ethnicity, and Class

Three analytical approaches can be discerned in the study of ethnic Chinese in Malaysia. The first approach focuses on the cultural dimension of globalization by highlighting the dynamics of Chinese transnationalism across Southeast Asia. As Malcolm Waters points out, cultural globalization is a dual process of differentiating and homogenizing through the rapid mediation of ideas by electronic communication and personal mobility. Globalization transforms all the territorially bounded national cultures into a global culture. The implication is that globalization "weakens the putative nexus between nations and states thereby releasing absorbed ethnic minorities and allowing the reconstitution of nations across former state boundaries" (1995: 136–137). The effects of cultural globalization are best seen in Thailand. The state had long assimilated ethnic minorities into the Thai national identity, but there was a resurgence of ethnic culture and identity at the popular level since the past decade (Jory, 2000). Aihwa Ong and Donald Nonini (1997: 326) argue that the identity of overseas Chinese is created through transnational systems. As some overseas Chinese capitalists do extremely well in the global economy, they create a discourse of Chinese transnationalism that revives Confucianism and romanticizes traditional Chinese culture (Chan, ed., 2000; Weidenbaum and Hughes, 1996; Redding, 1993). This discourse argues that some specific elements of Chinese culture contribute to the rise of entrepreneurial spirit such as *guanxi* (close interpersonal relations) and "bamboo network." Nonini (1997) points out that this new discourse of Chinese transnationalism has given the nonelite Malaysian-Chinese an alternative identity as opposed to the idea of multiethnic citizenship imposed by the Malaysian state. This Chinese transnational identity recasts the existing class, gender, and ethnic differences in new ways.

The second approach explores the problems of communalism and ethnic rivalries in Malaysia as legacies of British colonialism (Crouch, 1996; Bowie, 1991; Jesudason, 1990). The British saw the Malays as rice-growing peasantry, and they imported Chinese and Indians to Malaya to deepen the territorial exploitation (Alatas, 1977). The classic colonial policy of divide and rule created a division of labor along racial lines. As a result, ethnic cleavages emerged between the Chinese and Indian urban mercantile and the rural Malay peasantry (Abraham, 1997). At the economic level, the British relied on the ethno-class divisions in order to control the Malays and to undermine the Communist ideology that could easily transcend racial boundaries and mobilize the people against the colonial rulers (Brown, 1994: 214). But during decolonization, the British co-opted the Malay ruling classes to maintain its governance (Kahn, 1996: 54–55). This policy institutionalized ethnic divisions in national politics. The ongoing ethnic tensions and conflicts in postindependent Malaysia resulted from the imposition of political and economic divisions along ethnic lines. The ruling Malaysian elite continued to manipulate the concept of ethnicity to pursue their own interests. Scholars have highlighted the failure of an inclusive Malaysian national identity (Watson, 1996), the conflicting visions of nationhood within each ethnic group (Shamsul, 1996), and the ambiguities of the newly constructed notion of *bumiputra* (Means, 1985; Nagata, 1993). Clearly, it is important to understand the complex political economy of Malaysia and the changing power relations between Malays, Indians, and Chinese.

The third approach explores the class dimension of intra- and interethnic politics in Malaysia. The middle-level Malay bureaucrats and businessmen played an important role in formulating Malaysia's New Economic Policy (NEP) (Jomo, 1990: 469–471). The NEP deliberately affirmed the "superiority" of ethnic Malays at the expense of Chinese and Indians. But not all Chinese suffered under the NEP (Brown, 1994: 247–248; Jesudason, 1990: 139). Many well-connected ethnic Chinese capitalists benefited from the protection of senior Malay politicians (Lim, 1983). Wealthy Chinese and ruling Malay elites seemed to have more in common, and the interests of the economic and political elites became identical. As with the British colonial rulers, the Malay ruling elite and state managers are keen to reinforce ethnic boundaries in order to avoid structuring the Malaysian society based on class differences. Against this background of political economy and ethnic relations, this study looks at how a group of nonelite Malaysian-Chinese students in China draw on their transnational experience to recast their national, ethnic, and class identities in new ways.

The Conflicting Notions of "Chineseness"

Since it was founded in 1906, Jinan University has sought to evoke patriotism among overseas Chinese (Xia and Liang, 2004). Today, its mission is to "promote the superior traditional culture of the Chinese nation and to unite overseas Chinese into contributing to the nation" (Sun, 2004: 73). Jinan University is located in Guangzhou, the capital of Guangdong province and one of the most cosmopolitan cities in China. The patterns of urbanization and development in globalizing Guangzhou are comparable to that of New York in the United States (Li, 2002). The Malaysian-Chinese have always made up the largest group of overseas Chinese students from Southeast Asia at

Jinan University.[1] There were 79 Malaysian-Chinese undergraduate students in 2005. Four sessions of group interviews were conducted among fifteen–sixteen students, and forty-three Malaysian-Chinese students completed questionnaires. Most of these students self-claimed themselves belonging to lower middle class families in Malaysia. As such, they could not afford the expensive tuition fees in Western and Taiwanese universities. For example, three interviewees decided to major in clinical medicine at Jinan because the alternative was to pay seven times more to enroll in a Taiwanese medical school. In addition, these students' proficiency in English language was an obstacle toward their applications for admission into Western universities.

Because of the growing demands for higher education among overseas Chinese, Jinan University has enlisted alumni's efforts to recruit less well-off Malaysian-Chinese students. Most Malaysian-Chinese students were impressed by the prosperity of Guangzhou, but they did not intend to pursue a transnational career in mainland China as their parents had wished. The students had a poor impression of Chinese society. They complained about mainland Chinese people's notorious habit of spitting in public places, and they considered the mainland Chinese to be less civilized than the Malay-Muslims. Surrounded by the hustle and bustle of Guangzhou, they missed the slower pace of life in the suburban areas of Malaysia.

Furthermore, the Malaysian-Chinese students found it hard to identify themselves as ethnic Chinese, even though they spoke fluent Mandarin and had a better knowledge of Chinese history and culture than the local students. They felt they were being treated as "outsiders" by the administration of Jinan University, the local authorities, and fellow Chinese students. As a result, there was an invisible wall built between the Malaysian-Chinese and mainland Chinese students. A Malaysian-Chinese student once participated in a debate in which the motion statement was derived from a piece of classical text written by the famous literate Tao Qian (AD 365–427). The student knew everything about this Chinese text and tried to explain it to his Chinese teammates, who had little knowledge of the subject. But the teammates did not think that this "Malaysian" would have any knowledge of classical Chinese literature. They ignored him and spent hours doing research on Tao Qian in the library. On many other occasions, the Malaysian-Chinese students learned that their local peers seldom celebrated the Dragon Boat Festival and practiced ancestral worship. Classmates were also reluctant to accompany the Malaysian-Chinese to visit major historical sites in Guangzhou. In these episodes, the Malaysian-Chinese students strongly felt that they had a firmer attachment to traditional Chinese culture than the local students.

Lack of cultural sensitivity among local Chinese was another problem facing the Malaysian-Chinese students. Most mainland Chinese students thought Malaysia to be backward and less civilized.[2] A Malaysian-Chinese student once joked among his Chinese colleagues, "Most Chinese in Malaysia are still living in suburban tree houses." A local Chinese student took him seriously and replied, "Well, I knew it." In fact, Chinese students often referred to the relatively dark-skinned Malaysian-Chinese as *turen* (aborigines) and laughed at their fluently spoken Mandarin as *tuyu* (aborigines' language). Mainland Chinese students preferred Hong Kong classmates as friends because of the influence of popular culture. They admired Hong Kong students' better taste in fashion as well as their advanced computer apparatus and other electronic equipment.[3] Two group interviews with the Malaysian-Chinese students were conducted in a local restaurant with a big TV set near the dining table. During the interview, several students (most in their second or third year at Jinan) were distracted by a Hong Kong TV drama, and they explained that they needed to know about these dramas in order to converse with their mainland classmates. Knowledge of Hong Kong popular culture had become an important topic of conversation between the Malaysian-Chinese and local students.

What made the situation worse was Jinan University's policy of segregation. The Malaysian-Chinese students were *huaqiao* (overseas Chinese). But the university administration emphasized the students' status as *qiao* (living and coming from abroad) at the expense of their ethnic Chinese status (*hua*). The administration made no effort to integrate the Malaysian-Chinese students with mainland Chinese in the university curriculum and student activities. In fact, the university helped these students organize a Malaysian Students' Association and segregated them from the mainland Chinese students' unions at Jinan. The Malaysian-Chinese lived and studied separately from the mainland Chinese, and they felt that such an arrangement completely segregated them from the university community at large. This experience reminded them of the Malay-Chinese ethnic relations back home. As one Malaysian-Chinese remarked, "Of course, we can live peacefully with the Malays. However, doing something more than daily routine interactions, like greetings and casual conversation, will be difficult. You see, we have different cultures, religious beliefs, and outlooks (in life)." Most Malaysian-Chinese students did not consider ethnicity to be an obstacle toward the peaceful coexistence between Malays and

Chinese. The elite Malay and Chinese had more in common. They learned English as their mother tongue; they studied in the West; and they invested in global and national businesses. But the students were more concerned about class divisions between Malays and Chinese because it was the ruling elite that made government policies, and the ordinary people had no say in the process. According to Antony Milner (1998: 168–169), "The majority community in Malaysia, therefore, is to be seen, at least in part, as the product of ideological work. The innovative Malay ideologues...operated in the context of the challenge of dynamic Chinese minority, and in some situations they actually defined Malayness with reference to Chineseness." The Malaysian-Chinese students realize Jinan's administration defines their Chineseness as thin, but their status as "outsiders" as thick, similar to the political environment of Malaysia under Milner's analysis.

Although the Malaysian-Chinese students were dissatisfied with the Malaysian government's discrimination against ethnic Chinese, they still identified themselves as Malaysian when asked whether they were Malaysian, Malaysian-Chinese, or Chinese. Only two students referred to themselves as Malaysian-Chinese and one identified herself as Chinese. It was their family upbringing that had the most impact on their identification with the Malaysian state. Most students' parents identified strongly with Chinese culture, and they encouraged their children to study in mainland China in order to establish long-term transnational economic ties, but they did not embrace Chinese patriotism. Only two of the Malaysian-Chinese students' families had extensive business contacts and experience in China. All the other students' families were only acquainted with China through the Malaysian news reports about China's economic growth. Prior to their arrival in Guangzhou, the students knew nothing about the social, economic, political, and environmental problems in China today. In addition, the students had no intention to pursue their careers in mainland China after graduation from Jinan University. Neither did they care about any social and cultural capital that they had acquired in Guangzhou.

The students' mindset can also be seen in the results of the questionnaires. First, 72 percent of the students felt good about Malaysia as a country and 28 percent considered their country to be excellent. Second, the majority (81 percent) of the students had a very good or good impression about the Malay population, while only 5 percent had a negative view of the Malays and 14 percent remained neutral.[4] However, less than one-fifth of the respondents (19 percent) completely accepted the Malay lifestyle. More than half (63 percent) could only accept it partially, while the rest were equally split between neutral and unwilling to accept it. The acceptance of the Malays and their culture has to do with the social compartmentalization between the Malay and Chinese ethnic groups. Among the respondents, only 35 percent had Malay friends or acquaintances, while the rest (65 percent) seldom interacted with the Malays; thus, there was no conflict between the two groups. Their identification with Malaysia also explained their feelings. When asked to choose from a number of identities that fit them best, 46.5 percent chose Malaysian while 53.5 percent chose Chinese Malaysian. None of them chose overseas Chinese or ethnic Chinese as their desired identity.

These statistical findings are not surprising. As Jonathan Kent (2005) has commented, while some Malaysian-Chinese see themselves as more Chinese than the mainlanders, others see their perspectives, values, and tastes as more Westernized than mainland Chinese. The younger generations born after Malaysian independence completely identify themselves as Malaysians. China is only the abstract homeland of their ancestors. Even though all the students surveyed at Jinan thought of themselves as Malaysian or Chinese Malaysian, less than half wanted to stay in Malaysia permanently; 23 percent of them wanted to migrate to the West; and 30 percent had no idea about their future home.[5] The lure of cosmopolitan lifestyle and global capital may help to explain why these young people were not keen to settle down in Malaysia, while the failure of the Chinese assimilation into the Malaysian political and social structure may also be one of the reasons why they were not keen to settle down in Malaysia.

But it is interesting to note that none of the students saw China as a destination for migration. Almost half of them (46.5 percent) felt no attachment to China; 28 percent of them even felt negatively about staying in China, and only 25.6 percent had a favorable impression about the country. None of the students preferred to work in China after graduation, 46 percent wanted to go back to Malaysia while 56 percent favored working in both China and Malaysia. The students' impressions about the mainland Chinese were worse; 62.8 percent of them were very negative about the mainlanders; 32.6 percent neutral and only 4.7 percent felt fine about them. Their negative impression resulted from their exclusion from Chinese society. Less than one-third of the students (30 percent) thought that they could integrate into Chinese society, but 42 percent thought otherwise, while the rest (28 percent) remained neutral. Evidently, the Malaysian-Chinese students thought that they could not use their

Chinese linguistic skills and heritage to take advantage of the economic expansion of China.

In fact, some students regarded the mainland Chinese as competitors, and they worried about the influx of Chinese goods into the Malaysian market (Kent, 2005). When asked whether a strong China would help raise their political and social status in Malaysia, 54 percent of the students thought so, but a sizable 37 percent thought not, and 9 percent remained neutral. But when this question was cross-tabulated with the place-of-work question, an interesting psychological struggle emerged for these Malaysian-Chinese. Among the nineteen students who preferred working in Malaysia, 90 percent believed that a strong China would help them domestically. For the twenty-four students who preferred a transnational career, only 25 percent believed in the positive benefits of a strong China. It is indeed a paradox that those students who considered a strong China to be beneficial to them politically, socially, and economically would prefer working in Malaysia, not China. These students only treated China instrumentally and subjectively, and hoped for a strong China to lessen Chinese discrimination in Malaysia.

The Illusion of Chinese Transnationalism

Instead of surrendering to the totalizing impact of globalization as an economic rationality, other sociologists have emphasized the importance of the local and of multiple modernities (Ong, 1999: 4). Arjun Appadurai argues that such a "global production of locality" happens because the transnational flow of people, goods, and knowledge become imaginative resources for creating communities and "virtual neighbourhoods" (1996: 178–179). Multiculturalism has gained its status as a worldwide currency because it argues that not only is the world a heterogeneous cultural mix, something that everyone already knows, but that the world includes the cultures of individual nation-states. Therefore, multiculturalism appears to be capable of maintaining diversities and unifying a nation (Thomas, 2004: 136). This study of the Malaysian-Chinese students shows some of the difficulties with creating a transnational identity of "Chineseness" across national boundaries.

As far as the Chinese state is concerned, it has been keen on attracting foreign capital for its modernization program (Guo and Nie, 2004; Xia, 2004). Two decades since the onset of Deng Xiaoping's economic reform, more than 70 percent of foreign investments have come from overseas Chinese; a total equivalent to US$160 billion. In Guangdong province during the 1980s and 1990s, officially approved donations from overseas Chinese amounted to 15 billion RMB, and overseas Chinese implemented more than 26,304 charitable projects (Liu, 2005: 49). As time passes, the management of overseas Chinese capital will shift from the elder generation comprised of immigrants originally from mainland China to the younger generation of local-born nationals abroad. Against this background, the Chinese government has been eager to cultivate a transnational identity of "Chineseness" in order to attract the new generation of overseas Chinese to China (Zhao, 2004: 9). The government is also keen on engaging overseas Chinese in a united front to achieve unification with Taiwan. Beijing hopes to instill patriotism toward mainland China among overseas Chinese in order to isolate Taiwan (Shi, 2004: 82). Evidently, there is a geostrategic dimension in Beijing's overseas Chinese policy, and this coincides with the new rhetoric about China's "peaceful rise" under President Hu Jintao's administration (Ngok, Cheng, and Cheng, 2004: 175, 182).

But the younger Malaysian-Chinese students in Guangzhou do not subscribe to Beijing's pragmatic vision of "Chineseness." Most Chinese policymakers, including the university administrators, fail to understand the complexities of these overseas Chinese students' mindset and identity. For example, Jinan University has a long tradition of educating overseas Chinese, but it has not yet nurtured a new sense of Chinese cultural transnationalism on its campus. A scholar at Jinan criticized the university administration's failure to create a multicultural learning environment with the help of its multiracial student population (Wen, 2005: 93). Most mainland Chinese students are shown to have poorer knowledge of Chinese history, literature, and arts than the overseas Chinese students from Southeast Asia (90–91). In addition, the mainland Chinese students at Jinan regard Western and Japanese popular cultures as the model of modernity through the influence of Hong Kong and Taiwanese media. They tend to exclude the less-Westernized and less-wealthy "others" in their mindset. This explains why they look down upon the Malaysian-Chinese students as outsiders, even though the latter spoke fluent Mandarin and showed good knowledge of Chinese history and culture. The Chinese government's policy of making Jinan University the cultural hometown for overseas Chinese students appears to have failed.

It is equally important to explain this failure from the perspective of nationalism. Craig Calhoun argues that nationalism is a rhetorical system for pursuing "projects of large-scale collective identity" (1994: 304–336), while generally, dignity is a powerful term in the rhetorical system of nationalism. In recent years, much has been written about dignity in East Asia. There seems to be something culturally specific about dignity in the cultural legacy of East Asia. The intraregional dynamics of East Asian nationalism bears out this particular legacy. National equality and national dignity take root across different political vocabularies and cultures of the region. There have been repeated efforts over the past century to engineer panregional coalitions against Western imperialism (Fitzgerald, 2006: 5–6). Regrettably, one cannot see the shared legacy of East Asian nationalism from the experience of the Malaysian-Chinese students in Guangzhou. But one can identify this shared East Asian legacy in the case of Chinese-African student conflicts in Nanjing two decades ago.[6] The Han Chinese had long regarded the dark-skinned peoples of Africa and Southeast Asia as barbarians, morally and philosophically inferior.

Guangzhou was known as the major trading port for dark-skinned slaves after the early twelfth century. Referred to as *Kunlun*, Africans and other dark-skinned peoples were cast as subhuman savages. This negative imagery was established and remained an important cultural phenomenon into the twentieth century (Sullivan, 1994: 440–441). Furthermore, modern nationalism came to East Asia from Europe and America. The Chinese response to Western imperialism was characterized by a synthesis of racially determined attitudes toward non-Chinese people. Influential and reform-minded intellectual leaders spanning the period from the late Qing period to Republican China perceived the Chinese race as technologically inferior to the white race, but culturally superior to the black barbarians in India, Africa, and Southeast Asia,[7] and therefore looked down upon them (Dikötter, 1992: 82). The neonationalism engineered by the Chinese Communist Party regime does not correct this dichotomy fundamentally (Callahan, 2005). The Chinese discrimination against African students in Nanjing during the 1980s is similar to the mainland Chinese students' prejudice toward the Malaysian-Chinese at Jinan today. In the final analysis, the remarkable economic transformation of Guangzhou and the expansion of Jinan University have not created a new Chinese transnational identity among the overseas Chinese.

The Malaysian-Chinese Students' Identity Politics

The current Malaysian prime minister, Abdullah bin Ahmad Badawi, claims that the ruling coalition is composed of parties representing all ethnic groups (Beech, 2007: 31). But many non-Malays dispute this claim and their sense of alienation emerges from their time in public elementary schools. Malaysian public schools used to be essentially secular, but they now feature Islamic prayer halls. Today, only 6 percent of Chinese parents send their children to the public schools, while in the 1970s, more than half of the Chinese parents did so (31). Nevertheless, the less well-off Chinese families are not as strongly concerned with upward social mobility as are the wealthy ones (Mu, 2005). Their experience of the Malaysian government's anti-Chinese policy is less bitter than that of the Chinese upper class. Since the New Economic Policy was implemented three decades ago, well-educated Malays have earned more than the well-educated Chinese, but the poor Malays have earned less than the poor Chinese (Mazumdar, 1981: 201). Some socio-political activists believe that the young generation of Malaysian-Chinese seem to accept this reality and, sooner or later, the term "Chinese-Malaysians" will replace "Malaysian-Chinese" in the discourse of Malaysia's identity politics. The new generation's national identity is firmly rooted in Malaysia; hence, they will become one of the hosts of society and the ambiguous identity of *huaqiao* (overseas Chinese) will be further eroded (Tang, 2005: 101). Such a view is positively echoed by Malaysian anthropologists such as Tan Chee Beng (2000). Young Malaysian-Chinese are tolerant of Malaysian government policies, with special empathy for ex–Prime Minister Mahathir Mohammed's good will to the ethnic Chinese during his twenty-two years' rule (Phoon, 2004: 78–84). While the Malaysian government still upholds its pro-Malay policy, it has put in place new plans for addressing inequality and ethnic tensions (Fenton, 2003: 135). The Malaysian-Chinese students at Jinan University were dissatisfied with the pro-Malay policies, but they appreciated the leeway for preserving their "Chineseness" in Malaysia. This study reveals a certain degree of prudence from the young generation as their parents and country in general try to cultivate closer relations with China.

Conclusion

The economic success of overseas Chinese in Southeast Asia throws light on the transnational entrepreneurial drive and dynamism of the Chinese people (Mackie, 1998: 129). Such economic transnationalism probably produces certain political and economic benefits for Beijing (Baginda, 2002: 244). But it is unlikely that this economic transnationalism has changed the cultural identity of the younger ethnic Chinese in Southeast Asia. The young Malaysian-Chinese students in this study, who pursued their education in one of the most cosmopolitan cities in China, were treated by the mainland Chinese as outsiders, and were utterly disappointed with the notion of "Chineseness" they encountered on a daily basis. Their transnational experience in Guangzhou did not help them develop a new global Chinese identity. Instead, it reinforced their sense of political, social, and cultural identification with Malaysia.

Notes

The authors thank Professor Cao Yunhua at the Institute of Southeast Asian Studies as well as Mr. Peter Ngu and his fellow-members of the Malaysian Students' Association of Jinan University for their support of our fieldwork in Guangzhou. The authors also thank all the respondents of the questionnaires and the participants of the group interviews.

1. Interview with Professor Cao Yunhua in January 2005.
2. Mainland Chinese students' perception of Malaysia is misleading. Malaysia's impressive US$10,000 per capita annual income is highly appraised by the World Bank. Poverty has been reduced from half the population at the time of its independence in 1956 to just 5 percent today. In Asia, only Singapore, Japan, South Korea, and Brunei rank higher than Malaysia in the UN's Human Development Index (Beech, 2007: 29–31).
3. Although Cantonese is the prevailing local dialect in Guangzhou, Mandarin is the major language medium at Jinan campus. A large proportion of students and professors at Jinan are non-Cantonese speakers. Malaysian-Chinese students speak fluent Mandarin, and most of them speak good Cantonese. Relatively, proficiency of Hong Kong students' Mandarin is the lowest. However, language ability does not translate into an advantage for Malaysian-Chinese students in campus life, while the "language gap" of Hong Kong students does not undermine their superiority too much.
4. A similar survey on Jinan's Malaysian-Chinese students was conducted in 1999 by Cao (2004). Our survey's findings from these questions are similar to Cao's findings in 1999.
5. In 1999, Cao (2004: 39) found that 70 percent respondents would like to stay in Malaysia permanently, only 1 percent wanted to migrate to the West and 1 percent wanted to migrate to China, while 14 percent had no idea.
6. In the last week of 1988, hundreds of Chinese students took to the streets in Nanjing to protest against the government's inadequate handling of the alleged murder of a Chinese student by an African student in Hehai University. This situation escalated into serious racist anti-African protests and conflicts. For details, see Sullivan (1994: 444–456).
7. Some of these intellectuals had assimilated black "barbarians" to orangutan in Malaysia (Dikötter, 1992: 81–82).

Bibliography

Abranam, C. E. R. 1997. *Divide and Rule: The Roots of Race Relations in Malaysia*. Kuala Lumpur: INSAN.
Alatas, Syed Hus. 1977. *The Myth of the Lazy Native*. London: Frank Cass.

Appadurai, Arjun. 1996. *Modernity at Large: Cultural Dimensions of Globalization*. Minneapolis, MN: University of Minnesota Press.

Baginda, A. R. 2002. "Malaysian Perceptions of China: From Hostility to Cordiality." In Herbert Yee and Ian Storey, eds. *The China Threat: Perceptions, Myths and Reality*. London: RoutledgeCurzon.

Beech, H. 2005. "Deals and Diplomacy." *Time* (May 30): 14–21.

———. 2007. "Identity Crisis." *Time* (December 29): 28–32.

Bowie, Alasdair. 1991. *Crossing the Industrial Divide: State, Society, and Politics of Economic Transformation in Malaysia*. New York: Columbia University Press.

Brown, David B. 1994. *The State and Ethnic Politics in Southeast Asia*. New York: Routledge.

Callahan, William A. 2005. "Nationalism, Civilization and Transnational Relations: The Discourse of Greater China." *Journal of Contemporary China* 43, 269–289.

Cao, Y. H. 2004. *Political Participation of Southeast Asian Chinese*. Beijing: Chinese Overseas.

Chan, Kwok Bun, ed. 2000. *Chinese Business Network: State, Economy and Culture*. Singapore: Prentice Hall.

Cohen, David. 2000. "At Colleges in Malaysia, Chinese Need Not Apply." *Chronicle of Higher Education* (June 16): A47–A49.

Crouch, Harold A. 1996. *Government and Society in Malaysia*. Ithaca, NY: Cornell University Press.

Dikötter, Frank. 1992. *The Discourse of Race in Modern China*. Hong Kong: Hong Kong University Press.

Fenton, Steve. 2003. "Malaysia and Capitalist Modernisation: Plural and Multicultural Models." *International Journal on Multicultural Societies* 5, no.2, 135–147.

Fitzgerald, John. 2006. "Introduction: The Dignity of Nations." In Sechin Y. S. Chien and John Fitzgerald, eds. *The Dignity of Nations: Equality, Competition, and Honor in East Asian Nationalism*. Hong Kong: Hong Kong University Press.

Gellner, Ernest. 1983. *Nations and Nationalism*. Ithaca, NY: Cornell University Press.

Guo, X. N., and J. Nie. 2004. "An Investigation of Deng Xiaoping's Thoughts on Overseas Chinese Affairs." *Journal of Southwest University for Nationalities (Humanities and Social Sciences Edition)* 25, no.5, 421–423.

Jesudason, James V. 1989. *Ethnicity and the Economy: The State, Chinese Business, and Multinationals in Malaysia*. Singapore: Oxford University Press.

Jomo, K. S. 1990. "Whither Malaysia's New Economic Policy?" *Pacific Affairs* 63, no.4, 469–499.

Jory, Patrick. 2000. "Multiculturalism in Thailand: Cultural and Regional Resurgence in a Diverse Kingdom." *Harvard Asia Pacific Review* 4, no.1, 18–22.

Kahn, Joel S. 1996. "Growth, Economic Transformation, Culture, and the Middle Classes in Malaysia." In Richard Robison and David S. G. Goodman, eds. *The New Rich in Asia*. New York: Routledge.

Kent, Jonathan. 2005. "Chinese Diaspora: Malaysia." *BBC News, Kuala Lumpur*. Retrieved on September 15, 2006 from http://news.bbc.co.uk/go/pr/fr/-/1/hi/world/asia-pacific/4308241.stm

Lee, M. N. N. 2002. "Educational Change in Malaysia." *Monograph Series 3*. Penang, Malaysia: School of Educational Studies, Universiti Sains Malaysia.

Li, S. H. 2002. "New York and Guangzhou: A Kind of Historical Perspective of Urban Transition." *To Investigate*, 134.

Lim, M. H. 1983. "The Ownership and Control of Large Corporations in Malaysia: The Role of Chinese Businessmen." In Linda Y. C. Lim and L. A. Peter Gosling, eds. *The Chinese in Southeast Asia*, vol. 1. Singapore: Maruzen Asia.

Mackie, Jamie. 1998. "Business Success among Southeast Asian Chinese: The Role of Culture, Values, and Social Structures." In Robert Hefner, ed. *Market Cultures: Society and Morality in the New Asian Capitalisms*. Boulder, CO: Westview Press.

Mazumdar, Dipak. 1981. *The Urban Labor Market and Income Distribution: A Study of Malaysia*. Oxford: Oxford University Press.

Means, Gordon P. 1985. "The Orang Asli: Aboriginal Policies in Malaysia." *Pacific Affairs* 58, no.4, 637–652.

Milner, Antony. 1998. "Ideological Work in Constructing the Malay Majority." In Dru C. Gladney, ed. *Making Majorities*. Stanford, CA: Stanford University Press.

Mu, M. 2005. *Research on Malaysian Chinese and Ethnic Relationship*. Retrieved on May 18, 2005 from http://members.fortunecity.com.chikian/pol_mag/pol_mag010.htm

Nagata, Judith. 1993. "From Indigene to International: The Many Faces of Malay Identity." In Michael D. Levin, ed. *Ethnicity and Aboriginality: Case Studies in Ethnonationalism*. Toronto, Canada: University of Toronto Press.

Ngok, Kinglun, Patrick Cheng, and Joseph Y. S. Cheng. 2004. "China's Overseas Chinese Policy in the Globalization Era: Challenges and Responses." *Journal of Comparative Asian Development* 3, no.1, 157–182.

Nonini, Donald M. 1997. "Shifting Identities, Positioned Imaginaries: Transnational Traversals and Reversals by Malaysian Chinese." In Aihwa Ong and Donald M. Nonini, eds. *Ungrounded Empires*, 203–227. New York: Routledge.

Ong, Aihwa. 1997. "Chinese Modernities: Narratives of Nation and of Capitalism." In Ong and Nonini, eds. *Ungrounded Empires*, 171–202.

Phoon, W. K. 2004. "Protest and Compliant: Malaysian Chinese Politics under Mahathir Era." *Journal of Overseas Chinese and Southeast Asian Studies* 4, no.2, 54–86.

Pong, Suet-ling. 1993. "Preferential Policies and Secondary School Attainment in Peninsular Malaysia." *Sociology of Education* 66, no.4, 245–261.

Redding, S. Gordon. 1993. *The Spirit of Chinese Capitalism*. Berlin: Walter de Gruyter.

Shamsul, A. B. 1996. "Nations-of-Intent in Malaysia." In Stein Tønnesson and Hans Antlöv, eds. *Asian Forms of the Nation*. Richmond, Surrey, UK: Curzon.

Sin, I. Lin. 2006. "Malaysian Students in Australia: The Pursuit of Upward Mobility." *Asian and Pacific Migration Journal* 15, no.2, 239–251.

Sullivan, Michael. 1994. "The 1988–89 Nanjing Anti-African Protests: Racial Nationalism or National Racism?" *China Quarterly* 138, 438–457.

Sun, Y. 2004. "Development Strategy of the Higher Education for the Overseas Chinese in the New Century." *Journal of Liaoning Normal University (Social Science Edition)* 27, no.3, 72–75.

Tan, Chee Beng. 2000. "Socio-cultural Diversities and Identities." In Lee Kam Hing and Tan Chee Beng, eds. *The Chinese in Malaysia*. Kuala Lumpur: Oxford University Press.

Tang, N. F. 2005. "From Malaysian Chinese to Chinese Malaysian: A Reflection of the Concept 'Overseas Chinese'." In May Tam, Hok Bun Ku, and Travis Kong, eds. *Rethinking and Recasting Citizenship: Social Exclusion and Marginality in Chinese Societies*. Hong Kong: Hong Kong Polytechnic University.

Thomas, Brook. 2004. "(The) Nation-State Matters: Comparing Multiculturalism(s) in an Age of Globalization." In David Leiwei Li, ed. *Globalization and the Humanities*. Hong Kong: Hong Kong University Press.

Waters, Malcolm. 1995. *Globalization*. New York: Routledge.

Watson, C. W. 1996. "The Construction of the Post-colonial Subject in Malaysia." In Tønnesson and Antlöv, eds. *Asian Forms of the Nation*.

Weidenbaum, Murray, and Samuel Hughes. 1996. *The Bamboo Network: How Expatriate Chinese Entrepreneurs Are Creating a New Economic Superpower in Asia*. New York: Free Press.

Xia, L. P. 2004. "An Attempt to Discuss the Three Developmental Stages of Deng Xiaoping's Thoughts on Overseas Chinese Affairs." *Bagui Journal* 4, 28–31.

Xia, Q., and Liang, B. 2004. "Overseas Chinese Academy with a Hundred Years" (Jinan University). *Jiangsu Higher Education* 3, 132.

Zhao, H. Y. 2004. "About a Few Points of Thinking on the Sustainable Development of the Overseas Chinese Resource." *Bagui Journal* 2, 8–10.

GLOSSARY

aixin	爱心
baau yih naai (Cantonese)	包二奶
baojia	保甲
benshengren	本省人
biuyihn (Cantonese)	表现
bomin jituan	搏命集团
caomang qiyejia	草莽企业家
Chang Jin	长今
Chaozhou	潮洲
Cheung Gum (Cantonese)	长今
chiku	吃苦
chuannan bu chuannü	传男不传女
dahksau (Cantonese)	特首
Dai	傣
Dan	蛋
doihbiu (Cantonese)	代表
doihbiu gwaanwaaih (Cantonese)	代表关怀
Gong'an bu	公安部
guakao danwei	挂靠单位
guanggun	光棍
guanxi	关系
guoji	过继
Hakka	客家
Heunggong luhkjunggaau lihngjauh johtaahmwui (Cantonese)	香港六宗教领袖座谈会
Houyang	后洋
Hua	华
huaqiao	华侨
huishi	会试

hukou	户口
Jinghong	景洪
Jung Gwok Muhng (Cantonese)	中国梦
Kunlun	崑崙
lanzai	烂仔
laogai	劳改
linshansheng	廪膳生
liudong	流动
liumang wulai	流氓无赖
lixiang renshi	离乡人士
lü	律
Lutianba	洛田霸
mangliu	盲流
meici	妹仔
Meng Hai	勐海
Meng Zhe	勐遮
Mianhu	棉湖
mihngyuh (Cantonese)	名誉
minsheng	民生
Niupadi	牛皮地
Nongjianü	农家女
qianyi	迁移
qiao	侨
qunzhong	群众
ruoshi qunti	弱势群体
sanpeinü	三陪女
sanwu renyuan	三无人员
sanzi aiguo yundong	三自爱国运动
shangyu	上谕
Shantou	汕头
shaohuang	扫黄
shaoshu minzu	少数民族
Sili	司理
sui	岁
suishi	岁试
suzhi	素质
suzhi cha	素质差
sushi	素质
syungeui waiyuhnwui (Cantonese)	选举委员会
tiben	题本
Tongde shiguan	同德试馆

tuhng Yehsou yauh kautung (Cantonese)	同耶稣有沟通
turen	土人
tusi	土司
tuyu	土语
waijianü	外嫁女
waishengren	外省人
Wu Yuzong	吴耀宗
xiagang zhigong	下钢职工
xiangshi	乡社
xiaokang	小康
Xishuangbanna	西双版纳
xingfu	幸福
xueben jingying	血本经营
Yunnan	云南
Zengguangsheng	增广生
zouzhe	奏折

INDEX

aboriginals, 6, 132
affirmative action, 9, 10
AIDS, 130–1
Akirakani Suru Kai, 68, 76–7, 80–2, 84–5, 89
All-China Women's Federation, 146–7, 152
anti-imperialism, 59
apathy, 86, 201
Arendt, Hannah, 97
Article 23, 190–1
Asia-Pacific War, 67, 71, 86
atrocities, 75, 79, 83, 85, 87–8
autonomous region, 112

banditry, 13, 35–47, 96
Baptists, 51, 53–4, 58–60, 63–4, 194, 222, 224
Basic Law, 170, 178, 180, 190, 214, 221, 227, 231
Bellah, Robert, 213
black economy, 109
blind floaters (*mangliu*), 105
bloody payment, 117
border, 89, 128, 197
border control, 138
border regions, 123, 127, 130, 138–9
borderlands, 124
Britain, 87, 215
brotherhood, 45, 96, 102–3, 108, 117
Buddhism, 214, 218–19
 Theravada, 128
 Tibetan, 217

Buddhists, 124–6, 131, 135, 200–1, 217–19, 228–30, 232
bureaucracy, 8
bureaucratic procedures, 8–9, 12–13, 16, 75, 168, 181
bureaucratic state, 10, 16

campaigns, 25, 61, 88, 154, 189, 199, 205
 of agricultural collectivization, 60
 antipoverty, 138
 antisex industry, 110
 of border control, 138
 denunciation, 57
 of government, 28, 69, 161
 health, 129
 leftist-feminist, 88
 Legislator Loh, 179–80
 marketing, 14
 mass, 61
 merchant, 44
 military, 44
 political, 13, 68
 propaganda, 32
 redress, 67–8, 87–8
 socialist, 13
Canton Delta, 38, 43–4, 46
capitalism, 96
 bureaucratic authoritarian, 102, 116
 global, 117
 jungle-like, 114
 mafia-style, 96, 114
 state-guided, 116

Catholic Diocese of Hong Kong, 215–16, 220–1, 223
Chaozhou, 13, 15–16, 28, 49–54, 57–60, 62–4
chief executive, 15, 211, 214, 222–4, 227–31
China's peaceful rise, 246
Chinese Muslim Cultural and Fraternal Association, 221, 224–8, 232
Chinese patriarchy, 180–1
Chinese-Malaysian, 248
Chineseness, 178, 181, 238, 240, 243, 245–6, 248–9
Chinese-style politics of recognition, 2, 15–17
Christian activism, 49–50, 64
Christianity, 50–1, 53–5, 60–3, 219
Christians, 10, 13, 15–16, 45, 49–52, 54, 56–65, 223, 230
church, 13, 49–50, 52, 54–60, 62–5, 217, 222–3, 232
  leaders, 51–2, 56, 58–61, 63
  members, 52, 54–5, 62–3, 222
  Protestant, 56, 213, 222
church-state interactions, 65
church-state mediation, 61
church-state relations, 50, 55–62, 213
citizens, 2, 6–8, 10, 13, 68, 75, 82, 86–9, 96, 99, 101, 148, 152, 194, 214, 216, 237
citizenship, 1, 2, 4–6, 11, 151, 189, 194
  graded terms of, 8–11
  multiethnic, 239
civil examination, 21–2, 24–32
civil society, 4, 95, 187
claims-making, 3, 14, 212
clan, 106, 166, 176–7
class, 1, 2, 7–8, 10, 46, 88, 95, 97–8, 100, 102, 128, 153, 156, 187–9, 192–6, 198–201, 203–4, 239–40, 243
  lower, 98, 100, 102, 109, 116–17
  middle, 95, 101, 241
  ruling, 98, 239
  working, 7, 11, 97–8, 116, 202
class enemies, 51–2, 55, 61

class struggle, 61, 77
collective action, 11, 166, 191
Colloquium of the Six Religious Leaders of Hong Kong, 219, 227, 229, 230
colonialism
  enlightened, 168
  British, 170, 239
comfort stations, 70–1, 81
comfort women, 13, 67, 70–1, 73–4, 77, 82, 85–9
communal surveillance (*baojia*), 9
communalism, 239
Communist Revolution, 49, 52, 56, 59, 64, 125
Confucian Academy, 215, 218, 229
Confucianism, 22–3, 150–1, 212, 214, 239
converts, 43–4, 54, 62
corruption, 1, 45, 61, 64
cosmological understandings, 123–4, 134
crimes, 36–43, 45–7, 96–7, 100, 105, 107–8, 115, 117, 195, 219
  drug-related, 111, 114
  organized, 14, 95–6, 102, 107, 109, 115
  predacious, 44, 47
  violent, 38, 44–5
  war, 70, 79–80, 86
criminal entrepreneurs, 108, 114
criminal underworld, 96, 100, 105, 109, 115, 118
criminality, 37, 39, 42, 70, 87, 100–1, 105, 107–8, 111, 118

Dai, 5, 14, 123–30, 134–5, 137–9
Dan, 12, 22, 30–2
Dashu, 171
decolonization, 239
democracy, 4, 8, 95, 153, 191, 212, 222
Deng A-Mei, 14, 17, 166, 171–6, 178–3
Deng Xiaoping, 116, 245
deprivation, 11, 42, 98, 101, 182

INDEX

development, 14, 38, 53, 55, 65, 93, 98–9, 102, 124–5, 130, 138, 145–7, 150, 158, 194, 197, 204–5, 240
dialogical process, 161, 165, 183
difference, 1, 3, 5–6, 9, 16–17, 23, 61, 128, 165, 182, 188, 193, 195, 204–5
　class, 198, 240
　cultural, 5–6, 28
　ethnic, 32, 212, 238–9
　gender, 193–5
discipline, 13, 101, 159
discourse, 7, 22, 146, 149, 153, 155, 160, 188, 239, 248
　global, 153
　Maoist, 51
　nationalist, 59
　public, 130
　statist, 155
discrimination, 3, 30, 71, 192, 204, 212, 243, 245, 247
diversity, 1, 3, 5–6, 12, 17, 127, 138, 165–6, 212, 220, 225, 245
drug abuse, 129–30, 139, 171, 197
drug trafficking, 107, 109, 112–13

East Asian Women's NGO Forum, 190, 193, 197–8
education, 6, 9–10, 30, 70, 109, 115–16, 129, 150, 156, 158, 195, 205, 212, 238, 241, 249
egalitarian thinking, 33
election, 169, 192–3, 198, 214–16, 221–3, 228
election committee, 211–15, 217, 221–4, 227–32
elite Malay, 243
empire, 32, 35, 138, 166
empowerment, 11, 51, 63, 98, 158, 192, 205
enterprise crime, 107–8, 114
ethnic tourism, 14, 128–30
ethnicity, 6, 8, 10, 22–3, 187–9, 193–6, 198–200, 202, 240, 242

exclusion, 100, 189, 192, 198, 244
exploitation, 7, 30, 50, 68, 117, 123–4, 136, 139, 239

faith, 53, 55, 218–20, 222, 231
family, 10, 17, 21, 25, 40, 52, 61–3, 71–3, 80–2, 85, 104, 108, 137, 154–6, 159, 161, 171–2, 174, 176–7, 179, 188, 191, 238, 241, 243, 248
family business, 112, 116
family estate, 172–3, 175
family land, 169, 171–2
farmlands, 99, 173, 175, 179, 183
feminine potency, 131–5
femininity, 123, 131
feminism, 86, 150–1, 161
feminization, 123–4, 128–31, 136–7, 146, 149, 196
Fifth East Asian Women's NGO Forum, 193–4, 196, 198–9, 204
floating population (*liudong renkou*), 6, 38, 42, 46, 97, 100
Ford Foundation, 102, 147, 153–4
freedom, 10, 59, 72, 82, 112, 130, 159, 188, 196, 198, 223, 232

gangs, 40–2, 44–5, 80–1, 96, 101–3, 106–7
gangsters, 108
gender, 3, 8, 10, 15–16, 88, 102, 150–1, 155, 157, 166, 169, 182, 187–9, 191–6, 198–9, 202–4, 226, 239
Giersch, C. Patterson, 124
Gladney, Dru C., 3, 6, 128, 131
globalization, 1, 6, 16, 101, 152–3, 188–9, 196–9, 201, 203, 239, 245
Goldman, Merle, 7, 11
Go-West strategy, 130
grassroots activism, 78, 198
gray economy, 109
Guangdong, 13, 21–2, 28–31, 35–6, 38–9, 41–7, 49, 51, 61–2, 109, 113–14, 240, 246

Guangzhou, 15, 29–30, 44, 105, 109, 238, 240–3, 246–7, 249
Gum Gum, 192, 196, 198

Hakka, 1–2, 13, 22, 28–30, 62
Han Chinese, 5, 247
Han people, 128, 130
Hanification, 124, 139
harmony, 4, 125, 130, 132, 134, 220
Hebei, 150
hegemony, 146
Heung Yee Kuk, 169, 177–8, 180, 182
hierarchy, 7, 22–4, 30, 32–3, 73, 128, 149, 213, 221
Hindus, 215, 231
Ho, Ping-Ti, 21
Hong Kong, 5–6, 8, 14–17, 28, 20, 25, 61, 64, 109, 162, 166–7, 169–70, 176–8, 180, 187–205, 211–33
  handover of, 176, 190, 192, 214
Hong Kong Bar Association, 214
Hong Kong Buddhist Association, 217, 221, 228–32
Hong Kong Christian Council, 214–15, 217, 219, 221–4
Hong Kong Special Administrative Region, 170, 188, 190, 211, 213–14, 227, 231, 233
Hong Kong Taoist Association, 215, 218, 229
Houcheng, 157
household registration (*huji*) in Ming China, 24–6
household registration (*hukou*) in contemporary China, 9, 99
Human Civil Rights Front, 192
human rights, 4, 10, 79, 83, 86, 89, 177, 189, 192, 194

identity politics, 2, 8, 214, 238, 248
identity-formation, 6, 8, 14, 145, 161
ideology, 1, 49–50, 55, 63, 65, 153, 187, 239
illiteracy, 147, 158
imperialism, 10, 57, 247

indigenous inhabitants, 169, 170
indigenous tradition, 167, 178
indigenous villagers, 14, 182
indigenous women, 165–6, 171, 177–8, 198
indirect rule, 127, 166–8, 170, 176–7, 181
inequality, 3, 5–8, 10–11, 16, 193–6, 205, 248
injustice, 189, 205
International Labor Organization, 89
intersectionality, 187–9, 194, 198, 202–5
Ishida Yoneko, 69, 76
Islam, 212, 214, 226–7, 232, 248
Islamic fundamentalism, 233
Islamic Union, 217, 224–5, 227
Islamic Youth, 224–5

Jang Geum, 201
Japanese Army, 69, 71–3, 85, 87, 89
Jewel in the Palace, 201
Jewish traditions, 215
Jinan University, 15–16, 238, 240–3, 246–7
July 1, 1898, 170
July 1, 1997, 211
July 1 demonstration in 2003, 190–2
justice, 4, 11, 17, 106, 152, 181, 189, 191, 199, 202, 216, 224

kinship, 53–4, 62, 168, 173
Kipnis, Andrew, 7, 146
Korean War, 57–8
Kuala Lumpur, 237

label, 12, 29, 51, 96, 138
  administrative, 28, 33
  class, 10
  ethnic, 6, 9, 30, 126
  political, 9
  state-imposed, 2
  state-produced, 12
labeling, 1, 3, 8, 12, 14, 17, 19, 51, 61, 96, 138

INDEX

labor, 41, 99, 113, 151–2, 157, 182, 196, 239
laboring poor, 13, 35, 38, 41–2, 47
land, 12, 14, 23, 28, 31–2, 43, 46, 72, 99, 113, 115, 124, 131, 157, 165–9, 171–2, 175–7, 179, 182, 189, 218
landlords, 9, 46, 60–1, 63, 116, 175
landowners, 60, 168
landownership, 14, 116, 167, 176
law, 25–6, 35–6, 39, 44–7, 60, 97, 100–1, 103, 115, 117, 152, 167, 108, 170, 174–8, 180, 183, 188, 190, 194–5, 198, 203, 205, 214–15, 221, 227, 231
Lee, Ching Kwan, 11
Legislative Council, 176–8, 182, 215
legitimacy, 8, 11, 14, 25, 32, 51, 59, 104
life chances, 2, 9–10, 12, 156
lineage, 168, 173
lineage elders, 54–5
lineage networks, 13, 50
lineage organization, 167, 169
Loh, Christine, 178, 180

Madsen, Richard, 65, 153
Malay Indians, 237
Malaysian government, 237, 243, 248
Malaysian-Chinese, 5, 15, 237–49
Mao Zedong, 9, 98, 109, 117, 146
Maoist state, 10, 49, 51, 55, 57, 63–5
marginality, 3, 11–12, 35, 42, 145
marginalization, 2, 7–8, 11, 13–14, 101–2, 196, 212, 226, 237–8
market, 7, 25, 30, 40, 58–9, 62, 108–9, 111, 113–14, 146, 148, 152–3, 155–6, 161, 245
market economy, 7, 14, 99, 108–9, 114, 146, 151, 153, 161
marketization, 6, 114
marriage, 40, 73, 133, 152, 171
Marx, Karl, 11, 97, 183
Marxist ideology, 1, 47
media, 68, 86, 131, 160, 178, 191, 200–4, 227, 246
migrant criminals, 107
migrant sex workers, 109

migrant women, 194–5, 202–3
migrant women workers, 189, 195
migrants, 21, 25–6, 99–107, 109, 194, 199, 217
migration, 6, 16, 25, 28, 99, 127, 146, 154, 189, 197, 202, 244
Ming dynasty, 21, 25, 27–8
minority politics, 2, 7–8, 11, 16, 213
missionaries, 51, 53–5, 57, 59, 60, 62
mobility, 1, 9–10, 13, 16, 22, 29, 32, 39, 41–2, 96, 239, 248
modernity, 146, 149, 153, 245–6
    alternative, 153, 160
    Chinese, 155
    state-imposed, 50
morality, 23, 97–8, 110, 153
multiculturalism, 245
Muslims, 217, 225–7, 232, 241

nation, 4, 9, 50, 55, 68, 71, 74, 86–8, 199, 239, 240
nationalism, 55, 85, 87, 192, 247
NEP (Malaysia's New Economic Policy), 240
networks, 13, 22, 50, 52–3, 62–5, 89, 114, 117, 189–90, 194, 226, 239
New Territories, 14, 166–71, 176–8, 180–3, 198
NGOs (nongovernmental organizations), 4–5, 8, 14–16, 77–8, 110, 145, 147–9, 152, 178, 187–90, 192–9, 201–5
nomadism, 42
Nongjianü (Rural Women), 14, 145, 147–62
non-Han people, 127–8, 138
North Korea, 56

One country, two systems, 179, 225, 230
Ong, Aihwa, 7, 17, 155, 239
Opium War, 137
Orientalism, 149
outsiders, 15, 21–2, 24–5, 32, 54, 60, 97, 130, 174, 241, 243, 246, 249
overseas Chinese, 246–8

patriotism, 240, 243, 246
peasants, 7, 9–10, 60, 77, 98–9, 104, 108, 111–16, 128
Perry, Elizabeth J., 7
pluralism, 5
political representation, 97, 215, 231
politics of recognition, 2, 11–12, 15, 17, 154, 165–6, 171, 181–2
poverty, 7, 30, 38–9, 41–2, 97–8, 112, 115, 118, 158–9, 194
prostitution, 107, 109–10, 113–14, 129–31, 139, 203

Qing dynasty, 21, 30, 36, 127
Qing government, 28–9, 31
Qing Law Code, 174–5, 180
quotas, 9, 26–30, 61

race, 22, 33, 88, 116, 187, 189, 247
racism, 70, 247
rebellions, 32, 39, 44, 47, 182
rebels, 130
recognition, 2–6, 8, 11–17, 22, 96, 118, 123, 138, 145, 149–50, 153–5, 160–1, 165–6, 171, 180–3, 190, 193, 198, 202–5, 215, 220
   formal, 4, 15, 17, 187–8, 190, 193–7, 204–5, 212
   informal, 15, 17, 193, 196–9, 202–5
   minority, 4–5, 16
   official, 26, 205
   socio-political, 195, 205
recolonization, 191
religions, 6, 10, 16, 50–1, 53, 55, 64, 211–16, 218–19, 220, 222, 227, 229–31, 233
representation, 2, 124, 138, 145, 149, 154, 160, 188, 203, 211–12, 217, 221–2, 224–7, 230–2
   political, 97, 215, 221, 231
   system of, 213, 220–1
repression, 37, 127
resistance, 4, 12, 14, 38, 46, 50, 61, 63, 65, 69, 85, 131, 148, 159, 166, 177–8, 192

rhetoric, 12, 32, 49, 59, 61, 78, 130, 155, 246
rights, 2–4, 10–11, 14–15, 32, 76, 102, 131, 148, 152, 169–70, 173–5, 179, 182, 189–90, 192–3, 196, 199, 201, 205, 212, 221
   collective, 11
   customary, 167
   economic, 11
   human, 4, 10, 79, 83, 86, 89, 177, 192, 194
   inheritance, 2, 152, 174, 177, 179, 193
   land, 5, 17, 166, 171, 182
   political, 177, 180
   property, 152
   sex worker, 203
   state-granted, 148
   territorial, 167, 170
   women's, 15, 86, 181, 187, 193–7, 199, 201–5
rights claims, 4, 187, 190, 196, 202, 205
rights consciousness, 10–11
Rowe, William, 32

salt merchants, 26, 28
SARS (Severe Acute Respiratory Syndrome), 230
secret societies, 40, 103, 108
September 11, 2001, 200, 227
sex slaves, 67, 69–70
sex workers, 71, 78, 83, 86, 89, 197
sexual orientation, 8, 88, 196
sexual slavery, 71, 78, 83, 86, 89, 197
sexual violence, 86, 88, 194–5, 197
Shanghai, 56, 71, 103–5, 216
Shantou, 51, 54–5, 57–64
Shanxi, 13, 26–8, 31, 67–71, 73, 75–80, 83, 85–6, 89
Shirk, Susan, 9
Singapore, 5, 64, 188, 205
Sinification, 124, 139
Sino-British Joint Declaration, 214, 227
Six Religions, 214–15, 218–20, 222, 227, 231